"PARIAH STATES"
& SANCTIONS IN THE
MIDDLE EAST

The Middle East in the International System

ANOUSHIRAVAN EHTESHAMI &
RAYMOND A. HINNEBUSCH,
SERIES EDITORS

"PARIAH STATES" & SANCTIONS IN THE MIDDLE EAST

IRAQ, LIBYA, SUDAN

TIM NIBLOCK

LYNNE
RIENNER
PUBLISHERS

BOULDER
LONDON

Published in the United States of America in 2001 by
Lynne Rienner Publishers, Inc.
1800 30th Street, Boulder, Colorado 80301
www.rienner.com

and in the United Kingdom by
Lynne Rienner Publishers, Inc.
3 Henrietta Street, Covent Garden, London WC2E 8LU

Library of Congress Cataloging-in-Publication Data
Niblock, Tim.
  "Pariah states" and sanctions in the Middle East : Iraq, Libya, Sudan / Tim Niblock.
    p.   cm. — (The Middle East in the international system)
  Includes bibliographical references and index.
  ISBN 1-55587-962-4 (alk. paper)
  1. Economic sanctions—Case studies.   2. Sanctions (International law)—Case studies.
3. Middle East—Politics and government—1979–   4. Economic sanctions—Middle East.
I. Title.   II. Series.

JZ6373.N53   2001
341.5'82'0956—dc21

                                                                                  00-045981

British Cataloguing in Publication Data
A Cataloguing in Publication record for this book
is available from the British Library.

Printed and bound in the United States of America

∞   The paper used in this publication meets the requirements
    of the American National Standard for Permanence of
    Paper for Printed Library Materials Z39.48-1984.

5   4   3   2   1

Contents

Part Two: The Case of Iraq

Part Three: The Case of Sudan

Tables and Figures

Figures

Preface

This book constitutes an objective attempt to examine the rationale, impact, and effects of UN sanctions imposed on Iraq, Libya, and Sudan. I must confess, however, that the motivations for the study have been a mixture of anger and shame. Those who make regular visits to Iraq, and to a lesser extent Libya, cannot fail to be appalled by the misery under which the peoples of those richly resourced countries have been living. And though Western governments may seek to blame the countries' leaders, the reality is that economic sanctions have inflicted immense damage on populations—all in retaliation for acts over which they have had no influence or control. Responsibility for sanctions policy lies squarely with the Western powers that have guided UN Security Council resolutions. There is, moreover, no justification in terms of any higher ends. As this book shows, sanctions do not enhance the stability of the international order when applied over a prolonged period. To experience the goodwill that people in the countries concerned continue to show to visitors from outside, and to know that their agony is caused by the policies pursued by one's own government, creates the sense of shame.

The three countries covered in this book have all been subject to differing sanctions regimes, with differing backgrounds and effects. Informed readers will come to the analysis with more knowledge of the background to sanctions in some cases than in others. The intense media coverage of events in Iraq in 1990 and 1991, for example, means that those events are well known; thus a detailed rehashing of them should be unnecessary. No attempt has been made, therefore, to impose a common format on the analysis of the three cases. Each part has been structured to convey the dynamics that I wish to highlight and to avoid detailing material that has been amply covered elsewhere.

The list of individuals who deserve my thanks is indeed very long. I hope that I may be forgiven for mentioning some broad categories without specifying names: my colleagues at the Institute of Arab and Islamic Studies at the University of Exeter; former colleagues at the Centre for Middle Eastern and Islamic Studies at the University of Durham; friends and associates at the University of Baghdad, Bait al-Hikmah (Baghdad), Garyounis University (Benghazi), the Academy for Graduate Studies and Economic Research (Tripoli), and the University of Khartoum. I must also give particular thanks to the Ph.D. students with whom I have worked in recent years for providing a continuing source of intellectual stimulation.

Some of the most valuable support, and the insights that give true understanding, have come from family and friends. My daughter Rebecca has done valuable work as my research assistant in the final stages of preparing the text. My sincere thanks go to her, and also to my other daughters, Sally and Kathleen, for their moral support. I have always benefited from the insights on Sudan of my wife, Rida, and her Sudanese family, and similarly of my friends El-Baghir and Ibtisam. My knowledge of Libya has been deepened greatly by Amal and her family over many years, as well as by my friends Mansur, Salih, Ahmad, and Zeinab. Iraqi society has been made more comprehensible to me by Ihsan, Nisreen, and their family and by Wamidh and Saad and their families. I have also benefited from the perceptions of Eisa, George, Haifa'a, and Mustafa. May they all feel that the time that they have spent in helping me has been worthwhile.

I am grateful to Nabil Adawy and Barrie Wharton of the University of Limerick for permission to republish a section of the chapter that I contributed to their *Limerick Anthology of Arab Affairs* (Limerick, 1998); and to Anoush Ehteshami and Ray Hinnebusch for allowing me to publish some analysis of Libyan foreign policy making that will also appear in my chapter in their *Foreign Policies of Middle Eastern States* (Lynne Rienner Publishers, forthcoming).

Tim Niblock

1

Introduction: The New World Order, Sanctions, and the "Pariah States"

The focus of this book is on the utility and effects of United Nations sanctions, with case studies of the three Arab countries that have been subjected to such sanctions: Iraq, Libya, and Sudan.[1] The perspective is that of the role of sanctions in fostering the creation of a stable international order. On the one hand, this involves an assessment as to whether sanctions are achieving the immediate goals envisaged in the UN Security Council resolutions, that is, forcing a state that is judged to have transgressed international norms to take specific measures in compliance with these norms.[2] On the other hand, it involves looking at the impact of sanctions on wider dimensions of the international order, as defined by the UN Charter and associated covenants and conventions. The wider dimensions cover both international stability—Have the sanctions contributed to, or detracted from, the stability of the region and the wider international system?—and the values deemed fundamental to a stable international order—Have the sanctions buttressed respect for human rights?

The Arab world's experience with UN sanctions is important from two points of view. First, one-half of the instances where the UN Security Council has applied mandatory economic sanctions on member states have been within the Arab world.[3] The only other states that have been subject to such sanctions are Haiti and the Yugoslav Federation. Any attempt to assess the utility of sanctions internationally is, therefore, bound to give substantial attention to the Arab experience. Second, the politics and economics of the Arab world have been substantially affected by sanctions. Whether or not individual Arab countries have been under sanctions, all have felt the effects. Some of these effects have been positive (as when neighboring states gain from the trade diversion brought

1

about by sanctions), but mostly the impact has been negative. Sanctions may have been a response to threats to the stability of the international order, but they have also stoked regional political tensions, intensified social divisions, and created regionwide economic disruption. An understanding of the politics and economics of the Arab world today, therefore, requires some knowledge of the dynamics set in motion by sanctions.

The Context: The New World Order

The use of UN sanctions must be viewed within the context of the world order that came into existence after the disintegration of the Soviet Union and the collapse of communist regimes in Eastern Europe. It was only with this so-called New World Order that the UN Security Council gained the practical ability to impose sanctions. Prior to that, the divisions between East and West had ensured that there was never sufficient common ground for such actions to be taken. The dynamics of international relations under the New World Order, in fact, have not only enabled sanctions to be imposed but also shaped the character, content, and sustainability of sanctions. Events in the Arab world, moreover, carry particular relevance to conceptions of the New World Order: much of the early debate on the New World Order was engendered by the international reaction to Iraq's occupation of Kuwait in August 1990. There is good reason, therefore, to be attentive to the links between the New World Order and UN sanctions.

The New World Order, pronounced by Western leaders in 1989, was projected by those same leaders as bringing into being a more stable and peaceful international order, one built on democratic values and the free market economy. The bitter antagonism between East and West, the nuclear confrontation, and the rivalry for strategic preeminence and ideological hegemony would all be left behind. In its place the Western powers would be able to work through the United Nations to create a world order reflecting democratic values and a deeper respect for human rights, wherein attempts to disrupt the new international harmony would be met by collective action channeled through international organizations. The so-called end-of-history thesis was sometimes built into this perspective. The world was seeing the victory of liberal democracy; beyond that there would be no further political system that could evolve. Wherever liberal democracy was not yet established, it would be within the foreseeable future. There was, ultimately, no alternative system that could challenge it.[4]

Although some of the optimism that pervaded Western government circles during the beginning of the 1990s may have diminished—replaced by a more realistic appreciation of the continuing problems in managing the world order—in some respects the earlier projections and hopes of Western governments have been realized. First, the threat of global war no longer dominates the consciousness of most Western publics. With the disintegration of the Soviet Union and the communist bloc, the continued holding of nuclear weapons by states of the former Soviet Union is no longer viewed with significant alarm. The international system is generally viewed in the West as being more benign, less subject to dynamics that could lead (whether through design or miscalculation) to a nuclear confrontation.

Second, liberal democracy has spread. The number of countries operating multiparty parliamentary systems has increased not only in Eastern Europe but also in Asia and Latin America. Moves toward liberal democracy in Africa and the Middle East have been more limited. In the case of the Middle East, indeed, the 1990s opened with new initiatives toward liberal democracy being taken yet closed with most such initiatives being constrained.[5] Questions may also be raised about the long-term prospects of some of the new democracies in Asia and Latin America. Nonetheless, the emergence of functioning liberal democracies in most of Eastern Europe, the opening up of the political systems of Taiwan, South Korea, and Indonesia, the disintegration of apartheid in South Africa, and the strengthened credibility of liberal democratic systems in Chile, Argentina, and some other Latin American countries support the perception that the values of liberal democracy have spread.[6]

Third, there has been a well-documented advance toward a global economic market. The 1990s saw the transformation to free market economies in the former Soviet Union and a worldwide trend toward economic liberalization, both of which have opened commercial and financial markets to greater competition, as well as the strengthening of global regulatory mechanisms that underpin and facilitate global trading. Trade throughout the international economy has enjoyed the spread of standards in pricing, quality, and efficiency, enforced through the international protocols concluded under the Uruguay Round of General Agreement on Tariffs and Trade (GATT) negotiations in 1994. Among the latter were agreements on trade-related investment measures (TRIMS) and trade-related intellectual property rights (TRIPS). The structures of the World Trade Organization established in 1995 promote and expand the regulatory framework of the global market.[7] These developments have involved what some writers have called the "internationalization of the state" wherein the state has become "the vehicle for transmitting the global market discipline to the domestic economy."[8] It is significant, moreover, that the realm within which international financial institutions have sought to promote policy changes has steadily widened. In the 1970s and early 1980s, the objective was to achieve structural adjustment (bringing the economy into balance); in the late 1980s and the early 1990s the objective was to achieve economic liberalization; in the mid- and late 1990s the concern was extended to cover good governance—deemed necessary if economic reforms were to achieve success. The criteria for entry into the global economic market have, in practice, been made more rigorous in many respects.

Fourth, human rights considerations play a more significant role in international relations than they did before. The body of international human rights legislation has expanded, and governments have become more intent than before to act upon the legislation. There has been a steady move toward expanding human rights legislation in cultural and economic fields, and an increasing recognition of the close interrelationship between human rights, peace, democracy, and development. The rights of minorities were given more specific recognition than before in the Declaration on the Rights of Persons Belonging to National or Ethnic, Religious, and Linguistic Minorities, adopted by the UN General Assembly in 1992.[9] The right to development also attracted more attention than before. The Declaration on the Right to Development had been adopted by the General Assembly in 1986, but it was not until the 1990s that it was put on the agenda of international conferences—such as at the UN Conference on Environment and Development in Rio de Janeiro (1992) and the UN Conference on Social Development in Copenhagen (1995).[10] The increased governmental concern with human rights was complemented by, and to some extent stimulated by, nongovernmental organizations playing a growing role in this sphere. Such bodies as Amnesty International, Human Rights Watch, and Article 19 have helped to ensure that human rights issues remain at the forefront of popular concerns and that governments must bear some cost in international esteem if they infringe upon basic human rights.[11]

Increasingly, human rights issues can be (and are) pursued in fora wherein national governments cannot limit or control the international legal process. The safeguarding of global human rights, in particular situations, has therefore been given precedence over national sovereignty. This was made explicit in the Pinochet case in Britain. Although the Convention Against Torture and Other Cruel, Inhuman, or Degrading Treatment or Punishment was adopted by the United Nations in 1984, and had been ratified by the British government through its Criminal Justice Act of

1988, it was not until 1999 that the convention was used to bring a case against the former Chilean president, Augusto Pinochet, during one of his regular visits to Britain. The point was made that courts in one country could have jurisdiction over acts of torture inflicted in another, even when the accused was a former head of state. A further instance of international jurisdiction overriding considerations of national sovereignty was the establishment by the UN Security Council of International Criminal Courts for Yugoslavia and Rwanda.[12] These were empowered to hold to account individuals accused of violations of human rights in the two countries concerned. The agreement to establish an International Criminal Court will in due course carry this international jurisdiction over wrongdoing much wider. Once the treaty, which was signed in July 1998,[13] has been ratified by sixty countries, measures will then be taken to set the new court up and enable it to exercise its authority to try those accused of genocide, aggression, war crimes, and crimes against humanity. It is expected that the court will begin operating some five years after the initial agreement.

Fifth, the United Nations has expanded its international peacekeeping, peace enforcement, and security roles, guided in part by the new concept of "humanitarian intervention." The three cases of economic sanctions that are covered in this book are themselves examples of the United Nations being used to achieve objectives that had seldom been pursued through the United Nations before. Economic sanctions had been imposed on white-ruled Rhodesia, but this was an exceptional case and the sanctions were mild in comparison with those imposed on Iraq. The military action against Iraq in 1991 was the first occasion since the Korean War that the Security Council had specifically authorized the use of military force against a member state.

The New World Order Viewed from the Underside

The positive view of developments in the international order, as sketched out above, tends to be held—and purveyed—by the governments of the major Western powers. A substantial part of the world's population, however, sees the New World Order in much less positive terms. And negative critiques of the political-economic order today are to be found in both Western and non-Western countries.

There is a significant difference, however, in the manner in which Western and non-Western critiques are expressed. The former tend to describe the developments as the product of global forces that have damaging effects on all societies: a process of globalization—set in motion by the characteristics of international capitalism—that is increasing social and economic inequality nationally and internationally, creating high levels of unemployment, polarizing society between the unemployed and the overemployed, forcing wide-scale migration, and leading to social disjunction. Non-Western critiques, in contrast, tend to associate the perceived negative aspects of the New World Order less with impersonal global forces and more with a rejuvenated Western dominance. The United States is seen as the guiding force in, and the main beneficiary of, this reassertion of Western hegemony, the loss concentrated in the non-Western world. The New World Order, then, represents a new Western dominance, an imposition of the values and interests of Western governments and corporations on the world, not a move toward the harmonization of the values and interests of the world's different population groups.[14] The new dominance, within which the United States is the critical hegemon, is not the "benevolent global hegemony" as purveyed by some Western writers but rather a malign hegemony.

The very existence of negative criticism of the New World Order is crucial to the theme and substance of this book. Attitudes toward sanctions are clearly conditioned by perceptions of the current global order. The Western powers that have orchestrated the imposition of UN sanctions portray sanctions as the instruments through which a peaceful world order can be built, where transgressions of international law are punished through the channels of international institutions. States that are the targets of sanctions, however, are able to mobilize a good portion of international opinion to their side by portraying a different perception, wherein sanctions are an instrument to establish and maintain the new Western hegemony and international institutions are used to provide a cover for the pursuit of Western (particularly U.S.) interests.

Resistance to sanctions, within the perspective of the negative critique, thus does not imply disregard for international law but rather a determination not to allow international law and international institutions to be used to promote Western/U.S. interests. The ability of states to withstand the effects of UN sanctions resolutions, by mobilizing international sympathy and support, is substantially strengthened by this perception. It shapes the dynamics of support for, and opposition to, the use of sanctions: the degree to which the Western powers can obtain backing for the sanctions regimes that they apply through the United Nations, as well as the possibilities that sanctioned states have for maintaining an intransigent rejection of demands made in UN resolutions.

The negative (predominantly non-Western) critique will be described here as the "view from the underside." Found mainly in the non-Western world and in poorer and less privileged societies, this view does not divide neatly according to cultural and social environments or cohere clearly with any established ideology or class groupings. It may be shared by traditional conservatives, Marxists, and Islamists but not all within each category. The New World Order and the process of globalization have blurred the dividing lines between cultures and societies. There is less commonality in the attitudes and approaches of those within each unit. The disappearance of the so-called Third World is not simply a function of the disintegration of the Second World (the communist bloc) or the shifts of economic well-being that have lifted some former developing countries to "newly industrializing" or "newly emerging market" status; global integration has created new patterns of identification and alignment within and among societies. Populations in less developed countries that look to the Western world for support and contact are no longer simply conservatively inclined elites (some of whom, indeed, may now feel alienated from the West by the impact of the New World Order). Many varied groupings may look toward Western frameworks of human rights, economic liberalization, and democratization to promote their own interests against oppressive regimes.[15]

The significance of the view from the underside as to the effectiveness of sanctions makes it important to identify its dimensions.[16] First, the Western governmental perception of a more peaceful world is rejected. The threat to populations from war, far from decreasing, is seen as having increased, often under the cover of humanitarian interventions carried out by Western powers. During the 1990s there were two major wars in which the armed forces of major Western powers dropped more explosives than in any conflict since the end of World War II. The bombings were conducted, moreover, by planes flying at high altitudes, with little danger to life on the Western side. To the Western powers concerned it was a "virtual war," but to the people below it was real enough.[17] The societies of the states attacked (Iraq and the Yugoslav Federation), and those of some of the surrounding states, felt the full impact of the military force exerted against them.

The sense of insecurity is given substance by the increasing U.S. use of "air strike diplomacy."[18] Initiated during the U.S. bombing of Libya in 1986, it was later used during the Gulf War and then at regular, prolonged intervals against Iraq throughout the 1990s. Sudan and Afghanistan suffered air strikes in August 1998 in the wake of the U.S. embassy bombing in Africa. In the former case the strikes targeted a pharmaceuticals plant alleged to be producing chemical weapons, in the latter alleged terrorist camps. Although it was soon acknowledged that the pharmaceuticals plant was producing nothing other than medicines, no apology for the bombing was issued. Air strikes were also used during the conflicts in Bosnia and Kosovo.

Second, the international position of most non-Western states is perceived as having weakened under the New World Order. During the Cold War, Third World countries could maneuver between the antagonists, leveraging Western fears that they might align with the East to secure enhanced diplomatic or economic support or, conversely, leveraging communist fears to obtain support from the Soviet Union. Since 1990 these countries have not been able to take advantage of this valuable diplomatic and political leverage. Their weakness in the international balance of power has been revealed more starkly than before.

The manner in which the United States has been able to lead the Western alliance has, moreover, left little room for countries outside the alliance to play one Western power off against another. Documentary evidence from the United States provides some backing for this perception. A Pentagon defense planning document, published in the *International Herald Tribune* in 1992, states that the overriding U.S. strategic aim has been to maintain U.S. global dominance by looking after the interests of other advanced industrial countries, "to discourage them from challenging our leadership or seeking to overturn the established political and economic order."[19]

This weakening is seen as the key factor in the so-called new interventionism practiced by the Western powers under U.S. leadership.[20] It has enabled NATO to widen its concerns from Europe to the rest of the world within the framework of the Partnership for Peace program. This new, wider role for NATO has also taken on a nuclear dimension. The policy of offensive counterproliferation, promoted by the United States within NATO in the late 1990s, envisions the use of nuclear weapons against non-NATO countries trying to build chemical, biological, or nuclear weapons if other attempts to prevent them from doing so fails.[21] Whereas the use of nuclear weapons had previously been envisaged purely within the context of fighting wars, such weapons might now be used against countries that were not at war.

This military interventionism is accompanied by an increase in other forms of interventionism. Former U.S. secretary of defense James Schlesinger has acknowledged this trend. In a 1997 issue of *National Interest*, Schlesinger pointed out that during President Bill Clinton's first term in office the United States imposed new unilateral economic sanctions, or threatened legislative action to do so, sixty times in thirty-five countries representing roughly 42 percent of the world's population.[22]

The edge of bitterness at the new U.S./Western interventionism is sharpened by the perception that principles associated with world peace are camouflage for maintaining the power of the United States and its closest allies. In the Arab world, concern focuses on the use of these principles to strengthen Israel relative to its Arab neighbors. Early in 1999, for example, the United States was reportedly intent on taking measures against Middle Eastern and Asian countries believed to be developing weapons of mass destruction (WMDs). A leaked report of the U.S. Central Intelligence Agency identified Egypt, Iran, Iraq, Syria, Libya, and Sudan as Middle Eastern countries suspected of WMD development and needing to be watched, together with India, Pakistan, and North Korea. The omission from the list of Israel, whose WMD development was considerably more advanced than that of any other state listed, was noted by Arab states. It was recalled, furthermore, that whereas considerable pressure had been exerted on all of the Arab states to sign the extension of the Nuclear Non-Proliferation Treaty in 1995, Israel was not asked to participate.[23] But it is not only the United States that gives Israel special treatment on the question of WMDs. When an El-Al airliner crashed into a tenement in Amsterdam in 1998, there was a cover-up by Dutch officials who concealed the fact that the plane was carrying sarin nerve gas and munitions, not flowers and perfumes as was announced.[24]

Third, the United Nations is seen as having become a vehicle for Western interests. The perception is that where the institutions of the United Nations can be exploited to provide legitimacy to Western actions—as with the measures that have been in force against Iraq since 1990—they will be used. Where they cannot be employed for Western purposes, they will be ignored, as when NATO decided to use force in Kosovo. In the latter case, NATO for the first time took major armed action against an independent state—without the support of all five members of the UN Security Council—over government-sponsored repression within a state's internationally recognized borders.[25] Security Council Resolution 1199 had simply referred to the Council as "considering further action" if its demand for an end to armed action by Serbian and Albanian nationalists was ignored. NATO had now become the tool of intervention, "underpinned by whatever UN authority can be achieved to create a sense of an international community consensus."[26] However just or unjust the cause may have been, the action relegated the United Nations to a support role, undermining and distorting its assigned role in the maintenance of international peace and security.

The Arab world has been particularly affected by perceptions that UN structures and resolutions are used selectively for Western purposes. The Security Council resolution (S/RES/687) that has set the framework for the sanctions regime in force on Iraq since 1991 reaffirms the Council's call for a nuclear-free Middle East, yet this matter has never been pursued with the only nuclear power in the Middle East: Israel. The rigidity displayed by the major Western powers in seeking the implementation of Security Council resolutions against Iraq and Libya is contrasted with the U.S. refusal to allow Israel to be subject to serious criticism in any Security Council resolutions.

Fourth, programs of economic liberalization are perceived as bringing more benefit to advanced Western economies than to the countries forced to adopt them. The factors that ensure such policies are adopted in developing countries are multifaceted. Economic failure has opened the way for direct pressures to be exerted by Western governments and conditionality to be imposed by the international financial institutions. Economic consultants from Western countries have come to play a major role in reshaping policies in the countries concerned.[27] The perceived results, seen from the underside, have been the effective destruction of some economies (e.g., in Russia), the widening of the gap between rich and poor nationally and internationally, and a new dependence of the poorer states on the richer. This may be described as the "globalization of world poverty."[28] The point is not simply that economic damage has been done to the economies concerned but that the Western economies have gained from the damage. One example is Russia. Prior to his resignation in February 1999, Russia's general prosecutor, Yuri Skuratov, produced a report documenting the improper transfer of the central bank's currency reserves to accounts in Western countries; some $40 billion of this, he said, had been placed in the accounts of a small company registered in the Channel Islands.[29] The 1998 World Development Indicators report also showed that whereas in 1990 some 14 million people in the transition economies of Europe and Central Asia had been living in poverty (defined as having less than $4 per day to live on), by mid-1998 some 147 million people had fallen into that category—approximately one-third of the population. And rates of adult mortality in the region were worsening, not improving.[30]

Fifth and finally, the manner in which human rights issues have been pursued is perceived as promoting U.S./Western hegemony. It is contended that Western powers have used their influence in international bodies to restrict the implementation of human rights legislation to those issues on which non-Western states are vulnerable[31] while neglecting rights that might impose obligations on Western governments (i.e., the right to development, peace, a healthy environment, and environmental protection—all of which form an integral part of international human rights legislation).[32]

The perception that the United States in particular is in a position to pontificate to others about human rights, moreover, is contested. Comparisons of human rights records, even those produced in the West, where primary attention is given to civil liberties rather than to the wider structures of human rights, do not rank the United States highly.[33] The Observer Human Rights Index of 1998 ranked the United States as the ninety-second worst offender out of a total of 196 states, sandwiched between Haiti and Lesotho. Among affluent states, the United States emerged as the second worst offender.[34]

The negotiation of the treaty establishing the International Criminal Court provides further evidence of U.S. governmental ambivalence toward human rights legislation. At the 160-nation conference, the United States was one of only seven states to vote against the final text of the treaty[35] (a U.S. amendment that would have given U.S. soldiers immunity for prosecution of war crimes had not been adopted). As it was, the document had already been watered down to gain U.S. support (a provision that would have allowed suspects whose governments refused to hand them over to be arrested elsewhere had been dropped, and it had been agreed that countries could exempt their governments and citizens for war crimes for a period of at least seven years from the date they signed the treaty). Despite U.S. objections, however, the court's jurisdiction under the resolution still covered crimes of aggression—a cause championed by the Non-Aligned Movement.[36] European Union humanitarian affairs commissioner Emma Bonino, in a clear reference to U.S. activity during the conference, denounced "activity of pure obstructionism that I am informed is happening."[37]

Sanctions and the Creation of a Stable International Order

The New World Order, therefore, has provided the opportunity for sanctions to be imposed and created conditions for them to prove ineffective. On the one hand, the dynamics of the New World Order are such that leading Western powers have been able to orchestrate the imposition of UN sanctions. On the other hand, negative reactions to the New World Order (i.e., the view from the underside) destroy the international credibility and perceived legitimacy of sanctions. The scene is set for prolonged struggles in which the populations of sanctioned states suffer massively.

The relevance of the global balance of power in this context is further demonstrated by the transformation of attitudes that occurred at the end of the 1980s. Prior to 1990, it was the Third World that espoused giving the United Nations a more central role in the resolution of international conflicts and advocated the use of economic sanctions to maintain international law and human rights. The perception was that problems of minority rule in southern Africa and the Israeli occupation of the West Bank and Gaza could be resolved only by international pressure on the recalcitrant governments concerned, that coordinated economic sanctions could lay the basis for change, and that the appropriate channel was the United Nations. The Western powers responded with skepticism. They maintained that international experience had shown sanctions to be ineffective (often citing the prewar sanctions on Italy in response to its invasion of Abyssinia) and that sanctions would harm populations more than they would the governments. On occasion they contended that sanctions in some situations would contravene the UN Charter by interfering with national sovereignty. Although Third World countries were successful in using the United Nations as a sounding board for attacks on lingering colonialism and minority rule, they were largely unsuccessful in their attempts to impose sanctions. The sanctions imposed on Rhodesia in 1965 were anomalous, insofar as the Rhodesian government did not enjoy international recognition.

Since the end of the Cold War, the roles have reversed. Today Western governments promote the use of the United Nations for imposing sanctions. They purvey these measures as the proper means through which international transgressors can be isolated and controlled. Governments elsewhere look on with concern.

The states at the forefront of Western concern have been described variously in Western governmental circles as "pariah states," "rogue states," and "states of concern." In the United States, "pariah states" was the most usual epithet while Ronald Reagan was president, moving to "rogue states" in the 1990s, then to "states of concern" beginning in mid-2000. Of all these terms, "pariah states" probably reflects most accurately the manner in which the U.S. government views them. Such states were deemed to be playing an international role that was not only disruptive to U.S. interests but was also contrary to the norms and values of the international order. The "pariahs" had to be restricted and contained until domestic political change removed the leadership that had inspired the state's delinquency. The normal patterns of economic and diplomatic relations had to be disrupted, with as many countries as possible drawn into the boycott. Negotiating with them would do no good, as they could not be trusted to abide by international commitments. Perceptions of pariah-hood, therefore, are of direct relevance to the imposition, implementation, and dynamics of sanctions regimes.[38]

The debates over the appropriateness of sanctions as an instrument of international order, as well as debates over the impact that sanctions have on the human and material conditions of populations, will powerfully influence international organization in the years ahead.

Notes

1. The term *pariah*, when used in quotes, indicates that it has been used by others (including governments that have crafted the UN Security Council resolutions imposing sanctions) to describe certain states. Because the term also represents accurately the manner in which the states have been treated, it seemed appropriate to retain the term without intending in any way to justify the validity of its use.

2. Chapter 7, Article 39 of the UN Charter states: "The Security Council shall determine the existence of any threat to the peace, breach of the peace, or act of aggression and shall make recommendations, or decide what measures shall be taken . . . , to maintain or restore international peace and security."

3. Mandatory sanctions were imposed on South Africa in 1977, but these were restricted to the supply of weaponry. Mandatory economic sanctions were imposed on Rhodesia in 1966, but Rhodesia did not enjoy international recognition and was not a member state of the United Nations. A mandatory arms embargo was imposed on Somalia in 1992, but it was aimed primarily at restricting the supply of weapons to warlords rather than bringing about a change in the policies of the Somali government (which itself barely existed at the time).

4. See F. Fukuyama, *The End of History and the Last Man* (Harmondsworth, U.K.: Penguin, 1993).

5. At the start of the 1990s, Algeria, Morocco, Tunisia, Jordan, Egypt, and Yemen all appeared to be moving toward liberal democratic systems. The elections that were held in all of those countries, except for Morocco, at the end of the decade were all judged by external observers to be less free and more government-managed than the elections at the turn of the 1980s/1990s.

6. For a discussion of the spread of liberal democracy, see L. Diamond, "The Globalization of Democracy," in F. Lechner and J. Boli, *The Globalization Reader* (Oxford: Blackwell, 2000), pp. 246–254.

7. See P. Hirst and G. Thompson (eds.), *Globalization in Question* (Cambridge: Polity, 1996), pp. 129–143.

8. See A. Hoogvelt, *Globalisation and the Postcolonial World: The New Political Economy of Development* (London: Macmillan, 1997), p. 134.

9. The International Covenant on Civil and Political Rights (Article 27) had phrased minority rights in negative terms ("minorities shall not be denied the right"), whereas the declaration puts the rights positively: "persons belonging to

national or ethnic, religious and linguistic minorities . . . have the right to enjoy their own culture." See J. Symonides, *Human Rights: New Dimensions and Challenges* (Paris: UNESCO, 1998), p. 89.

10. Ibid., pp. 5–6.

11. This is to some extent a result of media coverage. Of particular importance is the increased ability and willingness of television reporters to convey powerful images of people suffering human rights abuse in different parts of the world. Demands for action against governments mistreating their own populations follow from this.

12. United Nations, S/RES/827, 25 May 1993, and S/RES/955, 8 November 1994, respectively.

13. *Observer*, 19 July 1998.

14. Even some of those Western thinkers held in respect by government circles in the West have emphasized the extent of antagonism to the West—especially the United States—in the non-Western world. Samuel Huntingdon noted that in the eyes of much of the world the United States had become "the rogue superpower . . . the single greatest threat to other societies." Samuel Huntingdon, "The Clash of Civilisations," *Foreign Affairs* 72 (1993): 22–49.

15. An example of the change that has occurred can be seen in the attitudes of communist parties toward external intervention. Before 1990, Western intervention in non-Western countries was consistently condemned. Since 1990, there have been many occasions where some leading elements in communist parties have specifically called on Western governments to help remove oppressive regimes from power. Such calls have been made by some Sudanese and Iraqi communists while also being condemned by others.

16. Although the different arguments are put forward here as one collective critique, we do not suggest that those adhering to the view from the underside are united in all respects. In practice, although the attitude of suspicion toward the Western governments may be held in common, the emphasis placed on—or even agreement with—the different arguments will vary according to the individual and to his/her social, cultural, and geographical environment.

17. A useful discussion of the concept of "virtual war," as seen in the case of the Kosovo conflict, is found in M. Ignatieff, *Virtual War: Kosovo and Beyond* (London: Chatto and Windus, 2000). Ignatieff comments (p. 184): "We now wage wars and few notice or care. War no longer demands the type of physical involvement or moral attention it required over the past two centuries."

18. S. Milne and R. Norton-Taylor, "Airstrike Diplomacy Ups the Odds," *Guardian*, 14 October 1998.

19. *International Herald Tribune*, 9 March 1992.

20. For a discussion of new interventionism with regard to the role of the United Nations, see J. Mayall, *The New Interventionism* (Cambridge: Cambridge University Press, 1996).

21. See *Guardian*, 5 January 1998.

22. Quoted in N. Aruri, "The United States Versus the World," *MidEast Mirror*, 12 March 1998.

23. This view was expounded in the Egyptian newspaper *Al-Ahram* on 16 February 1999.

24. *Guardian*, 22 September 1999.

25. Despite the intervention in Kosovo being aimed at protecting the rights of Kosovar Muslims, a substantial part of opinion within the Muslim world (at least as reflected in Arab newspapers) was critical of the intervention.

26. Milne and Norton-Taylor, "Airstrike Diplomacy."

27. For a comment on this, see M. Haynes, "Bankrupt Advice: American and British Academics Should Take the Blame for Russia's Crisis," *The Times Higher*, 23 October 1998.

28. See M. Chossudovsky, *The Globalisation of World Poverty: Impacts of IMF and World Bank Reforms* (London: Zed Books, 1998).

29. Reported in *Guardian*, 5 February 1999. Over the period when intensive Western advice was being given to Russia to enable its transition to a free market economy, the Russian GDP declined by 13 percent in 1991, 14.5 percent in 1992, 8.7 percent in 1993, 12.6 percent in 1994, 4 percent in 1995, and 6 percent in 1996.

30. World Bank, *World Development Indicators 1998* (Washington, D.C.: World Bank, 1998).

31. This view is frequently expressed in Arab newspapers. See, for example, the critique of the U.S. Freedom from Religious Persecution Act put forward by the Egyptian writer Fahmi Howeidi, in the Saudi newsmagazine *Al-Majalla*, 26 April 1998.

32. Legislation in these spheres is covered in Symonides, *Human Rights*.

33. There has been substantial comment in the Arab world on the Observer Human Rights index. In the week following the publication of the 1998 report, articles discussing the implications of it appeared in a number of Arab newspapers, including the semiofficial Egyptian newspaper *Al-Ahram*.

34. *Observer*, 28 June 1998.

35. For an official European Union view of this, see E. Bonino, "The International Criminal Court: A Step Forward in Moralising International Relations," *The International Spectator* (Rome) 33, no. 3 (July–September 1998): 5–8.

36. *Guardian*, 18 July 1998.

37. *Observer*, 19 July 1998.

38. For further discussion of the ideas and practice underlying U.S. policy on pariah and rogue states, see E. Herring, "Rogue Rage: Can We Prevent Mass Destruction?" *Journal of Strategic Studies* 23, no. 1 (March 2000): 188–212; and N. Chomsky, *Rogue States: The Rule of Force in World Affairs* (London: Pluto, 2000).

PART 1

The Case of Libya

2

Libya's Challenge to the Western Powers, 1969–1992

The imposition of UN sanctions on Libya in 1992 can properly be understood only within the context of the hostile relationship that had grown between Libya and major Western powers over the two decades prior to that. First, we will analyze the dynamics that shaped Libya's foreign relations; then we will describe how Libya, by the mid-1980s, found itself locked into an intense conflict with the United States and, to a lesser extent, other Western powers.

Western observers have tended to regard Libyan foreign policy as erratic, devoid of coherent rationale, and possessed of a tendency to undergo sudden, inexplicable changes of direction.[1] This image, however, does not reflect reality. Libya's foreign policy since the Qaddafi regime came to power in 1969 has in fact been among the most consistent of Arab foreign policies, at least in terms of its underlying thrust and philosophy.[2] The foreign policy can best be described as being shaped by a mind-set rather than by clearly defined objectives. That mind-set, similar to that which inspired many other radical Third World regimes from the late 1950s to the mid-1970s, emphasizes the need for a radical assertion of local interests. It sees the freedom and well-being of Libyans and other Arabs (and, in a wider and perhaps less intense context, Muslims and Africans) as being assured only through radical promotion of their own interests and independence against the outside world. The perception is that the outside world, especially the major Western powers and Israel, will always seek to subvert that freedom and well-being and to harm the interests of Arabs, Muslims, and Africans so as to further their own interests. A preparedness to be confrontational in the defense of Libyan, Arab, Muslim, and African interests, therefore, is integral to this foreign policy mind-set.

Libya differs from typical Third Worldist lines in its preparedness to flout the conventions of international relations and diplomacy in the wider system. The Libyan regime has, at times, been involved in international terrorism, providing support for organizations that strike (whether directly or indirectly) at those who oppose the regime's objectives. The targets of such actions have been the major Western powers, regional governments unsympathetic to the regime's transformationist vision, and Libyan opponents of the regime abroad.

The Libyan foreign policy mind-set is, of course, closely identified with Qaddafi, the central figure in framing Libyan foreign policy since his regime came to power. No major decision is likely to be taken unless specifically approved by him. He has also set the operational style of foreign policy, insofar as he personally deals directly with foreign governments and representatives and articulates the key policy pronouncements.[3]

Qaddafi's ideology blends anti-imperialism, Arab nationalism, and Islamic radicalism. The link between nation and religion constitutes the thread that draws the three elements together, as religion is seen as forming the central element in the definition of national identity—and national identity determines the dynamics of a state's internal coherence and external role.[4] The Palestine issue has been central to Qaddafi's perceptions of Arab identity and Arabism, constituting the pole around which his Arabism has revolved and creating the most urgent need for Arab unity. Qaddafi's attitudes toward other countries, both within and outside the Arab world, have been shaped and conditioned by their official positions on Palestine.[5] The different ideological strands pull in different directions. Anti-imperialism, for example, has run counter to attempts to foster Arab solidarity when other Arab governments are perceived (by Qaddafi) as failing to defend Arab interests effectively against Western machinations.

Libya's preparedness to confront the major Western powers, and its attitude toward Israel, have (not surprisingly) encouraged those states to be confrontational toward Libya. Ever since the mid-1970s, Libya, perceived as a threat to Western interests and Western-purveyed stability in the Middle East and Africa, has found itself subject to Western measures of restriction and retaliation. The Libyan expectations that Western powers are prepared to damage the interests of Arab states in defense of their own interests, therefore, have been realized. Libya has found itself the target of more Western governmental hostility than any other Arab country except Iraq.

Yet relations with other Arab countries have also sometimes been tense. The strength of Qaddafi's commitment to Arab nationalism has complicated and often damaged relations with Arab states. The latter's failure to share his Arab nationalist vision, their unwillingness to join Libya in confronting external powers supporting Israel, and their lack of solidarity with a Libya under pressure all provide the basis for a feeling of betrayal—not just a rational difference of policy. The result can be bitter confrontations, including occasional Libyan support for movements committed to overthrowing other Arab regimes. The strength of Qaddafi's Arabism also explains his turn toward Africa in 1998. His public praise for the preparedness of African countries to resist pressures from Western imperialism is, in part, intended to mobilize Arab opinion against what Qaddafi regards as the supine international position adopted by Arab governments.[6]

The Phases in Libya's Foreign Relations

Notwithstanding the dynamics of confrontation, relations between Libya and the major Western powers and those between Libya and other Arab countries have not been uniformly hostile since 1969. The overall character of these relationships has been affected by three main factors that have conditioned the effects following from Libya's pursuit of its ideological objectives. These are: (1) the changing dynamics of Libya's domestic politics; (2) the policies that major powers (especially major Western powers) have pursued toward Libya; and (3) developments in the regional politics of the Middle East, particularly with respect to Palestine and how other Arab countries (especially Egypt) have handled the issue. We describe each phase in turn below.

Between 1969 and 1973, despite Libya's militant support for anti-imperialist objectives (including the expulsion of the British and U.S. military bases at Wheelus and el-Adam in Libya, support for radical Palestinian groupings and the Irish Republican Army [IRA], and nationalization of some British and U.S. oil interests in Libya), major Western powers sought to cooperate with the new regime for strategic and economic reasons. Strategically, the Western powers noted that the new regime was even more suspicious of and hostile toward the Soviet Union. The hope existed, therefore, that Libya would resist the general trend for Arab radicals to align with the Soviet Union. Economically, despite the nationalization of some Western oil interests in Libya, Western companies saw opportunity in the regime's intensive economic development.[7]

Between late 1973 and 1977, relations between Libya and the Western world, as well as those with some Arab countries, became increasingly antagonistic. Regional developments in the Middle East played the

major role. Qaddafi had initially based his strategy within the Arab world
on a close alliance with Egypt, which included an agreement in August
1972 to move toward a unified state.[8] Egyptian president Anwar Sadat,
however, was beginning to look toward the United States to broker a
peaceful settlement of the Arab-Israeli dispute, and Qaddafi's radicalism
was strongly at variance with Sadat's developing strategy. To Qaddafi's
dismay, he was excluded from the planning and coordination that led up
to the 1973 October War and was sidelined in the negotiations that followed.[9] He would, in any case, have rejected the limited operations that
Sadat envisaged, which were aimed primarily at initiating negotiations
leading to a settlement on the basis of Security Council Resolution 242
(which Libya rejected because it did not recognize Palestinian rights to
statehood). The Libyan government became a strong supporter of the
rejectionists, who saw the path that Sadat had taken as a sellout. Egypt and
those Arab states that supported Sadat's approach found themselves subject to verbal attack and subversion from Tripoli. Given that the United
States was, after 1973, working closely with Sadat in pursuing a step-by-
step approach to an Arab-Israeli settlement, Libyan radicalism was now
viewed as a threat to U.S. interests. Moreover, in 1973 Libya began to
establish stronger links to the Soviet Union. The possibility of the Libyan
regime mobilizing anti-Soviet sentiment within the Arab world was now
discounted.[10]

Between 1977 and 1981, Libya's tense relations with Western and
Arab countries (excepting Egypt) relaxed. Again, regional developments
in the Middle East played the major role. Sadat's visit to Jerusalem in
November 1977 and the subsequent Camp David Accords of September
1978 meant that Libya was no longer regionally isolated in its confrontation with Egypt. Libya participated in unifying Arab ranks, that is, bringing all Arab countries besides Egypt into a common position to oppose
Egypt's bilateral negotiations and settlement with Israel. Libya, now welcomed into the circle of Egyptian critics, had a strong interest in avoiding
confrontation with other Arab states. Relations with the United States
became less antagonistic for different reasons, mainly President Jimmy
Carter's taking office in January 1977. Although Carter came to power
with a human rights agenda that identified Libya as a major transgressor
on human rights and a supporter of international terrorism,[11] Carter's tendency to pursue a problem-solving and, where possible, nonconfronta-
tional approach to international relations ensured that contacts with Libya
remained open. The Libyan government exerted some effort (albeit incon-
sistently) over this period to persuade U.S. policymakers that Libya

should be taken seriously and was committed to working within the framework of international law.[12]

Between 1981 and 1989, Libya was confrontational vis-à-vis much of the international system. Relations with the major Western powers (to varying degrees, depending on the power), several Arab and African countries, and some others (e.g., the Philippines due to the Muslim separatists struggling there) were tense and antagonistic. Critical to this development was the new determination on the part of the administration under U.S. president Ronald Reagan to confront Libya's radicalism and Soviet links. Although this trend in U.S. policy had begun under Carter as a result of the weakening of the U.S. position in the Middle East after the Iranian revolution and the Soviet invasion of Afghanistan, the major change occurred after Reagan took office in January 1981. From the outset President Reagan was intent on curbing what he saw as Libya's destabilizing role in the region and in the wider international system. On the day after his inauguration he presided over a meeting of the National Security Council wherein Libya was a main issue. It was decided that Libya would be challenged and controlled, possibly paving the way for Qaddafi's downfall.[13]

The Libyan reaction to the new U.S. stance itself buttressed the move toward a more intense confrontation. Libya again began supporting radical organizations that used violence (from the IRA[14] to Abu Nidal's organization), and Libya became increasingly hostile toward Arab and African governments that maintained close links with the United States.[15] The trend was encouraged, and to some extent made possible, by the militant role that the revolutionary committees played in Libya and abroad. They inspired Libya's destabilizing international policies and became the instrument through which those policies were carried out. They were also used by the Libyan regime to hunt down and assassinate opponents abroad.[16]

Much of the 1980s, therefore, was spent in open military and diplomatic conflict with the United States. Clashes occurred between the U.S. Navy and Libya's air and sea forces in the Gulf of Sidra, where U.S. insistence on its right to navigate was met by Libya's assertion that these waters fell within its territorial sovereignty.[17] Attempts by European countries to maintain (usually profitable) relationships with Libya were undermined by the combination of U.S. pressure and Libyan militancy. Britain, for example, was able to maintain a strong economic relationship with Libya, and a substantial diplomatic presence there, through 1984. Relations were severed, however, following the shooting of police constable Yvonne Fletcher outside the Libyan people's bureau (i.e., its embassy) in

London, apparently from within the bureau.[18] The European Community (EC) was eventually persuaded to impose diplomatic sanctions on Libya in April 1986 in the wake of U.S. air strikes against Libya.[19]

At the end of the 1980s, domestic developments within Libya, and regional developments in the Middle East, appeared to lay the basis for Libya to establish more settled relations with the Western world and with regional states. Domestically, Qaddafi took measures in 1988 and 1989 to restrain the role of the revolutionary committees.[20] In the international arena, they began to lose the ability to play an independent role. At the regional level there was also change. The end of the Iran-Iraq War, the outbreak of the Palestinian intifada, and the Soviet Union's waning ability to support regional allies created more harmonious inter-Arab relations. Libya followed this trend, establishing cooperative relations with most other Arab governments, including Egypt.

Qaddafi and President Husni Mubarak of Egypt held a conciliatory meeting during the Arab summit meeting at Casablanca in May 1989, and that June Qaddafi described Egypt as "the true mainstay of the Arab peoples." He called on Arabs to give support to Mubarak, whom he described as "an honest and sincere man."[21] In October Qaddafi undertook a successful visit to Egypt, which was followed by a visit to Libya by Mubarak.[22] The latter was intended to allay Western suspicions that Libya was producing chemical weapons at the al-Rabta industrial plant. The intent to cooperate closely with other countries in North Africa was made clear in February 1989, when Libya became a founding member of the new Arab Maghreb Union.[23] The possibility of better relations with the United States was also raised when Qaddafi described the newly elected president, George Bush, as "more prudent and knowledgeable than his predecessor"; he expressed the hope that Reaganite policies against Libya would be reversed.[24] In an interview with the Egyptian magazine al-Musawwar, Qaddafi indicated that Libya would terminate its support for "groups which sought to achieve their aims by using acts of terrorism and that had harmed their cause."[25]

A less confrontational role for Libya within the international system, however, did not come to fruition. Its international relations through the 1990s would be shaped by the bombs that exploded on two international airliners at the end of the 1980s: Pan Am flight 103, which exploded over the Scottish town of Lockerbie on 21 December 1988 with the loss of 270 lives, and that on UTA flight 772, which crashed in Niger on 19 September 1989 with the loss of 179 lives. The finger of suspicion over Lockerbie was first pointed at Libya in October 1990.

Notes

1. This is true not only of the press comment but also of books written by academics and other researchers. For an example of the latter, see B. Davis, *Qaddafi, Terrorism, and the Origins of the U.S. Attack on Libya* (New York: Praeger, 1990). Notable exceptions to this approach, however, are R. St. John, *Qaddafi's World Design* (London: Saqi Books, 1987), and M. ElWarfally, *Imagery and Ideology in U.S. Policy Toward Libya* (Pittsburgh: University of Pittsburgh Press, 1988).

2. A more detailed discussion of the dynamics that have shaped Libyan foreign policy is T. Niblock, "Libyan Foreign Policy," in A. Ehteshami and R. Hinnebusch (eds.), *The Foreign Policies of Middle Eastern States* (Boulder: Lynne Rienner, 2001).

3. The centrality of Qaddafi in Libyan foreign policymaking, however, should not be taken to mean that no other bodies or individuals within the state have a role in making policy. As this writer has contended elsewhere, policy appears to be developed in interaction between Qaddafi and an inner circle of his closest associates, with significant roles also being played by the Liaison Committee of the Revolutionary Committees (which itself is closely linked to the inner circle), and the secretariat for foreign liaison (which would in most other countries be called the ministry of foreign affairs) whose expertise is important in ensuring that policies are effectively implemented. The basic people's congresses and the General People's Congress, although given prominence in the regime's own literature on decisionmaking in the Jamahariya, appear to play no more than a legitimizing role in foreign policy making. See Niblock, "Libyan Foreign Policy."

4. See M. Qaddafi, *The Green Book (Part Three): The Social Basis of the Third Universal Theory* (Tripoli: Public Enterprise for Publishing, n.d.), p. 88.

5. Two weeks after coming to power, Qaddafi gave expression to his views on Arabism and Arab unity and the link with Palestine, in a manner that was to remain constant over the years. He stated: "Arab unity is the decisive historical answer to the challenges of both imperialism and zionism. It is the safe basis and the solid land from which the great masses of the Arab people will surge forward to liberate the holy and emancipate what the enemy has taken from us." "Address Delivered by Col. Muammar Qaddafi, 16 September 1969" (Tripoli: National Cultural Centre, 1969).

6. Observers in the West have tended to portray Qaddafi's denunciations of Arab countries in the second half of 1998 for their failure to uphold Arab nationalist principles as being a totally new element in Libyan foreign policy. Much the same denunciations can be found, however, in statements made by Qaddafi in 1992. The latter statements also envisaged Libya withdrawing support from Arab causes in light of the inadequacy of Arab support for Libya. *Guardian*, 24 June 1992.

7. A useful account of Libya's foreign relations at this time can be found in ElWarfally, *Imagery and Ideology*, pp. 43–51.

8. For the Libyan-Egyptian relationship in the early 1970s, see M. Heikal, *The Road to Ramadan* (London: Collins, 1975), pp. 185–197.

9. Despite this, Libya made a substantial contribution to the Egyptian and Syrian war efforts once the war had started. Heikal estimates the value of the contribution to Egypt as being "no less than $1,000 million." Heikal, *The Road to Ramadan*, p. 197.

10. For an official U.S. account of the changing nature of the relationship in the mid-1970s, see Statement by David Newsom Before the Subcommittee to Investigate Individuals Representing Interests of Foreign Governments, Judiciary Committee, United States Senate, 4 August 1980, *Department of State Bulletin* (October 1980).

11. ElWarfally, *Imagery and Ideology*, pp. 115–135.

12. In early 1978, Libya signed three international conventions on airplane hijacking, and the provision of support for the IRA was discontinued. A number of delegations of prominent U.S. citizens, including the president's brother Billy Carter and mother, Lilian, went on visits to Libya at the invitation of the Libyan government.

13. See *Washington Post*, 14 January 1986; and U.S. Department of State, *Libya Under Qadhafi: A Pattern of Aggression*, Special Report 138 (Washington, D.C.: U.S. Department of State, 1986).

14. *Guardian*, 19 June 1986.

15. An account of these developments can be found in E. Haley, *Qaddafi and the United States Since 1969* (New York: Praeger, 1984).

16. See H. Mattes, "The Rise and Fall of the Revolutionary Committees," in D. Vandewalle (ed.), *Qadhafi's Libya, 1969–1994* (New York: St. Martin's, 1995), pp. 89–112.

17. See Davis, *Qaddafi, Terrorism, and Origins*, ch. 3.

18. See D. Blundy and A. Lycett, *Qaddafi and the Libyan Revolution* (London: Corgi, 1988), pp. 196–202.

19. Under these diplomatic sanctions Libyan diplomatic representation in EC countries was cut, and the representation of EC countries in Libya was reduced to a minimum. See Davis, *Qaddafi, Terrorism, and Origins*, p. 160.

20. See Mattes, "The Rise and Fall," pp. 107–108.

21. See Summary of World Broadcasts, ME/0487 A/4, 20 June 1989.

22. *Guardian*, 17 October 1989.

23. *Guardian*, 17 February 1989.

24. Summary of World Broadcasts, ME/0487 A/5, 20 June 1989.

25. *Al-Musawwar*, 25 October 1989.

3

Unilateral U.S. Sanctions Against Libya

Although UN sanctions were not imposed on Libya until 1992, this was not the beginning. The United States applied its own sanctions to Libya well before that, and some sanctions were applied by European Community countries as well.

Libya's experience with sanctions began in 1973, with measures taken to prohibit certain types of military sales to Libya. The U.S. government blocked the delivery to Libya of eight Lockheed C-130 Hercules planes, which the Libyans had already paid for, and took the decision not to sell to Libya military weapons and equipment that "could add significantly to Libya's military capabilities."[1] These measures were in part a response to Libya's alleged involvement in international terrorism, but they were also linked to the perception that Libya was becoming less accommodating to U.S. interests: The U.S. ambassador had left the country at the end of 1972, frustrated by the refusal of senior members of the regime to see him; and the shares of four U.S. oil companies were nationalized in September 1973.[2] The U.S. reluctance to supply any military-related materials to Libya strengthened following the 1973 October War, reinforced not only by Libya's militancy on the Arab-Israeli issue but also by Libya's growing links to the Soviet Union (an arms agreement was signed at the end of 1974).[3] In January 1975 the United States delayed the sale of a $200 million air-defense system to Libya, confirming in August of that year that the sale would not be made, and refused to allow Libyan air force trainees to enter the United States for training in aircraft maintenance.[4]

Even so, U.S. trade relations with Libya during the 1970s were generally strong. U.S. imports from Libya (almost exclusively oil) grew from

27

$215.8 million in 1973 to $7.8 billion in 1980, such that by the end of the period more than 10 percent of U.S. imported oil came from Libya. U.S. exports to Libya over the same period grew from $103.7 million to $426.2 million.[5]

At the beginning of the 1980s, U.S. policy moved from low-key opposition to determined constraint and restraint. In 1980 President Carter substantially reduced the diplomatic relationship between the two countries, in part a response to changes in the global environment and in part to Libya-specific developments. Soviet military involvement in Afghanistan, South Yemen, and the Horn of Africa, seen in the West as creating an arc of crisis around the all-important oil-producing Gulf area, together with the weakening of the U.S. position in the Middle East as a result of the Iranian revolution, had created a perception in Western capitals that a new Cold War had started—focused very much on the Middle East and its oil resources. This in turn meant that Libya's Soviet ties, which had been growing steadily stronger through the late 1970s, now looked more threatening. Within Libya, the challenge to the United States was highlighted in December 1979 when the U.S. embassy in Tripoli was sacked and burned by some 2,000 demonstrators responding to the siege at the Grand Mosque at Mecca and the burning of the U.S. embassy in Pakistan. There was also concern over alleged Libyan involvement in an attempt to stage an armed uprising in the southern Tunisian city of Gafsa in January 1980 and over reports that Libyan revolutionary committees were launching an assassination campaign against regime opponents overseas. During 1980 the United States withdrew its remaining diplomats in Tripoli and expelled six members of the Libyan people's bureau in Washington. It was made clear, however, that diplomatic relations had not been severed.

From the outset Reagan clearly intended to intensify the pressure. He came to power determined to "implement assertive, forceful policies to reverse the decline in America's position in the world."[6] His particular concern was to ensure that the U.S. weakness shown in Iran—standing on the sidelines while a ruler closely allied to the United States was removed from power and U.S. diplomats were kept hostage—would not be allowed elsewhere. This required taking a tough and uncompromising stand toward states opposing U.S. interests in the region. Libya was of key importance in the new policy, and the policy that emerged saw Qaddafi as "a cancer that had to be removed."[7] A State Department spokesperson said that "overthrowing Col. Qaddafi would be the world's most popular crusade," which was also implied by Reagan when he declined on diplomatic grounds to respond to a question as to whether he would like Qaddafi overthrown.[8] Brian Davis, a writer sympathetic to the Reagan administration, wrote that "the Reagan administration recognized that Libya was not the entire problem but felt that it was the most appropriate place to begin drawing the line."[9]

On 6 May 1981, the U.S. government closed the Libyan people's bureau in Washington, D.C., alleging that the Libyan regime was supporting international terrorism, subverting African governments (especially that of Chad), and operating a hit squad to assassinate Libyan opposition figures in the United States.[10] On the following day, the U.S. government warned its citizens that travel to Libya was hazardous and urged U.S. oil companies to begin an orderly withdrawal from Libya. On 12 June the U.S. administration announced that "the U.S. would support all African nations that want to resist 'interventionism' from Libya."[11] In October the U.S. government formally ordered all U.S. citizens to leave Libya and invalidated U.S. passports for travel to Libya. In March 1982 the U.S. government ordered a ban on all future imports of Libyan oil and, in addition, expanded controls on most U.S. exports to Libya such that all exports except for food and agricultural and medical supplies would require licenses.[12] It was made clear that no licenses would be issued for exports of oil and gas equipment, high-tech equipment deemed sensitive, and weapons and other military items. U.S. imports from Libya declined from $5.5 billion in 1981 to $1.5 billion in 1982, with exports declining from $809 million to $533 million. By 1985 U.S. imports from Libya had fallen to no more than $9 million, exports to less than $200 million.[13]

The U.S. government's perception that Libya was disruptive to U.S. interests and the stability of U.S. allies was accurate between 1981 and 1986. At this time Libya was intent on countering U.S. influence and positions and was prepared to use both conventional diplomatic instruments (such as its substantial financial resources) and instruments outside international law (e.g., the support of groups that would carry out campaigns of violence and assassination) in order to confront the United States and its allies.[14] The confrontation was thus willed by both sides: the United States was eager to strike at a regime that was undermining its influence, and the Libyan regime was eager to confront the growing U.S. involvement and military presence in the Middle East. Furthermore, the Libyan regime by its own admission sought to assassinate prominent Libyans who were opposing the regime from the outside,[15] and the United States beginning in June 1981 was supporting "authorized clandestine political work with Libyan exiles in order to form a legitimate opposition to Qaddafi."[16]

The confrontation intensified through the early 1980s and included clashes between Libyan and U.S. aircraft over the Gulf of Sidra, conflicts between Libya and U.S. allies in the Middle East and Africa (often involving claims that Libya was interfering in the internal affairs of these countries), allegations that Libyan hit squads were seeking to assassinate not only Libyan opponents of the regime but also senior U.S. public figures (including the president) and politicians elsewhere identified as friendly to the United States, and indications that the United States was actively seeking to remove Qaddafi from power.[17] This was followed by a strengthening of existing U.S. sanctions against Libya.

The Intensification of Sanctions and Military Confrontation

The triggers for new U.S. sanctions were the bomb attacks on the Rome and Vienna airports on 27 December 1985; U.S. citizens were among the twenty dead and 110 injured. Responsibility was claimed by the Abu Nidal Palestinian grouping, and subsequent investigations by Italian and Austrian authorities suggested that planning and organization were orchestrated by Abu Nidal from the Syrian-controlled Bekaa Valley in Lebanon.[18] Nonetheless, Abu Nidal had also been in close contact with the Libyan regime, and President Reagan claimed to have "irrefutable evidence" of Libyan complicity in the airport attacks.[19] In a news conference on 7 January, Reagan announced the imposition of economic sanctions, banning U.S.-Libya trade (except for the import of news materials and the export of humanitarian supplies), banning credit on loans to Libyan state-controlled entities, forbidding U.S. citizens to work in Libya, prohibiting economic transactions between U.S. citizens and the Libyan government, freezing all Libyan assets in U.S. banks, and banning transactions related to travel between the two countries (except for those undertaken for journalistic purposes).[20] The possibility of military action, should further acts of terrorism be attributed to Libya, was also raised. On 11 January, Reagan told an interviewer that the withdrawal of U.S. citizens from Libya was necessary so as to "untie our hands with regard to whatever action might be necessary in the future."[21]

Up to this point, other Western powers had not followed the U.S. lead in imposing sanctions or other restrictive measures on Libya. To the annoyance of the U.S. government, indeed, European governments had ignored U.S. diplomatic pressures to move in that direction.[22] This applied even to the British government, despite the close and collaborative friendship between Prime Minister Margaret Thatcher and Reagan and the absence of diplomatic relations between Britain and Libya. Relations between Great Britain and Libya had been broken off in 1984 after the killing of police officer Yvonne Fletcher. Substantial trade between Britain and Libya had continued: Britain remained the third largest exporter to Libya through most of the mid- and late 1980s.[23] Two days after President Reagan's statement of 8 January, Thatcher expressed her opposition to economic sanctions on the grounds that they "don't work" and said that retaliatory strikes against terrorism were against international law and were likely to cause "much greater chaos."[24]

In the spring of 1986 Libya came under increasing pressure as the confrontation with the United States took a decidedly military edge. In the first three months of the year the United States moved parts of the 6th Fleet into the Gulf of Sidra, including three aircraft carriers, twenty-seven accompanying vessels, some 200 airplanes, nuclear-powered attack submarines, and almost 25,000 personnel.[25] In part, the action was intended to reassert the right of the United States to navigate in those waters, but there was also the belief that any military conflict that ensued could be used to weaken Qaddafi. It had been decided that any Libyan attack on U.S. ships would be met with a substantial counterattack against Libyan naval vessels and aircraft. In the event, the Libyan military fired a number of missiles in the direction of U.S. planes overflying the Gulf, and some patrol boats were sent out armed with antiship missiles. The U.S. Navy responded by destroying radar sites on the Libyan mainland and by sinking a number of Libyan patrol boats.

Another terrorist attack on 2 April 1986—the bombing of a Berlin disco frequented by U.S. service personnel—caused the United States to move from sanctions to military action and the European Community to impose some limited sanctions on Libya. The U.S. military action involved air raids on targets within Libya, including Qaddafi's residence in the Azizia barracks in Tripoli. The clear intent was to assassinate the Libyan leader from the air.[26] Qaddafi narrowly avoided injury, but his adopted daughter died in the attack.[27] Although President Reagan referred to there being "incontrovertible evidence" linking Libya to the Berlin bombing, later evidence suggested that Libya may not have been implicated.[28] There were some indications that the incident was in fact the work of a Palestinian group working under the general direction of Syrian intelligence. The expression of U.S. anger at Libya, the belief that the evidence against Libya must indeed be strong, and outrage over an attack being staged on European soil led the European Community, for the first time, to impose its own sanctions on Libya. On 21 April a meeting of foreign ministers of the European Community agreed that all EC member states would reduce the number of Libyans serving therein in official capacities (whether in people's bureaus or for press agencies, airlines, etc.) and would make it more difficult for nondiplomatic Libyans to obtain visas. Trade policy with Libya would also be reviewed, especially with regard to reducing export credits and ending the sale to Libya of subsidized goods from the EC.[29]

For three years following the 1986 bombing of Libya, there were few new allegations of Libyan complicity in terrorism and no new military or economic measures taken by the United States. In the 1990s, however, the United States tightened sanctions against Libya. These were directed at Libya's ability to operate within the international economy. In 1991, the U.S. Treasury Department blacklisted forty-eight businesses that it claimed were controlled by the Libyan government,[30] and in 1992 forty-six additional companies were blacklisted.[31] Economic exchange between U.S. organizations and companies and the blacklisted companies was forbidden. In August 1996, the U.S. Congress adopted the Iran-Libya Sanctions Act (also known as the D'Amato Act, after the senator who guided the legislation through). The act imposed punishment on non-U.S. companies that invested more than $40 million in any one year in the oil and gas sectors of Libya or Iran.[32]

The extent to which the United States was undertaking a sanctions campaign against Libya is evident from two paradoxes regarding the Iran-Libya Sanctions Act. The first paradox was that the United States had in another context strongly opposed the imposition of secondary sanctions of this nature. The Arab League's practice of blacklisting companies that invested substantially in Israel was consistently rejected by the United States as running counter to international law. The second paradox was that Libya found itself subject to the act by accident. The act was initially intended to be concerned solely with Iran. As the act was passing through Congress, however, the question was raised as to why such a measure was not also implemented against Libya. Given the overall U.S. posture against Libya, there was no rationale for not including Libya—which soon found itself subject to the same policy framework imposed against Iran.[33]

Notes

1. See Statement of David Newsom before the Senate Subcommittee.
2. Ibid.
3. ElWarfally, *Imagery and Ideology*, pp. 59–62.
4. Ibid., p. 91.
5. See International Monetary Fund, *Direction of Trade Statistics*, 1970–1980 (Washington, D.C.: IMF, various years).
6. Davis, *Qaddafi, Terrorism, and Origins*, p. 38.

7. This was the reported view of Secretary of State Alexander Haig; see *New York Daily News*, 17 May 1981.

8. ElWarfally, *Imagery and Ideology*, pp. 167–168.

9. Davis, *Qaddafi, Terrorism, and Origins*, p. 39.

10. Ibid., pp. 40–41.

11. Quoted in ElWarfally, *Imagery and Ideology*, p. 168.

12. U.S. Congress, *Congressional Quarterly Weekly Report*, no. 40, 13 March 1982.

13. Figures taken from a U.S. State Department briefing on 2 January 1986; reported in *Guardian*, 3 January 1986.

14. See, e.g., reports of a press conference given by Qaddafi on 31 December 1985, *Washington Post*, 1 January 1986.

15. See Qaddafi's speech to the General People's Congress in March 1985; reported in *The Times*, 11 March 1985. The Libyan opposition has published details of some of the assassination attempts in *Document for the Day of Solidarity with the Libyan People* (no place of publication: Committee for the Day of Solidarity with the Libyan People, June 1983).

16. See Davis, *Qaddafi, Terrorism, and Origins*, p. 41.

17. See ibid., pp. 62–77, and *Observer*, 24 November 1985.

18. Davis, *Qaddafi, Terrorism, and Origins*, pp. 78–81.

19. *Guardian*, 8 January 1986.

20. Ibid.

21. *Observer*, 12 January 1986.

22. The position of the West German government, for example, was that the federal government would envisage action of this kind only within the framework of a coordinated European Community policy. See *Guardian*, 4 January 1986. The European Council of Ministers then rejected collective EC sanctions. *Guardian*, 9 January 1986. The critical need on the part of the United States to bring Europe into the sanctions regime against Libya is indicated by the 1985 trade and revenue statistics for Libya: 90 percent of export earnings were from sales of crude oil, and 80 percent of that oil went to Western Europe.

23. Organization for Economic Cooperation and Development, *Monthly Statistics of Foreign Trade* (Paris: OECD, 1980–1990).

24. *Washington Post*, 11 January 1986.

25. For the developments covered in this paragraph, see Davis, *Qaddafi, Terrorism, and Origins*, pp. 101–110.

26. A well-authenticated report to this effect was written by Seymour Hersh and published in *Sunday Times*, 22 February 1987.

27. *Guardian*, 16 April 1986.

28. An early report of how the West German evidence on the disco bombing in Berlin differed from the U.S. evidence is found in *Observer*, 27 April 1986. Suspicion of complicity in the incident moved back toward Libya in the mid-1990s after evidence emerged of the involvement of a Libyan diplomat in East Berlin in the incident.

29. *Guardian*, 22 April 1986.

30. Economist Intelligence Unit (EIU), *Libya Country Report*, no. 3 (London: EIU, 1991), p. 8.

    31. Economist Intelligence Unit, *Libya Country Report*, no. 3 (London: EIU, 1992), p. 16.
    32. Economist Intelligence Unit, *Libya Country Report*, no. 4 (London: EIU, 1996), pp. 10–12.
    33. *Guardian*, 19 February 1996.

4

Lockerbie and the Imposition of UN Sanctions

For two years following the bombing of Pan Am 103 over Scotland on 21 December 1988, the suspicions of British and U.S. investigators centered on the involvement of radical Palestinians linked to Syria and/or Iran.[1] The first suspicions of Libyan involvement were made public in early October 1990. The detonator that had exploded the bomb (the detonator was hidden inside a Toshiba radio–cassette player) was found to be the same as ten detonators found on two Libyans arrested in Senegal in February 1988. The two Libyans had been carrying the detonators, together with nine kilograms of Semtex plastic explosive, onto an Air Afrique flight from Benin to Abidjan. The Lockerbie detonator and the Samsonite suitcase in which the mechanism had been carried were of the same type used in the bombing of UTA flight 772 over Niger on 19 September 1989. French investigating magistrates were said to have found evidence that the explosives and the detonator for the UTA bombing were taken into the Congo, from where the plane took off, in late August 1989 in the Libyan diplomatic bag.[2] The clothing that had surrounded the bomb was of Maltese origin, and British and U.S. investigators eventually pieced together an account of how the suitcase carrying the bomb originated from Malta, was conveyed on flights from Malta to Frankfurt, and then Frankfurt to London, before being placed on Pan Am 103.[3] The clothes that enclosed the bomb were traced to a shop in Malta, and the son of the shopkeeper claimed to have remembered selling the clothes to two individuals who were later identified as Abdul-Basat al-Magrahi and Khalifa Fheimah.[4] The former had worked at the Libyan Arab Airlines office at Luqa airport in Malta, and the latter was known to work for Libyan security. Of critical importance in giving credence to the account was evidence from a

Libyan defector, Abd al-Majid Giacha. The latter was said to have been a Libyan intelligence officer who had been working as assistant station manager for Libyan Arab Airlines at Luqa airport.[5]

The appearance of the evidence pointing to Libyan officials came at a convenient time for British and U.S. diplomacy. The Iraqi invasion of Kuwait and the subsequent Gulf War left the Western powers badly in need of regional allies. If Western opposition to Saddam Hussein was to be legitimated within the region, it was essential that key regional powers should not oppose it. Iran and Syria, by virtue of their geographical positions as well as their regional weight, were of critical importance in this strategy. As noted above, the first press report indicating that Western suspicions were falling on Libya was published on 10 October.[6] That same week, the United States and Britain were working on the text of a new UN resolution that would permit the use of military force against Iraq.[7] Two days before the report, Western hopes for Arab support against Saddam had been thrown into doubt by developments in Palestine (Israeli forces had opened fire on demonstrators on Temple Mount, with the loss of twenty-one Palestinians).[8] Casting suspicion upon Libya helped the Western powers improve relations with Iran and Syria, ensuring that they would not support Iraq. Paradoxically, Qaddafi himself was highly critical of the Iraqi move into Kuwait but tempered his criticism in light of domestic Libyan support for Iraq.[9]

After completed investigations and simultaneous indictment proceedings in the United States and Britain, an indictment was issued on 27 November 1991 specifically naming the two Libyan suspects. The indictment claimed that between 1 September and 21 December 1988 they had run a shell company known as Medtours from a Malta address as a cover for Libyan intelligence; that during December they had unlawfully acquired luggage tags at Luqa airport and elsewhere in Malta; that on 7 December they had bought clothing at a shop in Sliema, Malta; that on 20 December Magrahi had entered Malta using a false passport and the alias Ahmad Khalifa Abd al-Samad; and that on 21 December they had the suitcase, containing an explosive device concealed in a radio, placed on Air Malta flight KM18 to Frankfurt. The device was, it was alleged, programmed to be detonated by one of the timers obtained from the Swiss firm MEBO AG, and the suitcase had been tagged so that it would be placed on Pan Am flight 103 from Frankfurt to New York via Heathrow. In a statement to the British House of Commons, Foreign Secretary Douglas Hurd said: "This is a mass murder, which is alleged to involve the organs of government of a state."[10] Two weeks prior to the British and U.S. indictments, arrest warrants had been issued in France for four

Libyan officials suspected of involvement in the bombing of UTA flight 772 in September 1989.

The Libyan response to the indictments came in a statement from the secretariat for foreign liaison one day later. The secretariat denied "categorically any Libyan involvement in the mentioned incident or any knowledge by the Libyan authorities of it." It called on the United States and Britain to "resort to the logic of law, wisdom and reason by referring the issue to neutral arbitration panels or the International Court of Justice."[11] This insistence on a legal process outside those of the United States and Britain was to remain the cornerstone of the Libyan position for seven years. On the same day that the Libyan statement was issued, a U.S. spokesperson rejected the possibility of an international body being involved.[12]

On 27 November the United States, Britain, and France issued a tripartite declaration demanding that Libya hand over the two suspects for trial in Scotland or the United States and that Libya satisfy the requirements of French justice over the UTA bombing. The declaration also demanded that Libya "take complete responsibility for the actions of the Libyan officials" and that it "disclose all it knows about the crime...and allow full access to all witnesses, documents and material evidence, including the remaining timers [of the type used in the bomb on the Pan Am flight] and that it pay compensation."[13]

The Libyan government rejected handing over the accused, asserting it would be incompatible with Libyan sovereignty. The tripartite declaration was described as revealing an agenda that was political and not judicial in character, as it demanded the payment of compensation from Libya before the guilt of the accused had been established and without evidence of Libyan state involvement. On 8 December the Libyan secretary for foreign liaison announced that Libyan judicial authorities would undertake their own investigation into the case against the two accused, who had been taken into custody for this purpose.[14] Western judges were invited to discuss the issue with the Libyan judiciary, and Britain and the United States were asked to produce the evidence against the two accused. On 18 January the Libyan government informed the UN Security Council that it was invoking the 1971 Montreal Sabotage Convention in defense of its position.[15] Article 7 of the convention (Libya, the United States, Britain, and France were all signatories) states that "the contracting state in the territory on which the alleged offender is found shall, if it does not extradite him, be obliged, without exception and whether or not the offence was committed in its territory, to submit the case to its competent authorities for the purpose of prosecution."[16] The Libyan government contended that it had, on this basis, carried out its obligations under international law.

Libya also at this stage emphasized its own rejection of international terrorism. In a statement, the secretariat for foreign relations on 15 November reiterated its "condemnation of all forms of terrorism" and expressed "the sympathy of the Libyan people for and solidarity with the families of the victims caused by the destruction of Pan Am flight 103."[17] The British minister of state for foreign affairs, Douglas Hogg, disclosed that Libya had offered to disclose details of its past relationship with the IRA.[18]

Moving to UN Sanctions

Notwithstanding Libya's attempts to justify its refusal to hand over the accused, the United States, Britain, and France brought the issue before the UN Security Council. On 21 January 1992, the council passed Resolution 731, which strongly deplored "the fact that the Libyan Government has not yet responded to the . . . requests to cooperate fully in establishing responsibility for the terrorist acts . . . against Pan Am flight 103 and UTA flight 772" and urged the Libyan government "immediately to provide a full and effective response to those requests so as to contribute to the elimination of international terrorism." The UN Secretary-General was asked to seek the cooperation of the Libyan government to provide a full and effective response.[19]

The Libyan government's initial reaction to Resolution 731 was conveyed to the United Nations at a meeting between the Secretary-General's special envoy, Vasiliy Safronchuk, and Qaddafi on 26 January.[20] At that meeting, Qaddafi stressed Libya's willingness to cooperate in finding those responsible for the Pan Am and UTA bombings but insisted that the case against the two Libyans be handled by Libyan courts. He suggested that the Secretary-General invite judges from the United States, Britain, and France and representatives of relevant international bodies to observe a trial of the accused. He informed the special envoy that the Libyan judges would require further information and requested that the U.S. and British governments provide it. If the latter were dissatisfied with the Libyan judges, he said, then they should send their own judges. After the special envoy returned to UN headquarters in New York, the Libyan representative to the United Nations held direct talks with the UN Secretary-General, and there was some further development in the Libyan position. On 11 February the representative informed the Secretary-General that Libya now accepted the French demands insofar as they conformed with international law and did not infringe on Libyan sovereignty.[21] With regard to the wider aspects of Resolution 731, he said that Libya was ready to cooperate fully with the Security Council in a way that would not infringe on the sovereignty of the state or violate the UN Charter and the principles of international law. Libya believed that a mechanism should be created for the implementation of Resolution 731 and suggested that negotiations be held to set up such a mechanism.

The precise character of the Libyan proposals became clearer after Safronchuk visited Qaddafi on 24 and 27 February.[22] Qaddafi stressed the constitutional obstructions preventing any handover of the accused in the absence of an extradition treaty. The Libyan law that covered such cases had been in force since the 1950s (i.e., under the monarchical regime and subsequently) and specified that Libyan nationals could not be extradited in the absence of an extradition treaty. The obstruction could perhaps be removed if the General People's Congress so decided, but this would need time and proper consideration. Qaddafi raised the possibility of the accused being tried in a third country, suggesting that Malta or an Arab country might be appropriate.

The core of the case that Qaddafi advanced was that the lack of trust between Libya and the United States made it inappropriate to try the case in the United States or Britain, the closest U.S. ally. If there was a general improvement in the relationship between the United States and Libya, he intimated, handing over the two suspects might be possible. There was no objection to handing over the suspects to France, if so requested. Qaddafi also promised his cooperation in putting an end to terrorist activities and gave an assurance that Libya would sever its relations with all groups and organizations that targeted innocent civilians. Although it was premature to discuss the question of compensation, which could only result from a civil court decision, Libya would guarantee the payment of compensation awarded as a result of actions for which its citizens were responsible, if they were themselves unable to pay it. With regard to the French case, Qaddafi confirmed that Libya would agree to the French proposal, such that a French judge should travel to Libya to investigate the case. The French judge would be given a copy of the minutes of the investigation carried out by the Libyan judge.

Two letters addressed to the UN Secretary-General by the Libyan secretary for foreign liaison and international cooperation, dated 27 February and 2 March, introduced additional flexibility in the Libyan position.[23] It was suggested that the UN Secretary-General form a legal committee made up of judges whose probity and impartiality were well-attested in order to ascertain whether the charges made against the two suspects were well-founded. If the charges were shown to be well-founded, then Libya would agree to hand over the suspects to a third party (while stressing that they should not thereafter be handed over to any other party). The UN Secretary-General should "endeavour to provide all legal and judicial guarantees for the conduct of a just and fair trial based on the International Bill of Human Rights and the principles of international law." The letters also affirmed Libya's "outright condemnation" of terrorism in all its forms and offered to provide all the facilities and information that the Secretary-General or his representative might need to ascertain that Libya was not involved in terrorism. The Libyan government undertook "to cooperate in any matter that may put an end to terrorist activities and to sever its relations with all groups and organisations which target innocent civilians."

It would seem that Boutros Boutros-Ghali, the UN Secretary-General, was not unimpressed by the Libyan position. In his report to the Security Council on 3 March, he noted that although Resolution 731 had not been complied with "there has been a certain evolution in the position of the Libyan authorities"; he suggested that "the Security Council may wish to consider this in deciding on its future course of action."[24] The Libyan position also won the support of the Council of the Arab League, which, at a meeting convened on 22 March specially to consider the issue, welcomed Libya's readiness to cooperate with the UN Secretary-General regarding the legal aspects of Resolution 731 in an "impartial inquiry or an impartial or international tribunal." The Arab League urged the UN Security Council to avoid adopting any decision to take economic, military, or diplomatic measures that "might increase the complications and have an adverse impact on the region."[25]

Despite the efforts of Libya and of the Arab League, the Security Council proceeded, on 31 March 1992, to pass a resolution enabling international sanctions to be imposed on Libya. Resolution 748 instructed members of the United Nations to impose a series of measures against Libya beginning 15 April.[26] The measures were mandatory, as the resolution was passed under Chapter 7 of the UN Charter; they were to remain in force until the Libyan government had "complied with requests to cooperate fully in establishing responsibility for terrorist acts against Pan Am flight 103 and UTA flight 772." UN members were required to cut air links with Libya, except those based on humanitarian needs; to prohibit the supply of parts or servicing to Libyan aircraft; to prohibit the provision of arms-related material, advice, or assistance; to significantly reduce the level of Libyan diplomatic representation in their countries; to prevent the operation of all Libyan Arab Airlines offices; and to deny entry to or expel Libyan nationals suspected of involvement in terrorist activities. A committee of the Security Council was established to oversee the implementation and operation of the sanctions. Among other tasks, the committee would "decide upon the approval of humanitarian flights, consider information concerning violations of the resolution and recommend appropriate responses to such violations." The Security Council would review, every 120 days, the measures contained in the resolution. Although no states voted against the resolution in the Security Council, five of the fifteen states represented abstained, including China and most of the African and Asian states on the Council.

It is important to note that the resolution placed no restrictions on the sale of Libyan oil. Any such move would have met with opposition from those European countries that were most dependent on imports of Libyan oil—Italy, Germany, and Spain.

In the absence of any change in the Libyan position during 1992 and 1993, the United States, Britain, and France sponsored a new resolution tightening the sanctions on Libya at the end of 1993. Security Council Resolution 883, passed on 11 November, provided for the freezing of Libyan financial assets abroad and banned the export to Libya of selected equipment for downstream operations in the hydrocarbon sector.[27] The frozen financial assets excluded funds that were derived from the sale of oil, gas, petroleum, and agricultural products, so Libya was still able to export its oil without restriction. Nonetheless, the ban on "selected equipment for downstream operations" raised the possibility that Libya might encounter difficulty in maintaining the level of its oil exports: the ban covered all equipment that was needed for the extraction of oil and its transport to the exporting terminals.

Notes

1. For information on the initial investigations, see *Independent*, 30 October 1989, *Sunday Times*, 3 December 1989, and *The Times*, 1 December 1989. Reports of Iran having instigated the bombing continued long after suspicion had moved to Libya. A senior Iranian security officer, who had defected to the West, was reported by the German magazine *Der Spiegel* in 1997 as having given a detailed account of how the bombing was carried out. See *Der Spiegel*, 7 July 1997.

2. *Guardian*, 11 October 1990.

3. For a critique of the evidence against the two Libyans, see the article by Paul Foot and John Ashton in *Guardian*, 29 July 1995.

4. The shopkeeper had previously identified someone else as having purchased the clothes in question. This was Muhammad Abu Talb, a Palestinian associated with the PFLP–General Command. *Sunday Times*, 3 December 1989.

5. There were reports that Abd al-Majid Giacha was paid $4 million by U.S. authorities for his evidence and then was able to live in the United States under the U.S. federal witness protection program. See C. Flores, *Shadows of Lockerbie* (Malta: Aedam Publishing House, 1997), p. 54.

6. *New York Times*, 10 October 1990.

7. *Guardian*, 5 October 1990.

8. *Guardian*, 9 October 1990. The *Guardian* headline on the following day ran "Arab Anger Threatens Iraq Action," and the text of the article that followed noted that all of the Arab speakers in the Security Council discussions on the Temple Mount killings compared the Israeli occupation of Palestine with the Iraqi occupation of Kuwait. Britain had a further reason at this time for welcoming a shift of blame away from Syria: it was relying on Syrian help to ensure the release of hostage Terry Waite from his incarceration in Lebanon.

9. The divisions within the Libyan leadership over the issue of Iraq's occupation of Kuwait were expressed in the middle of January 1991. On 16 January, Major Abd al-Salaam Jallud called for "infidels to be expelled from the holy land" (Saudi Arabia), and for Muslims to engage in jihad to bring this about. On 17 January, Qaddafi stressed that Libya was on the side of the international community, and on 20 January he gave permission for the Saudi ambassador to broadcast a statement that called on all Libyans to support right and justice and to condemn injustice and aggression. The ambassador's statement accused Saddam Hussein of having an obsession about leading the Arab world—to such an extent that he was prepared to destroy the Arab world. Libyan radio and television initially referred to the Coalition attacks on Iraq as actions by "United Nations forces," which implied the international legitimacy of what was being done. Major Abd al-Salaam Jallud was said to have been a moving force behind mobilizing mass demonstrations on 17 January that demanded the cessation of the bombing of Iraq. Information on these events is taken from *Al-Zahaf al-Akhdar*, 17–21 January 1991.

10. The terms of the indictments can be found in *Guardian*, 15 November 1991. In the foreign secretary's statement to the House of Commons he went to some length to stress that no other country besides Libya was suspected of complicity in the bombings.

11. Jamahaniyyah News Agency (JANA, the Libyan news agency), *Statement of the Secretariat for Foreign Liaison and International Cooperation*, 15 November 1991.

12. *Guardian*, 16 November 1991.

13. *Guardian*, 28 November 1991.

14. JANA, *Libya Denounces Accusations*, 8 December 1991.

15. Flores, *Shadows of Lockerbie*, p. 79.

16. The text is taken from Montreal Sabotage Convention, 1971: Convention for the Suppression of Unlawful Acts against the Safety of Civil Aviation, art. 7.

17. JANA, *Statement from the Secretariat for Foreign Liaison*, 15 December 1991.

18. *Guardian*, 5 December 1991.

19. United Nations, S/RES/731, 21 January 1992.

20. United Nations, *Report on the Libyan Crisis by UN Secretary-General Dr. Boutros Boutros-Ghali*, S/23574, 11 February 1992.

21. The French demands were that Libyan authorities should produce all material evidence in their possession and facilitate access to documents that might be useful for establishing the truth; facilitate contacts and meetings for assembling witnesses; and authorize the responsible Libyan officials to respond to any request made by the examining magistrate. The Libyan authorities were not being asked to hand over any suspects. See United Nations, S/23306, 20 December 1991.

22. United Nations, *Report on the Libyan Crisis*, S/23574.

23. The letters are given in an annex to Boutros Boutros-Ghali's report in ibid.

24. Ibid.

25. League of Arab States, Resolution 5161, 22 March 1992.

26. United Nations, S/RES/748, 31 March 1992.

27. United Nations, S/RES/883, 11 November 1993. Although the decision not to extend sanctions to the export of oil protected the economic interests of Western European countries, the economic interests of Russia were not protected. The freezing of Libyan assets abroad meant that Libya would not be in a position to repay its substantial debts to Russia.

5

The Libyan
Response to Sanctions,
April 1992–July 1998

Libya's policy during the six years that followed the initial imposition of UN sanctions in 1992 was to persevere within the framework of proposals Libya had put forward prior to the sanctions. The government continued to express eagerness to find a framework that would enable a judicial inquiry into the cases against the two Libyans accused of the Lockerbie bombing but stressed that it must be consistent with Libyan and international law. The accused would not be handed over to courts in Britain and the United States. And the willingness to cooperate with the French inquiry into the UTA bombing was repeated.

The proposals were further developed in February 1994 when the Libyan delegate to the Arab League, Ibrahim al-Bishari, proposed that the two suspects should be tried at the International Court of Justice (ICJ) in The Hague under Scottish law before a tribunal of Scottish judges.[1] He stressed that this proposal indicated that Libya was not trying to prevaricate but was intent on a judicial process that respected national sovereignty, one in which there was no political dimension. This proposal was given added weight when the Council of the Arab League, on 27 March 1994, passed a resolution supporting the idea of a trial at the ICJ under Scottish law and called on the UN Security Council to "take this new and constructive proposal into consideration with a view to arriving at a peaceful settlement and avoiding any escalation which might exacerbate tension within the region."[2]

Mobilizing International Opinion

In order to convince the international community of the justice of its case and to escape from the sanctions regime, the Libyan government conducted campaigns at three levels: it tried directly to persuade the Western powers to change their positions; contested the sanctions in international law; and sought to mobilize support in African and Arab countries.[3]

The first level focused on changing the place and nature of the proposed trial of the Lockerbie suspects. Libya initially seems to have believed that by taking actions that would be well regarded in London and Washington the two powers would change their stands on Lockerbie. At the end of 1991, as noted above, Libya had informed Britain that it would be prepared to pass along information on Libya's past connections with, and arms supplies to, the IRA.[4] In response, the British government submitted to Libya a list of questions drawn up by the British security organizations asking for details of the weapons and money supplied to the IRA, the dates of deliveries, and the names of recipients. A foreign office spokesperson in June 1992 said that "if the Libyans provide a full response to the questions we have asked about their links, this would be an indication of good intention and a step toward complying with the UN Security Council resolutions."[5] Meetings were duly held in Cairo and Geneva between British and Libyan officials during 1992, in the presence of a UN undersecretary-general, at which such information was handed over. The British side expressed its appreciation for the information provided, which was described as "positive and helpful,"[6] but did not change its position on sanctions. In June 1993 the Libyan government arranged for a group of 192 Libyans to travel to Jerusalem on pilgrimage, apparently believing that this initiative (with its inevitable acceptance of the practical interaction with Israeli officialdom) would soften opinion in the United States.[7] The U.S. reaction, however, was to see this as further evidence of erratic behavior on the part of the Libyan leadership. The conduct of the pilgrims while they were in Jerusalem—shouting slogans that "called on Muslims from all over the world to contribute to the liberation of Jerusalem, which must be the capital of the Palestinian state"[8]—emphasized the negative perception on the U.S. side.

The campaigns at the second level focused on the International Court of Justice. Failure to bring about any change in the British or U.S. positions led Libya in October 1997 to turn again to the ICJ. On 13 October 1997, Libyan lawyers at The Hague asked the ICJ to pass judgment on the claim that Libya, under the 1971 Montreal Convention, was not obliged to surrender the two accused for trial in Britain or the United States. The Libyan interpretation of the convention was that crimes of "international terrorism" could be tried in the courts of the country of the accused person's nationality. The Libyan side maintained that "the reactions of Britain and the United States after the tragic explosion at Lockerbie are explained by geopolitical and ideological reasons"[9] and repeated an offer by Qaddafi that a trial could be held in a neutral country under Scottish law. Legal advisers for the British and U.S. governments, in response, contended that the ICJ had no jurisdiction on matters that had been determined by the Security Council.[10] The first stage in the ICJ's deliberations, therefore, was to reach a judgment as to whether it had jurisdiction enabling it to hear Libya's claim.

On 27 February 1998, the ICJ ruled that it did indeed have jurisdiction to hear the Libyan claim. Although Britain and the United States dismissed this ruling as a technicality, insofar as the substance of the Libyan case was still to be examined, the judgment did raise the possibility that Libya might find itself buttressed by international legitimacy in its struggle with Britain and the United States.[11]

It is worth noting that Libya, in seeking to use the International Court of Justice to counter British and U.S. demands, was not a novice to ICJ procedures. Indeed, Libya had a record of dealing effectively through the ICJ and of respecting ICJ judgments. The most important case that Libya had pursued through the ICJ was its dispute with Chad concerning sovereignty over the Aouzou Strip on their common border. This was taken to the ICJ by Libya and Chad in 1992, with both sides agreeing to be bound by the ICJ's decision. In 1994 the ICJ decided in Chad's favor, and Libya duly withdrew from the Aouzou Strip and recognized Chad's sovereignty over it.[12]

The campaigns at the third level, aimed at mobilizing support among Arab and African countries, registered steady progress, although more clearly on the African than on the Arab side. As noted above, the Arab League had opposed the imposition of sanctions when they were first imposed in 1992. On 19 April 1993, the Council of the Arab League, meeting in Cairo, proposed that the trial of the two accused should take place either in a neutral country or at the ICJ. This was consistent with the proposals put forward by Libya in 1992.[13] At the meeting of the Arab League Council on 27 March 1994, it urged the UN Security Council to take into consideration the Arab League secretary-general's proposal that the two suspects be tried at the ICJ under Scottish law by Scottish judges.[14] A further resolution on 14 September 1994 gave responsibility to an "Arab committee of seven" to "contact the parties concerned to . . .

accept the new proposals as a basis for settlement of the crisis."[15] Nonetheless, the Arab countries incurred the displeasure of the Libyan government by refusing to break the sanctions.

The Organization of African Unity (OAU) was slower to champion the Libyan case but ultimately pressed its support for Libya further than did the Arab League. Resolutions of the OAU Council in 1993 and 1994 expressed general solidarity with Libya but were not specific as to how the problem should be resolved.[16] Resolution 1566, adopted by the OAU Council on 27 January 1995, called for the trial of the two accused in a neutral country and for the lifting of sanctions. On 4 June 1997 the meeting of OAU heads of state and government suggested three options for bringing the Lockerbie crisis to an end: trying the two accused in a neutral country to be determined by the UN Security Council; holding the trial at the ICJ according to Scottish law and before Scottish judges; or establishing a special criminal tribunal at the ICJ. More significant, however, the meeting marked the beginning of a direct challenge by the OAU to the sanctions regime, raising the possibility that OAU countries might decide to break sanctions unilaterally. The meeting called for lifting sanctions, described as being "imperative as the sanctions are having an increasingly devastating effect on the people of Libya," and warned that "continued imposition of sanctions might lead African countries to devise other means of sparing the Libyan people future suffering." The OAU secretary-general was mandated to "prepare a practical plan of action."[17]

The implicit threat in the 1997 OAU declaration was made specific at the meeting of OAU heads of state and government held on 18 June 1998. The meeting determined that African countries would stop implementing UN sanctions on Libya unless Britain and the United States agreed to trial in a neutral country.[18] Following up this resolution, the OAU Council of Ministers at the end of that month determined that the decision to stop implementing sanctions would take effect beginning 1 September unless the UN Security Council had responded by then to the neutral-country proposal.[19] Some African governments had in fact already started breaking the sanctions before the resolution was passed. The strong stand taken by the OAU seemed likely to encourage the Arab League to move in the same direction. On 19 June, the assistant secretary-general of the Arab League told reporters that "the Arab foreign ministers will consider swift steps toward doing away with the embargo in their next regular meeting."[20]

Western comment on OAU support for Libya has suggested that economic factors were shaping the positions that were adopted.[21] This, however, is not realistic. All African countries had substantially more to gain from their economic relationships with the United States, Britain, and

France. More significant was the long record that Libya had of support for African liberation movements in their struggles against white minority rule in southern Africa. The leaders of these movements were naturally appreciative of Libyan support, and by the 1990s several of these leaders—most prominently Robert Mugabe of Zimbabwe and Nelson Mandela of South Africa—had become the governmental leaders of their countries. It is significant that the 1997 OAU summit, at which the first move to break the sanctions was taken, was held in Zimbabwe.

Notes

1. BBC, *Summary of World Broadcasts*, 26 February 1994.

2. Council of the League of Arab States, Resolution 5373, 27 March 1994. The resolution describes the proposal as being that put forward by the secretary-general of the League, and it would appear that this is indeed where the proposal originated. The outlines of the proposal first began circulating in the international media at the end of 1993. See *Guardian*, 17 January 1994.

3. A Libyan account of the development of foreign policy making, which emphasizes these dimensions, can be found in Dar al-Jamahariya lil-Nashr, *Al-Thawra Libya fi 30 'Ama* [The Revolution in Libya over Thirty Years] (Tripoli: Dar al-Jamahariya lil-Nashr, 1999), pp. 207–248.

4. *Guardian*, 8 June 1992, 10 June 1992, 4 July 1992, and 15 August 1992.

5. *Guardian*, 10 June 1992.

6. *Guardian*, 15 August 1992.

7. *Guardian*, 1 June 1992. The decision to send the pilgrims to Jerusalem appears to have led to an intensification of divisions within the Libyan leadership. There were reports that Major Abd al-Salaam Jallud strongly opposed the move. Since then, Major Jallud appears not to have played any role in the country's leadership. *Al-Hayat*, 23 September 1994.

8. *Guardian*, 2 June 1993.

9. *Guardian*, 18 October 1997.

10. Ibid.

11. *The Times*, 28 February 1998.

12. JANA, *Statement from the Secretariat for Foreign Liaison and International Cooperation*, 10 March 1994.

13. *Al-Hayat*, 20 April 1993.

14. Council of the League of Arab States, Resolution 5373, 27 March 1994.

15. Council of the League of Arab States, Resolution 1082, 14 September 1994.

16. See, e.g., Council of the Organization of African Unity, Resolution 1527, 11 June 1994.

17. Organization of African Unity, Declaration of the 33rd Ordinary Session of the OAU Assembly of Heads of State and Government on the Dispute Between

the Libyan Arab Jamahariya and the United States of America and Great Britain, 4 June 1997.

18. Organization of African Unity, Declaration of the 34th Ordinary Session of the OAU Assembly of Heads of State and Government on the Dispute Between the Libyan Jamahariya and the United States and Great Britain, 18 June 1998.

19. *The Times*, 28 June 1998.

20. *Al-Hayat*, 20 June 1998.

21. Such allegations were made in early July 1998, when Britain, the United States, and France launched a diplomatic campaign warning African countries not to break the sanctions regime on Libya. See *Guardian*, 6 July 1998.

6

The British-U.S. Initiative of July 1998

On 24 August 1998, Britain and the United States put forward new proposals for trying the two Libyans accused of being responsible for bombing the Pan Am flight over Lockerbie. The accused would be judged in a specially convened court in the Netherlands, with three Scottish judges sitting in judgment, and with imprisonment being in Scotland if they were found guilty. The place of trial, though on Dutch soil, would be under temporary Scottish jurisdiction.[1] If acquitted, the accused would not face any other charges arising from any other evidence revealed in the court. The prospect of lifting sanctions was raised as part of the package.[2] The proposals were based on an agreement reached between the British and U.S. governments in early July, the content of which had been given publicity in the press later that month. Announcement of the initiative was delayed pending the formation of a new government in the Netherlands, whose approval was needed.[3]

The similarity of these proposals to those that Libya and the Arab League had put forward since 1992 makes clear the scale of the concession being made by Britain and the United States.[4] British foreign secretary Robin Cook, when putting the proposals forward, pointed out that they amounted to "the very terms which they [the Libyans] have said they would accept. For years Libya has promised that it would accept a court without a jury, meeting in a third country. That way is now open to them."[5]

The Reasons for the Sudden Change

There were a number of reasons why, after rejecting a third-country solution for six years, the British and U.S. governments changed their position. First, sanctions were in danger of becoming unsustainable. With African, and possibly Arab, governments intent on flouting the sanctions unless a third-country trial was agreed to, the sanctions regime might simply fall apart. The moral basis for flouting the sanctions was strengthened by the stand taken by President Mandela of South Africa. At the meeting of Commonwealth heads of state in Edinburgh on 24 October 1997, he asserted that "Britain can not be a judge and jury in the Lockerbie affair and allow justice to be done."[6] Russia and China, together probably with a majority of states on the Security Council, were critical of the inflexibility of the British and U.S. positions and might also be tempted to undermine the sanctions. Moreover, if the ICJ were to rule in Libya's favor with regard to the applicability of the 1971 Montreal Convention, then the legal basis of the British and U.S. positions would be removed.

Second, the sanctions regime had clearly not had its desired effect. Although Libya suffered economically, there was no evidence that the regime had moved toward accepting British and U.S. demands. Indeed, all of the indications were that no such concession was to be expected and that Libya—far from finding itself isolated on the international scene—was gathering support.

Third, the governments felt considerable pressure from representatives of families that had lost relatives in the Lockerbie tragedy (a factor that was particularly important on the British side). Paradoxically, the British Lockerbie families, led by Dr. Jim Swire, who had lost his daughter, Flora, in the Pan Am bombing, had come to adopt a position that was more in harmony with that of Libya. To these families, a trial should be held that (hopefully) would help to establish how the victims had died and who was responsible. The insistence that the trial should be held in Britain or the United States appeared to them as an unnecessary obstacle. Swire had held a number of meetings with Qaddafi and was convinced that he was genuinely intent on finding a solution that would meet the demands of the families.[7] Swire and the British Lockerbie families, moreover, were coordinating their activities with a parliamentary group that had emerged and was intent on pressuring the government to seek a resolution within the third-country framework. Thus the Lockerbie Justice Group, which gave formal expression to the established cooperation between Swire and some parliamentarians, was established in the summer of 1998.[8]

The change of government in Britain in May 1997 was also significant. Although the new Labour government was no more favorable to the
Libyan regime, there was less feeling that past positions had to be maintained. The new government was at least prepared to consider a change in
position, with the representatives of the Lockerbie families being invited
to Downing Street for a meeting. Former prime minister John Major had
taken a strong personal stand against any weakening in the government's
stand.[9] The new prime minister, Tony Blair, told reporters after the proposals had been announced that he "felt particularly for the relatives of
those killed in the bombing" and that "it was important for them to have
the possibility . . . of having those people brought to justice because it is
part of their continuing anguish."[10]

Although the British and U.S. proposals can be seen as testimony to
Libya's achievement, they also constituted a diplomatic achievement for
the British government. Just over three months before the British-U.S.
proposals were issued, U.S. president Bill Clinton had stated that the United States would never accept a third-country trial for the Lockerbie
accused. Intense British diplomatic effort was needed in order for this
position to be changed—and this effort was to continue in the period subsequent to the proposals, when the British Foreign and Commonwealth
Office had to convince the U.S. State Department of the appropriateness
of every assurance it gave to the Libyan side. Whereas the British Lockerbie families were supportive of a third-country solution, U.S. families
were not—and they were in support of their government retaining an
intransigent stand.

Notes

1. *The Times*, 25 August 1998.
2. This was made formal by Security Council Resolution 1127, which stated
that the sanctions would be suspended once Libya had handed over the two
accused. United Nations, S/RES/1127, 27 August 1998.
3. *Guardian*, 21 July 1998.
4. The British government in January 1994 had specifically rejected the possibility of holding a trial of the two Libyans in the Netherlands with Scottish
judges and using Scottish judicial procedures. The proposal at this stage, however, was that the trial would come under the International Court of Justice. *Scotland
on Sunday*, 16 January 1994.
5. *Guardian*, 25 August 1998.
6. *The Times*, 25 October 1997.
7. Swire gave a number of interviews over the years expressing this position.
See, e.g., *Guardian*, 2 May 1998.

8. *Newsletter of the British-Libyan Business Group*, 27 August 1998. The principal parliamentarians in the grouping were Lord Steel (Liberal), Sir Teddy Taylor (Conservative), Tam Dalyell (Labor), and Roseanna Cunningham (Scottish Nationalist). Whereas the first three were acting in an individual capacity, Cunningham was representing the position of her party.

9. The view that John Major was particularly strongly opposed to any change in the British-U.S. position, more so than his foreign secretary, Douglas Hurd, has been expressed to the writer by members of the Lockerbie Justice Group.

10. *Independent*, 29 August 1998.

7

Toward the Libyan Handover of the Accused, August 1998–April 1999

One day after the British-U.S. proposals were officially put forward, Libyan authorities formally accepted them. The secretariat for foreign liaison issued a statement announcing "acceptance of the new position of the United Kingdom and the United States."[1] The following day, Qaddafi, in an interview on CNN, confirmed this while making it clear that there needed to be agreement concerning procedures before the two accused were handed over. He cast some doubt on whether Britain and the United States were serious in their new initiative, suggesting that they might be intending to trick Libya. He stated: "More details have to be given. . . . You cannot say 'Give us these two people quickly'; they are not tins of fruit. They are human beings."[2] He raised, in particular, the issues of what would happen to the accused following either conviction or acquittal, the conditions under which they would be held, and possible procedures for appeal.

Negotiating the Procedures

In the months that followed, the two sides engaged in indirect contacts geared toward bringing about the trial. The British-U.S. position was that negotiating with Libya was not appropriate: The substance of the proposals was not negotiable, and there could be no question of further concessions. This position was underpinned in practice by the dynamics of the relationship between Britain and the United States and the manner in which they had agreed to the proposals going forward. Effectively Britain had persuaded the United States, against considerable resistance, to permit the new initiative to proceed. The United States had eventually agreed and had accepted that the British government would take the lead in carrying the matter forward—provided that further developments did not go outside the framework. One element was that there should be no direct contacts between the Libyan and British governments. The main channel for any communications would be the Secretary-General of the United Nations.[3]

Libya's position was that the proposals constituted a significant step forward but that further negotiations were needed. Britain and the United States had at last accepted the principle of a third-country trial, and Libya now needed to be assured of the details. It was not fair to expect the Libyan side to accept the proposals unconditionally, that is, without any assurance that procedures were fair and that the trial would be free of political prejudice. Libya suspected that Britain and the United States may have planned a political trick and that their real agenda would emerge once the two accused were handed over.[4]

In practice, the dealings leading up to the handover of the accused were indirect negotiations, carried out formally through the office of the UN Secretary-General. This channel was reinforced by contacts through individuals and governments that had access to both sides, most prominently South Africa, Saudi Arabia, and their representatives. In short, Libya sought clarifications and elaborations as to the proposals, and the British government (after consulting with the U.S. government) provided a series of assurances. The latter were intended, where possible, to meet Libyan concerns and to reassure Libya that no political tricks would be attempted.[5] The Libyan concerns were initially made explicit through a letter to the UN Secretary-General in early September 1998 containing twelve issues that were in need of clarification and elaboration. These were developed further by Libyan lawyers during meetings at UN Headquarters in New York on 4 October 1998.[6] The initial British assurances, in response, were conveyed through the UN later that month.[7] When the Libyan side sought more detail on some of the assurances, further assurances were given.

By the end of 1998, assurances had covered five major areas of concern. The first was the place of trial. In mid-September 1998, Britain and the Netherlands had signed an agreement enabling the trial to be held at Camp Zeist, part of Soesterberg Air Base between The Hague and Utrecht.[8] Libyan authorities stated that this raised suspicions that Britain and the United States were not genuinely intent on an independent and objective trial. The location, the Libyan side maintained, had been a U.S. air base, and the U.S. Air Force still had rights to use the base. This suggested that the location was a place of transit from which the accused could be flown to either the United States or Britain without the government of the Netherlands being able to prevent it. The British government's response was that this was a misunderstanding. Although the proposed site had indeed constituted part of a NATO air base, the area no longer had a NATO presence. The proposed site, in any case, was situated in buildings that had not been used for military purposes: a school and hospital that were used by the families of service personnel. There was indeed an airstrip in the vicinity, but this and the area surrounding it were all under Dutch government control. Britain and the United States would not be able to take action by themselves, as that would infringe Dutch sovereignty. The site had been chosen simply because the buildings were vacant, they occupied sufficient space for the purpose, and they could easily be equipped to provide the security needed for the trial.[9]

The second area of concern related to the conditions under which the accused would be held. The British government gave assurances that the families of the accused would be able to visit them during the trial and that the defense would be able to summon any witness to give evidence—including British and U.S. officials.[10]

The third area of concern was the link between the trial and the lifting of UN sanctions against Libya. Libyan authorities wanted assurance that its agreement to the proposals would be followed by the lifting of UN sanctions.[11] The British government's assurance, in keeping with the decision that had already been taken by the UN Security Council, was that sanctions would be suspended immediately after the accused were handed over to Dutch control. It was pointed out informally that the decision of the Security Council to suspend sanctions was in practice little different from withdrawing them completely. Any decision to reimpose sanctions would require the support of the Security Council, and it would be difficult to imagine that Russia and China—known to be highly antipathetic to the continuation of the sanctions regime—would not impose their vetoes to prevent such a decision being made. In response to continuing Libyan pressure for the sanctions to be formally withdrawn, the British side argued that this was not in the hands of Britain and the United States alone. The resolutions were also tied to the UTA bombing and to the wider issue of Libya's support for international terrorism and, thus, out of British and U.S. hands. The only acceptable procedure was for the matter to be brought before the Security Council within the framework of a report presented by the Secretary-General, which would be submitted within three months of the handover. The British government would play a "not unhelpful" role in ensuring that the formal withdrawal of sanctions was agreed.[12]

The fourth area of concern—perhaps the most crucial of all—was that the trial would become political, that it would turn into an attack on the whole Libyan system. To deal with this concern, the British government gave assurances that the British and U.S. governments saw the trial simply as a criminal justice trial involving two individuals; that they were not seeking to inculpate anyone other than the two accused; that the prosecution did not "at present" intend to call any witnesses from Libya; that if any witnesses were called from Libya they would be given immunity from arrest for any offenses committed in the past; and that the British and U.S. governments were not pursuing any hidden political agenda through the trial.[13]

The fifth area of concern was tied to events should the accused be found guilty. Libya's initial position was that imprisonment take place in Libya, possibly under UN supervision. This was later changed to include an acceptance that imprisonment could be in the Netherlands. For Libya, the arguments against imprisonment in Scotland were the same arguments for not holding the trial in Britain or the United States: the two governments could not be trusted to treat it as an objective matter of justice but would use it to political ends. In the case of imprisonment, the prisoners would become tools in the political campaign waged by the two governments against Libya. To meet these concerns, the British government gave the Libyan side the following assurances: The prisoners would not be interrogated by British security or police forces during their imprisonment; no security or police forces of any other country would be allowed to interrogate them; no inducement would be given to encourage the prisoners to provide any information; the place of imprisonment would be made open to inspection by such international bodies as were desired by the Libyan side and also by Libyan diplomatic officials (with visits taking place as often as desired); a Libyan consulate would be opened in Scotland so as to enable close contact with the prisoners to be maintained; the prisoners would be given humane conditions with regard to family visits, appropriate diet, prayer facilities, and the like; and there would be no extradition of the prisoners to the United States.[14]

By the end of January 1999, the main assurances that the British government felt able to give had been transmitted. Libya remained dissatisfied over Britain's failure to agree to imprisonment in Libya or the Netherlands, but there were indications that this would not impede a final agreement. The problem that remained was that Qaddafi, although acknowledging that the British side had covered the issues on which Libya had concerns, cast doubt on the trustworthiness of the assurances themselves. This was a reflection of the almost total lack of trust between Libya and the two powers. To the British and Americans, the Libyan side was devious, unreliable, and mendacious: it was seeking to escape from sanctions without fulfilling the requirements set by the United Nations. To the Libyans, the British and Americans were using the framework of UN resolutions to undermine and if possible destroy the Libyan regime: they would seek any pretext to forward their aims. Qaddafi pointed out in an interview with this writer that it was difficult to have trust in the British government when he was given no opportunity to meet British ministers face-to-face and establish a feeling of trust. He was convinced that Britain was not sincere about bringing the crisis to an end and was still intent on changing the regime, whether through his own assassination or through the gradual undermining of the system.[15] To the British side, this was simply an attempt to establish a direct diplomatic relationship with Britain without agreeing first to the conditions that Britain had placed on such a relationship: acceptance of the requirements of the relevant Security Council resolutions in their entirety.

The problem of mistrust was ultimately overcome through the use of intermediaries who were held in trust by both sides. The intermediaries added virtually nothing to the content of the assurances, although one final concession from the British-U.S. side—that UN observers could be stationed permanently in the place of imprisonment if the accused were found guilty—seems to have been left in the hands of the intermediaries to convey. But their credibility with Libyan authorities enabled Qaddafi and those around him to have the confidence in the British assurances that was necessary for the handover to proceed. The key intermediary was President Mandela, directly during his visits to Libya in October 1998 and March 1999, or indirectly through the head of his office, Professor Jakes Gerwell. Also of importance was Prince Bandar bin Sultan, the Saudi ambassador in Washington, who joined Gerwell on some of his visits to Libya. However, there were others who enjoyed the respect of Qaddafi and whose persuasion helped to convince him that the handover was indeed in Libya's interest. Jim Swire, representing the British Lockerbie families, was of particular importance in this regard. He retained contact with Qaddafi by letter and used his influence to encourage acceptance of the British-U.S. proposals.

The accused were flown to the Netherlands on a UN plane on 5 April 1999 and duly placed under arrest.

Notes

1. *Guardian*, 27 August 1998.

2. Reported in *Independent*, 29 August 1998.

3. This information is drawn from the writer's interviews with the Foreign and Commonwealth Office in December 1998 and January 1999.

4. This was Qaddafi's position as put to this writer in an interview in November 1998.

5. British foreign secretary Robin Cook on 25 October assured the Libyans that "our objective is to do justice in terms of a trial of two people who have been accused of mass murder. We are not in any sense seeking to stage some kind of political theatre here." Reported in *Guardian*, 26 October 1998.

6. *Guardian*, 5 October 1998.

7. *Guardian*, 26 October 1998.

8. *Newsletter of the British Libyan Business Group*, 25 September 1999.

9. Information from interviews with British and Libyan officials while the contacts were under way, December 1998 and January 1999.

10. Ibid.

11. It should be noted that Libya was not asking for the removal of U.S. sanctions against Libya, which were more extensive than the UN sanctions. The concern was only with the latter.

12. Information from interviews with British and Libyan officials while the contacts were under way, December 1998 and January 1999.

13. Ibid.

14. Ibid.

15. Interview with Qaddafi, November 1998.

8

The Economic Impact of Sanctions

The three chapters that follow cover the economic, social, and political impacts that sanctions have had on Libya. Accurately estimating the economic impact, which underlies the social and political impacts, is not easy. The greatest problem is attempting to separate out the effects of the sanctions from developments that might have occurred if sanctions were not in place. Moreover, although our concern here is the impact of sanctions imposed by the United Nations, the United States was applying comprehensive economic sanctions against Libya prior to 1992—making it even more difficult to assess the effects of sanctions imposed in 1992 and 1993. Nonetheless, we will consider a range of evidence from different sources, official and nonofficial.

This chapter will focus on the macroeconomic effects of sanctions on Libya. The social impacts of the sanctions and their economic effect on the Libyan people will be covered in Chapter 9.

Characteristics of the Libyan Economy Prior to 1992

This analysis must be set within the framework of the characteristics of the Libyan economy prior to 1992.

Ever since it began in the 1950s, oil production and its export have shaped the development of Libya's economy. Oil production reached a peak of 3.3 million barrels per day in 1970, gradually declining through the remainder of the 1970s, falling to around 1 million barrels per day through most of the 1980s.[1] This decline in production was intentional:

Table 8.1   Government Expenditures, 1981–1988 (in millions of Libyan dinar)[a]

	1981	1982	1983	1984	1985	1986	1987	1988
Admin. budget	1,095	1,255	1,520	1,440	1,200	1.360	1,240	1,243
Devel. budget	2,740	2,600	2,370	2,110	1,700	1,700	1,450	1,355

Source: Central Bank of Libya, *Annual Reports*, 1981–1989.

Note: a. From 1973 to March 1986, the Libyan dinar was pegged to the dollar at a rate of LD1 = $3.38. In 1986 this was abandoned in favor of a peg to Special Drawing Rights, with 47 percent fluctuation bands on either side of the central rate. In practice the rate remained between LD1 = $3.0 and LD1 = $3.38 for the remainder of the period up to 1992. Thereafter, there were a number of small devaluations that took it from LD1 = $2.8 in 1992 to LD1 = $2.58 in 1998. The black-market rate for the dinar was to diverge sharply from the official rate during the 1990s.

with sharply rising oil prices during the 1970s, the revenues coming from oil production had risen sharply, and the Libyan state adopted a conservationist policy aimed at saving the country's oil resources for the long term. A peak in oil revenues was reached in 1980, when Libyan oil exports brought in some $21 billion. During the remainder of the 1980s, the falling price of oil and the quota limitations imposed on oil exports through OPEC agreements (which Libya scrupulously respected) led to a sharp drop in revenues—such that oil exports were earning Libya only some $6 billion per annum in the latter part of the decade.[2] Throughout this period, oil accounted for more than 95 percent of exports.

Libya also has substantial gas reserves, but most of the production in this field has been for Libya's own use rather than export: some 75 percent of production has been consumed locally, mainly for industrial purposes. Gas production reached a peak of some 23.5 billion square meters per annum in 1979, falling to 12–13 billion per annum through most of the 1980s.[3]

Government expenditures were, not surprisingly, tied closely to the revenues coming from oil production. The funding of the development budget came almost exclusively from that source, and the major part of the administrative budget came from taxes and profits from activities that oil-generated developments had brought into being. The mid-1980s saw a steady decline in government expenditures, especially in the development budget (see Table 8.1).

Throughout the 1980s there was a relatively high level of expenditures for defense and for supporting international activities. It is, however, difficult to accurately estimate these expenditures, as figures for allocations to the armed forces were not made public after 1984, and support for foreign organizations would appear to have been subsumed under a general "miscellaneous" category. In 1984, expenditures on the armed forces came to LD340 million (dinar), constituting some 48 percent of the allocations for central government expenditures in the administrative budget (a total of LD709.2 million, with the remaining LD731 million in the administrative budget being allocated for municipal expenditures). The allocations for miscellaneous expenditures in 1984 came to LD58 million, and the allocations for the foreign liaison secretariat came to LD22 million.[4]

Despite the heavy defense expenditures, substantial expenditures on agricultural, industrial, and infrastructure development did continue through the 1980s. Through the mid- to late 1980s, some 20 percent of the development budget was going into industrial development, with about 13 percent going to agricultural development, 13 percent to communications, 10 percent to utilities, 9 percent to electricity, 9 percent to housing, 7 percent to education, and 3 percent to health. The impact of the industrial and agricultural investments, however, was relatively limited. During the 1970s and 1980s, the share of agriculture in Libya's gross domestic product grew from 2.6 percent in 1970 to roughly 6 percent at the end of the 1980s, and the share of industry over this same period grew from 1.7 percent to roughly 10 percent.[5]

Over most of the 1970s and 1980s, the public sector proportion of the economy grew steadily as the private sector proportion shrunk (see Table 8.2). By the mid-1980s, virtually all manufacturing, foreign trade, banking, and insurance, together with most agricultural production and domestic trade, was in the public sector. From 1987 onward, however, there began a gradual liberalization of the economy. On 27 March 1987, Qaddafi presented to the General People's Congress a plan for liberalizing the economy, acknowledging that the existing economic structure was not providing the population with the goods it wanted and that there was discontent among farmers at the prices paid by the municipally controlled purchasing organizations.[6] During the two years that followed, the state monopoly on the import and export trade was lifted, regulations restricting privately owned retail trade were lifted, the *suq* (market) areas of the cities were reopened, some of the smaller state industrial undertakings were handed over to self-managing cooperatives (wherein the management controlled the operation of the plant, but the workers were also members of the cooperative), and private companies could be started (although they were not permitted formally to employ labor).[7] By the end of 1991 some 10,223 *tasharikat* (self-managing cooperatives) were in existence.[8] The impact of these changes was that the availability of consumer goods for the population improved, but the balance of public as against private sector econom-

Table 8.2   Comparison of Public and Private Sector Investment, 1970–1997 (percentages)

	Public	Private
1970–1972	69.1	30.9
1973–1975	79.1	20.9
1976–1980	87.2	12.8
1981–1985	91.7	8.3
1986–1990	90.2	9.8
1991–1997	75.4	24.6

Source: Dar al-Jamahariya lil-Nashr, *Al-Thawra Libya fi 30 'Ama* (Tripoli: Dar al-Jamahariya lil-Nashr, 1999), p. 255.

ic activity was not substantially changed. The major change occurred after, and as a result of, the imposition of UN economic sanctions.

Structure and Development of the Economy After the Imposition of UN Sanctions, 1992

An official assessment of the economic impact of sanctions on Libya, prepared under the auspices of the Libyan secretariat for foreign liaison at the beginning of 1998, put the cost at about $24 billion.[9] An Arab League report, prepared in mid-1998 and covering the period up to the end of 1996, put the figure at $23.5 billion. The main areas of loss, according to the latter report, were the energy sector ($5 billion), the commercial sector ($5.8 billion), the industrial sector ($5.1 billion), the transportation and communications sectors ($2.5 billion), and the agricultural sector ($337 million).[10] Although these figures may represent accurate estimates of the scale of damage done, they will not be used here to evaluate the economic impact of sanctions. The real effects have been more complex and nuanced and cannot be conveyed by simple monetary figures.

Since 1992, a central element of the Libyan economic strategy has been to ensure that the all-important oil industry continues to produce and to export oil at the level of Libya's quota under OPEC. Priority has also been given to ensuring that the major infrastructure project, the Great Man-Made River, continues and that basic supplies continue to be made available to the population. This strategy has been broadly successful: the core of the Libyan economy, therefore, remained intact throughout the sanctions period.

There is, however, a paradox about the impact of sanctions. Although it can (and will) be shown that the core of the Libyan economy continued

Table 8.3   Libyan Oil Production and Oil Exports, 1980–1998

Year	Crude oil production (in millions of barrels)	Crude oil exports (in millions of barrels)
1980	1.827	1.765
1981	1.109	1.125
1982	1.017	1.052
1983	1.030	1.016
1984	0.957	0.990
1985	1.024	0.885
1986	1.034	0.750
1987	0.973	0.770
1988	1.030	0.836
1989	1.101	0.940
1990	1.372	1.265
1991	1.483	1.410
1992	1.400	1.302
1993	1.361	1.227
1994	1.390	1.130
1995	1.399	1.105
1996	1.394	1.072
1997	1.395	n.a.
1998	1.385	n.a.

Source: Production figures are taken from Dar al-Jamahariya lil-Nashr, *Al-Thawra Libya fi 30 'Ama* (Tripoli: Dar al-Jamahariya lil-Nashr, 1999), p. 343. Export figures are taken from National Corporation for Information and Documentation, *Statistical Yearbook 1998* (Tripoli: NCID, 1998), p. 29, and from earlier issues of the same yearbook.

to operate after sanctions much as it had before 1992, it can also be shown that the living conditions of the Libyan population deteriorated sharply after sanctions were imposed. This section will seek to explain this paradox: how and why the Libyan population has been so negatively affected by sanctions when the central core of the economy has survived without major damage.

The figures for Libyan oil production indicate the success that Libyan authorities achieved in maintaining this key sector. The sanctions did not forbid the sale of oil, but the 1993 measures did ban the export to Libya of equipment that could be used for extracting oil and transporting it to export terminals. Oil production might also have been damaged by the freezing of Libyan assets abroad, as the Libyan state faced difficulties in investing in the development of the oil sector. However, Libya was producing and exporting more oil in the mid-1990s than it had been in the 1980s (see Table 8.3). The major changes in Libyan oil production were caused by variations in the OPEC quota, not by production difficulties on the Libyan side. In March 1983, OPEC set a production limit for Libya at 1.1 million barrels per day, which remained in force for most of the period through to 1993, when it was raised to 1.39 million barrels per day. In 1997 it was raised further to 1.52 million barrels per day.[11] Therefore, only in 1997 and 1998 was there any shortfall on the OPEC quota, and the shortfall was not expected to last: the development of the Murzuq field would enable Libya to reach its quota.[12] Gas production followed a pattern similar to that of oil, maintaining a production level of 12–13 billion square meters per annum through most of the 1980s, rising to some 15 billion square meters per annum through most of the 1990s.[13]

Despite the success of the Libyan state in maintaining production and exports, oil revenues declined. This, however, was due to global developments in the oil market and did not reflect any problems specific to Libya. The oil price fell in the early 1990s and did not recover fully until 1997. The OPEC meeting in July 1990 (held shortly before the Iraqi occupation of Kuwait, which brought considerable turbulence to the oil market) set the reference price for oil at $21 per barrel, but by June 1993 this had dropped to less than $18 per barrel. In practice the average import price for Organization for Economic Cooperation and Development (OECD) oil fluctuated between $13 and $16 per barrel during the 1993–1995 period, before reaching $20 per barrel again in late 1996.[14] Libya would therefore have received lower revenues from its oil exports than it had received at the beginning of the decade. The secrecy in regard to figures on oil income since the imposition of sanctions, however, makes it impossible to provide realistic estimates on the decline in revenue.[15]

Another aspect of success in protecting the core economy was in ensuring that no significant part of Libya's foreign assets were frozen following the passage of the 1993 sanctions measures. Anticipating the UN resolution, Libyan authorities moved their liquid assets (some $3 billion) into safe havens in mid- to late 1993. Statistics from the Bank of International Settlements indicate that Libya's assets in OECD-based banks declined from $4.428 billion to $1.611 billion between March and December 1993.[16] The funds that remained in OECD banks could be identified as stemming directly from the sale of Libyan oil, and Libya retained access to these funds under the UN sanctions. The money that had been moved was transferred to institutions that were outside the purview of UN sanctions. Libya's holdings in OECD-based banks increased again after 1993, but this stemmed from the establishment of special bank accounts to receive payments for Libyan oil. By 1996, Libya's assets with OECD-based banks had risen to $5.688 billion, all of which was outside the scope of UN sanctions.[17] Other measures were taken to change the ownership structure of some Libyan-owned companies in Europe to ensure that they did not run afoul of the sanctions regime.

Libyan authorities were also successful in carrying forward the Great Man-Made River, the major infrastructure project of the 1980s and 1990s.[18] Feasibility studies on the project had been initiated in 1974, and the decision to go forward was taken by the General People's Congress in October 1983.[19] The objective was to bring supplies of freshwater from southeast Libya to coastal regions in the east, and from the central-western region to coastal regions in the west. The first phase of the project, bringing freshwater to Benghazi and Sirte, was completed on schedule in 1994, and the major part of the second phase, bringing freshwater to Tripoli, was completed on schedule in 1996. One element envisaged for the second phase, a pipeline to supply water for agricultural purposes to Kufra in the south, was postponed until the third phase. An agreement for proceeding to the third phase was reached in 1996 with the South Korean construction firm Dong Ah Consortium, which had also been responsible for the first two phases. The third phase involved linking up the eastern and western water systems through a pipeline between Sirte and Tripoli; building a pipeline linking Tobruk and Ajdabiyah that would enable water to reach the extreme east of Libya's coastal region; and proceeding with the postponed pipeline to Kufra. Construction on these pipelines began in 1997, and the work is due to be finished in 2005.[20] The first two phases involved expenditures of some $25 billion; the last phase was expected to cost a further $5.1 billion.[21]

Three factors explain Libyans' deteriorating standard of living despite the regime's success in protecting the core elements of the economy. First, Libya was not only receiving less oil revenues due to the falling price of oil but also seeking to increase its foreign reserves and assets. The Libyan leadership expected that the major Western powers might in due course intensify sanctions against Libya, expanding them to ban the export of Libyan oil. Libya therefore needed reserves and assets that it could draw upon in that event.[22] Due to the necessary secrecy with which Libya needed to proceed in building up its assets in different parts of the world,[23] it would be impossible to put an accurate figure on the assets and reserves thus accumulated. Nonetheless, there are some indications of the character and scale of the operation that was undertaken. Clearly the roughly $3 billion withdrawn from OECD-based banks in late 1993 became part of the accumulated funds; the assets held with OECD-based banks, having declined to $1.608 billion at the end of 1993, had risen again to $5.688 billion at the end of 1996;[24] assets worth $4.67 billion were being held in a special reserve account at the central bank, known as Moujannab; the Libyan Arab Foreign Investment Company at the end of 1998 had assets valued at $559 million; and there was another overseas portfolio invest-

Table 8.4   Value of Manufacturing Production in Food and Cement, 1992–1996 (in millions of dinar)

	1992	1993	1994	1995	1996
Food manufacture	255.6	222.90	124.94	132.36	78.69
Cement and cement products	105.94	102.03	80.93	79.16	67.60

Source: National Corporation for Information and Documentation, *Statistical Yearbook 1998* (Tripoli: NCID, 1999), p. 28.

ment fund, Mahfazah, whose assets were probably worth $4–$5 billion at the end of 1998.[25]

Second, Libya experienced severe inflation over the sanctions period. This stemmed in large part from the indirect effects of sanctions, combined with greater dependence on the private sector to import goods. Goods that were subject to sanctions (such as those for the downstream operations of the oil industry) were thus acquired by indirect means, which meant substantial payoffs to third parties. The higher prices for imported goods, however, were not restricted to those banned by sanctions. Without air links to the outside world, and with international businesses and institutions wary about conducting business with Libya, there was a general upward pressure on prices. Prior to sanctions, some 30 percent of Libyan imports reached the country by air.[26] Shortages, created by the inability of Libyan authorities to respond quickly to consumer needs, meant that goods soon commanded prices above the levels set by the government. The impossibility of obtaining by air the spare parts needed for industrial machinery, moreover, led to a decline in the production of key goods for the domestic market and placed further pressure on prices. Production in food manufacturing and cement, for example, both declined sharply over the four years that followed the imposition of sanctions (see Table 8.4).

The ability of the government to control prices was weakened by the liberalization of the economy, which had occurred in the late 1980s, and by further measures of liberalization introduced in the wake of sanctions. The latter stemmed from the government's realization that merchants and private entrepreneurs could be more adept than the government in supplying consumer needs in light of sanctions. Law No. 9 of 1992, introduced in September, laid the basis for the privatization of state enterprises engaged in production, distribution, trade, services, agriculture, industry, education, health, commercial tourism, transport, real estate, and finance. It allowed for private practices to be established by lawyers, medical doctors, financial and economic consultants, civil engineers, notaries, carpenters, and black-smiths.[27] In 1993, wholesale trade as well as retail trade was opened up to the private sector. In practice the major growth that occurred in the private sector was in commerce, with only limited investment in other fields. The shift in the balance between the private and public sectors was nonetheless substantial. As indicated in Table 8.2, the proportion of investment account-ed for by the private sector grew from 9.8 percent of total investment between 1986 and 1990 to 24.6 percent between 1991 and 1997.

Although private entrepreneurs were given an expanded role in the economy, the government intended to retain control over prices for the sale of goods. So-called purification committees, operating under the control of the Liaison Committee of the Revolutionary Committees, were instituted in 1996 to enforce price controls and to close down shops that ran afoul of the regulations.[28] This, however, proved ineffective. In practice, the gains that merchants could enjoy by selling goods at market-driven prices gave them a strong incentive to find ways to evade the restrictions (sometimes selling from the back door of the shop while the main entrance was shut, or even trading from home). The purification committees, tempted by the substantial bribes that merchants were willing to pay, in due course became party to the evasion of price controls. New "volcano committees" were then created to oversee the activities of the purification committees. The overall impact of these measures was to create an unsettled atmosphere for the conduct of business and a circle of individuals drawing illicit benefit from high prices. Prices were not kept under control.[29]

The rate of inflation, as a result of the factors just discussed, was sub-stantial. Although it may not be possible to put an accurate figure on the rate, the *Worldwide Cost of Living Survey* produced by the Economist Intelligence Unit suggests an average rate of 35 percent over the 1993–1997 period.[30] The most substantial inflation occurred in the two years immediately after the imposition of sanctions (42 percent in 1993, 50 percent in 1994), with rather lower rates being recorded in subsequent years partly as a result of actions taken by the government to control prices (30 percent in 1995, 35 percent in 1996, and 25 percent in 1997). This coheres with the impression held by many Libyans. The impacts of inflation on the standard of living of the Libyan population, on the gap between the rich and the poor, and on the dependence of the mass of the population on government subsidies to remain alive have been massive and critical (see Chapter 9).

A third factor explaining the deteriorating living standard is the prior-ity given to maintaining the oil industry and the construction of the Great Man-Made River, both of which required cuts in expenditures in other fields. Declining oil revenues (stemming mainly from falling global oil prices), coupled with the rising cost of obtaining equipment for the oil industry and the Great Man-Made River, meant that there were fewer resources available to support agriculture and industry, health, education, and other parts of the social and economic infrastructure. It is difficult to quantify the drop in resources to those sectors, insofar as Libya since 1993 has not made public the breakdown of government expenditures. Nonetheless, there is ample evidence that expenditures in these fields were reduced, probably in absolute terms (i.e., in dinar spent) as well as in real terms as a result of inflation. Through the mid-1990s, expenditures on the Great Man-Made River were absorbing around 15 percent of total government expenditures,[31] and the government introduced a series of measures that would reduce expenditures in other spheres. Proposals were made for public servants to work on reduced salaries (or without salary) over extended periods, in return for subsequently being given privileges to establish private consultancies or practices. Studies were made of the possibility of privatizing some roads, such that users would pay tolls and the entrepreneur-purchaser would maintain it. The possibility of introducing an income tax was discussed but rejected by the General People's Congress on the grounds that the value of salaries was already declining sharply through inflation. Measures to reduce overall state employment by 20 percent were examined, although reductions occurred more through attrition than outright cuts. Fees were introduced for university students.[32]

Although these three factors provide the basic explanation for the deterioration of living standards, there is another reason why the Libyan population did not fare better. The Libyan economy has over a prolonged period been poorly managed. Although the core economy clearly benefited from effective administration and good strategic planning, the rest of the economy suffered from lax administration, a weak legislative framework in which regulations are unclear and liable to sudden change, and inefficient use of resources. This dimension does not in and of itself explain the deteriorating conditions, insofar as it was present before sanctions, but it does help explain why the economy did not respond more effectively to the challenge of sanctions.

The elements of poor management in the Libyan economy were in part structural, stemming from the character of Libya's political system. Paradoxically, it was precisely the more positive social dimensions of the system of popular congresses that helped to create incoherence in economic policy. The logic of *jamahiri* (mass-based) rule was that authority rested with the popular congresses, such that demands coming from the basic people's congresses for improved local facilities were difficult for

the central authorities to resist. On major national issues, the basic people's congresses could be guided effectively by the revolutionary committees, but the latter were in no position to prevent congresses from raising
demands for new schools, health centers, and other social and economic
infrastructure in their local areas. The demands from the congresses would
then be taken to the General People's Congress, where the leadership
would find it politic to include the desired projects in plans for government expenditures. The result was that even the smallest communities felt
entitled to a full range of services from the state (electricity, schools,
health centers, access roads, etc.). Thus resources were spread thinly in a
highly uneconomic and inefficient manner. This political dimension
ensured that projects were undertaken but that resources to maintain the
projects were not available. There was, therefore, a tendency for roads to
go unrepaired, schools to be without sufficient teachers and books, and
medical centers to lack necessary medical equipment and medicine.

Besides this structural problem, there was a large element of simple
mismanagement. Economic policymaking in Libya has had an off-the-cuff
character. Decisions are taken to meet pressing problems without due
thought to the long-term effects. When these consequences arise, a new
decision will be taken to cope with the situation, which will bring unfore-
seen consequences that necessitate yet another change. A good example is
the government decision in 1997 to import a large number of Korean Daewoo cars, which would be sold at the heavily subsidized price of LD6,000
(equal to roughly £10,000 at the official rate of exchange but only £1,200
at the black market exchange rate on the streets). The objective of the
measure was commendable—to enable many families to purchase cars. In
practice, the gains made by purchasing and reselling cars to foreigners resident in Libya (or else seeking to take them outside of the country for sale)
were such that many Libyan families registered several family members
to acquire cars. When this became clear to the government, it responded
by forbidding the resale of cars for two years after purchase. That restriction, however, was widely ignored, so the authorities took to confiscating
any Daewoo being driven by a foreigner. The changing governmental regulations in this matter became known to Libyans by word of mouth rather
than public announcement. The result of such off-the-cuff policymaking
has been economic confusion: policies have changed day to day, depriv-
ing economic entrepreneurs of the ability to plan effectively and thereby
discouraging long-term investment.[33]

In effect, the sanctions partly absolved the government for its mismanagement. The government was able to blame deteriorating economic

conditions on the sanctions regime, and many in the population accepted that perspective. Sanctions were indeed partly to blame, and the population was acutely aware of some of the direct effects of sanctions (such as the difficulty of traveling abroad, or even of traveling by air within Libya). The authorities therefore had a strong basis upon which to project this perspective.

Notes

1. Dar al-Jamahariya lil-Nashr, *The Revolution in Libya*, p. 341.
2. Economist Intelligence Unit, *Libya Country Profile, 1989/90* (London: EIU, 1990), pp. 19–23.
3. Dar al-Jamahariya lil-Nashr, *The Revolution in Libya*, p. 345.
4. Central Bank of Libya, *Annual Report: 1984* (Tripoli, 1985).
5. The figures in this paragraph are taken from Dar al-Jamahariya lil-Nashr, *The Revolution in Libya*, chs. 5–7.
6. *Al-Zahaf al-Akhdar*, 28 March 1987.
7. Vandewalle, *Qadhafi's Libya*, pp. 212–213.
8. The law that made possible the establishment of *tasharikat* in fact dates from 1985, but the rapid development of the *tasharikat* did not occur until after 1987. See Dar al-Jamahariya lil-Nashr, *The Revolution in Libya*, pp. 435–439.
9. See Economist Intelligence Unit, *Libya: Country Report, 2nd Quarter 1998* (London: EIU, 1998), p. 14.
10. See Economist Intelligence Unit, *Libya: Country Report, 3rd Quarter 1998* (London: EIU, 1998), p. 17.
11. Economist Intelligence Unit, *Libya: Country Profile, 1998/99* (London: EIU, 1999), pp. 25–26.
12. Ibid.
13. Ibid., p. 37; and Dar al-Jamahariya lil-Nashr, *The Revolution in Libya*, p. 345.
14. Figures from OPEC, *Statistical Bulletins*, 1990–1996.
15. Figures on revenues in official Libyan government publications end in 1992.
16. See Economist Intelligence Unit, *Libya: Country Report, 4th Quarter 1995* (London: EIU, 1995), p. 19.
17. See Economist Intelligence Unit, *Libya: Country Profile, 1998/99* (London: EIU, 1999), p. 42.
18. "Success" here relates simply to the carrying forward of the project and does not necessarily imply that the project itself was useful. Some have criticized the project on grounds of it absorbing too large a proportion of Libya's resources, with too uncertain a result. Nonetheless, this writer does personally believe the project to be valuable provided (as seems realistic) that it does make available supplies of water over at least a fifty-year period.

19. For a good description of the conceptions underlying the project, see Management and Implementation Authority of the Great Man-Made River, *The Great Man-Made River Project* (Tripoli: MIAGMMR, 1989).

20. Dar al-Jamahariya lil-Nashr, *The Revolution in Libya*, pp. 287–311.

21. Economist Intelligence Unit, *Libya: Country Report, 4th Quarter 1996*, p. 20.

22. This strategy, and the perception on which it was based, was made clear to this writer in a number of interviews with senior Libyan officials in December 1996. The position adopted was realistic: the United States had consistently sought a tightening of sanctions to include oil revenues—a stand that was repeated as late as February 1999. See *Guardian*, 19 February 1999.

23. The International Monetary Fund publication *International Financial Statistics* has not provided information on Libya's reserves since 1993, presumably because the relevant information has not been made available by Libya. In 1993, the IMF reported Libya's foreign reserves as standing at $7.103 billion.

24. Economist Intelligence Unit, *Libya: Country Profile, 1998/99* (London: EIU, 1999), p. 42.

25. Economist Intelligence Unit, *Libya: Country Report, 1st Quarter 1999* (London: EIU, 1999), p. 19. It may be presumed that the $3 billion withdrawn from the OECD-based banks was placed either in the Moujannab account or the Mahfazah fund. The estimation of the size of the Mahfazah fund is the responsibility of the writer alone and is based on the fact that some $200 million was being drawn from the fund annually in profits and interest.

26. Information provided to the writer by the Libyan secretariat for foreign liaison and international cooperation, December 1996. It is interesting that imports by sea did not increase after air sanctions were imposed but actually declined. This in part reflects the shift from state-controlled importing to private-sector importing (with the private sector less equipped to organize large-scale imports and more inclined to make more limited arrangements through Egypt or Tunisia), but it may also stem from the nature of goods that were previously imported by air. It seems likely that a significant part of the latter imports were perishable or were needed urgently and, hence, could not be sent by sea. For the statistics on sea trade, see National Corporation for Information and Documentation, *Statistical Book, 1998* (Tripoli: NCID, 1999), pp. 18–20.

27. A full description of Law No. 9, and the effects that followed from it, can be found in Dar al-Jamahariya lil-Nashr, *The Revolution in Libya*, pp. 432–444.

28. The government had first sought to introduce purification committees in 1994, but this was delayed by opposition within the General People's Congress.

29. The observations in this paragraph are based mainly on observations made by the writer on his visits to Libya between 1996 and 1999.

30. See Economist Intelligence Unit, *Libya: Country Profile, 1998/99* (London: EIU, 1999), p. 17.

31. This is an estimate based on information in the reports by the Libyan Central Bank. A similar figure was given by Qaddafi in his speech to the General People's Congress in March 1997. See *Al-Zahaf al-Akhdar*, 28 March 1997.

32. The information about cost-cutting measures and proposals is drawn from interviews conducted by the writer with Libyan officials in the secretariat of planning, January 2000.

33. Information drawn from conversations the writer had with Libyan and foreign businessmen in Tripoli during visits in 1998 and 1999.

9

The Social Impact
of Sanctions

The most influential impact on social conditions has been through inflation. To understand its importance, we must bear in mind that wages and
salaries in the Libyan public sector have remained static since 1982. Wage
and salary levels were set by Law No. 15 of 1982 and have not been
changed since. During the 1980s, Libyan standards of living benefited
from a small measure of negative inflation. World Bank figures suggest
that prices were falling by 0.3 percent per annum between 1980 and 1985,[1]
and the extension of subsidies to more products than during the late 1980s
suggests that a similar trend persisted through the end of that decade. This
pattern shifted abruptly after the imposition of sanctions. Between 1993
and 1997 inflation was running at about 35 percent per annum.

The inflation was reflected in (and to some extent resulted from) a fall
in the exchange rate of the Libyan dinar against international currencies.
Although the change in the official dinar-dollar rate was limited (from
$1 = LD0.27 at the end of 1990 to $1 = LD0.45 at the end of 1998), the
fall of the dinar on the black market was more dramatic. The sterling
pound had been exchanged on the black market at parity with the dinar in
1990, but by 1998 the rate was about £1 = LD5. The black market
exchange rate for the dollar in 1998 valued the dinar at about one-seventh
of the official value.[2]

Most Libyan salaries and wages in the public sector under Law No.
15 of 1982 were in the range of LD150–LD600 per month. An unskilled
manual worker generally earned an income of between LD150 and LD250
per month (at the black market rate of the mid-1990s, about $50–$80). In
higher-status, professional occupations, incomes were higher but still not
substantial. A university lecturer would begin at LD270 per month (at

Table 9.1   State Subsidization of Consumer Necessities, 1992–1997 (in millions of dinar)

Year	Subsidization cost
1992	23.0
1993	41.0
1994	36.0
1995	98.0
1996	144.0
1997	160.0

Source: Dar al-Jamahariya lil-Nashr, *Al-Thawra Libya fi 30 'Ama* (Tripoli: Dar al-Jamahariya lil-Nashr, 1999), p. 356.

point 10 on the government scale, relevant to those with Ph.D.'s) and could expect, after a few years teaching, to be earning about LD350 per month.[3] Well-established academics, able to add to their basic salary through part-time and overtime teaching, might be able to earn LD600 per month. At the black market rate of exchange of the mid-1990s, the latter sum came to roughly $200, whereas at the end of the 1980s the salary (at the black market rate available at that time) would have been worth roughly $800. Given that almost 80 percent of the Libyan workforce was employed within the state sector,[4] the fall in the real value of wages and salaries, by some 35 percent per annum in the mid-1990s, inevitably damaged living standards.

This led to three associated changes to social conditions and the social balance. First, the livelihood of most Libyans became much more dependent on direct state support, through rationed subsidized goods. Given that it was not possible for most Libyans to live on their wages and salaries, they increasingly depended on subsidized goods, which they obtained from their local cooperative societies. The state provided families with ration books bearing different entitlements according to the number of people in the family. Families had to be registered with specific cooperatives and, by the end of 1997, some 750,000 Libyan families (in effect, almost the whole Libyan population) were registered in a total of 5,598 cooperatives.[5] Although the rationing system had been in operation before sanctions, the number of cooperatives and the scale of state subsidization grew sharply after the imposition of sanctions (see Table 9.1).

Rations varied month to month depending on the availability of goods, but they were generally sufficient to meet a family's requirement, at least in basic goods. In late 1997, monthly rations for an average family included a sack of sugar (fifty kilograms for LD6), a tin of vegetable oil (twenty kilograms for LD8), and reasonable quantities of tea, milk, flour,

rice, cheese, soap, and baby milk.[6] Given that it would have been very difficult for many families to survive without rations, the rationing system
gave the authorities an extra dimension of control over the population.

A second aspect of change stemming from the high inflation was the
trend toward secondary employment. Given that state salaries were insufficient to ensure a reasonable standard of living, public sector employees
in all spheres took second jobs or engaged in private commerce. Professionals might act as consultants to publicly and privately owned companies or nongovernmental organizations, while both the educated and the
uneducated might engage in commerce. At the higher end, this might
involve opening a shop, developing an agricultural smallholding, traveling abroad to bring in goods for resale, or undertaking petty manufacturing. At the lower end, it meant reselling goods that larger merchants had
brought into the country. Although the gains from some such activities
were not always substantial, often they exceeded wages and salaries
earned through formal employment. The public sector, therefore, began to
suffer increasingly from a lack of commitment among employees. The
duties performed would be barely sufficient to ensure that an individual
retained his or her job, but the workers' main energies were put into activities outside the principal workplace. Schools, universities, and hospitals
all suffered, as did government ministries.[7]

A third aspect of inflation was an increase in corruption. Whereas
there was relatively little corruption in Libya during the 1980s, the economic pressures and the growing gap between rich and poor (discussed
below) meant that bribery came to characterize interactions between public institutions and private individuals. The regulations on private sector
activities were, in any case, usually so restrictive that it was possible to
function commercially only if some regulations were disregarded—and
that usually meant paying off some official. One example is the purification committees, which were established to prevent merchants from over-
charging but themselves became a party to, and a beneficiary of, the evasion of price controls. Even in education, money could influence the
results obtained by students.[8]

Corruption was, to some extent, a reflection of the more general com-
mercialization of society. The need to make money ensured that most
social groupings became more oriented to commercial values. Popular
esteem for the value of disinterested work for the benefit of others, which
had previously figured as a key value in the Libyan system, declined and
made room for more individualistic values. To attribute this shift entirely
to sanctions would be wrong. The trend was evident in other Arab countries (indeed, Libya can perhaps be seen as a latecomer to the spread of

more individualistic consumerist values), and it was clearly associated with wider global processes that have spread Western values. The reception of satellite television was not restricted in Libya, and given the poor quality of Libyan television and newspapers, many depended more on Arab and other international broadcasts for their news and entertainment than they did on Libya's own media. Nonetheless, the rapid pace of the change of values, and the manner in which corruption and commercialism came to be interlinked in social practice, stemmed to a significant extent from inflation's impact on living standards.[9]

The Growth of Social Inequality

Libyan society has also been transformed by growing social inequality. Although inflation was a contributing factor depressing the standard of living of those on fixed salaries, it was not the only factor. The emergence of a commercial class was made possible by the economic liberalization put in motion beginning in the late 1980s. Yet the wealth that this class could accumulate depended centrally on the sanctions regime. Until the early 1990s, Libya had been one of the most egalitarian societies in the Middle East. Egalitarianism was the key value the regime used to justify its rejection of Western-style economic and political freedoms. The effective prohibition on private investment that was in force through most of the 1980s—including restrictions on owning more than one house and employing labor—meant there was no legitimate means for acquiring individual wealth. Even those few who grew rich through corruption could do little with their gains. Ostentatiousness and conspicuous consumption would have drawn attention to their corruption, and there was no opportunity for them to use their capital so as to acquire yet more wealth. Special treatment (i.e., at private schools or health facilities) could not be purchased. Of course, people close to or within the regime leadership and those in senior administrative positions were better off, but the gap in socioeconomic conditions was not wide. Between the richest and poorest, the gap in wages and salaries was about 5:1[10]—substantially less than in other states in the Middle East. The lowest-paid workers, moreover, were entitled to a range of welfare payments and state housing, which were not available to wealthier workers.

All this changed after sanctions were imposed. Those who had the international contacts and foreign currency that enabled them to import goods found themselves in a very favorable situation. The reduced role of the state in the commercial sector, and the limited number of merchants who had the necessary currency and contacts to negotiate contracts with foreign companies, put those who did have such currency and contacts in a semimonopolistic position. Despite the regime's attempts to control prices, such merchants could charge much higher prices. Thus there developed a parallel economy that was not under state control[11] and was therefore not affected by the state's attempts to promote equality. Indeed, the state itself had a somewhat ambivalent attitude toward this parallel economy, as it did bring in consumer goods the population needed.[12] By the mid-1990s, most major consumer products available in Europe could be bought in Libya. The wealth resulting from this parallel economy went not only to the merchants but also to those in the administration who were willing to look the other way.

The new commercial elite came from varied backgrounds. Access to foreign currency and international contacts were the keys. Outside companies were not permitted to establish a direct presence in Libya (except in specialized fields such as the oil industry) and would, in any case, have probably been loath to do so. Commercial intermediaries, therefore, were crucial. Among them were people who left the country when the monarchy fell in 1969. There were even members of the pre-1969 al-Sanussi ruling family who returned to Libya and undertook some commercial activity. Others had left at the end of the 1970s, when much of the old commercial elite lost their businesses and property through outright dispossession and/or regulations that removed the basis upon which business could operate. Some had, during the intervening period, become established commercial entrepreneurs in Europe and were now ideally situated to benefit from the new economy—often cooperating with family members who remained in Libya or cementing links with individuals in the state administration. State officials who benefited from facilitating the new commercial activity, and who then had the means to enter business themselves, became part of Libya's new commercial elite.

The major shopping districts in Tripoli and Benghazi reflected the wealth and tastes of the new commercial elite. Shops displayed the latest fashions of Italy and the most modern electronic equipment, sold at prices beyond the dreams of ordinary Libyans. At the end of 1998, for example, mobile telephones were being sold in Libya for about LD3,000—five times the monthly salary of a senior academic. Large new houses in the fashionable suburbs of Tripoli (such as Girgarsh, Sarraj, and Janzur) and Benghazi (such as El-Fuwayyat and an area that came to be known as "Hai al-Dollar," in recognition of the provenance of the wealth that was to be found there) reflected the riches of the new commercial elite.

Education and Health

Social conditions were also changed by the spending limits on education and health. Cuts occurred even as needs increased in these fields. Population growth in Libya through the 1980s was 3.3 percent per annum—one of the highest rates in the world. The balance of the population, as a result, was very much skewed toward youth: only 4.9 percent of the Libyan population in 1996 was over sixty (compared with 20.7 percent of the population of the United Kingdom).[13] Table 9.2 details the growth in student numbers in primary and secondary schools between 1990 and 1996. The increase of student numbers at the university level was even more dramatic, rising from 55,600 in 1990 to 138,346 in 1998.[14] In the health sector, demands on medical services were increasing not only because of population growth but also due to the sharp drop in the number of patients able to travel abroad for treatment. Sanctions on air travel meant that it was no longer practicable for most seriously ill patients to go abroad, thereby burdening the local medical services. A document from the Libyan secretariat for foreign liaison assessing the impact of sanctions, prepared at the beginning of 1998, estimated that some 17,000 Libyans would have been sent abroad for treatment during 1993–1997. This figure is consistent with the numbers being sent abroad before 1993.

Falling expenditures in education and health were, therefore, bound to have a damaging impact on the Libyan population, as the need to educate children and provide health care to all was paramount.[15] There are no sta-

Table 9.2   Numbers of Pupils in Primary and Secondary Education, 1990–1996

	Primary education	Secondary education
1990/91	1,175,229	113,683
1991/92	1,238,986	138,860
1992/93	1,254,278	150,625
1993/94	1,357,040	239,240
1994/95	1,364,900	264,092
1995/96	1,460,443	251,275

Source: National Corporation for Information and Documentation, *Statistical Yearbook 1998* (Tripoli: NCID, 1999), p. 24. The reasons for the rapid rise in numbers of secondary school pupils in 1993/94, and the small drop in 1995/96, is not explained in the source but may stem from changes in the designation of secondary schools (with some being shifted in 1993/94 from the Technical School category to Secondary General). Given that there was an increase in technical school students over the whole 1990–1996 period, however, the overall trend of student numbers was still sharply upward.

tistics to document the deterioration of education and health, but there was a widespread perception among the population that standards declined sharply throughout the 1990s. University academics saw the quality of students drop year by year; funding to purchase new books for university libraries was cut off completely between 1992 and 1996; schools were unable to spend money on new teaching resources; the state of repair of schools steadily worsened; medical equipment in hospitals broke down and was not replaced; medicines, apart from the most basic, became difficult to obtain within the public health sector; and hospitals were left without proper upkeep. Some of the deterioration may well have stemmed from poor management and administration, but there can be no doubt that falling expenditures constituted the most critical factor.

There have, in addition, been direct casualties resulting from Libyans' need to rely exclusively on road travel through Tunisia and Egypt for contacts with the outside world. A report by the Libyan mission to the United Nations in 1996 stated that during 1992–1995 there were 10,200 accidents on the roadways to Tunisia and Egypt, killing 2,560 people and seriously injuring 12,700.[16] It is, of course, impossible to estimate how many of these might have occurred in the absence of sanctions.

Notes

1. Economist Intelligence Unit, *Libya: Country Profile, 1989/90*, p. 14.

2. Information from writer's own experience.

3. Figures taken from Law No. 15 (1982).

4. The percentage has been worked out by the writer by the material on the Libyan labor force published in Dar al-Jamahariya lil-Nashr, *The Revolution in Libya*, pp. 672–710.

5. Ibid., p. 355.

6. Information from interviews by the writer, December 1997.

7. Ibid.

8. The extent and significance of corruption was recognized in a report written for the Libyan authorities in 1996. The report stemmed from discussions among a group of economists at Garyounis University in Libya. It gave a bleak but realistic view of the deficiencies in the economy and put forward recommendations. The report stressed that corruption was not only bringing illicit gains to individual administrators but was also distorting the pattern of economic policy. The report was later published outside of Libya, under the title *Al-Iqtisad al-Libii: Dirasat Mut'a-nia lil-'Azma wa al-Hulul* [The Libyan Economy: A Study of the Signs of Crisis and the Solutions] (Croydon: AAS Publishers, 1998); see pp. 49–50. The report's outspoken criticism of existing policy suggests that the room within which criticism could be tolerated by the regime was perhaps wider than some have suggested.

9. The material in this paragraph is necessarily impressionistic and depends on many conversations the writer had with Libyans and foreign businessmen in Libya over the 1990s. It should be stressed that despite substantial value change some traditional values and attitudes changed little. Libya remains one of the few countries in the Middle East where foreigners visiting shops and markets are never harassed. Shopkeepers and stall holders will not press their wares on visitors unless the latter show an interest in them. The difference between visiting a *suq* in Egypt and one in Libya is substantial.

10. This is the proportion between the top and bottom of the wages scale as given in Law No. 15 (1982).

11. The U.S.-based Heritage Foundation in 1999 produced a report that classified Libya as the third least free economy in the world, with only Cuba and North Korea scoring lower. Any visitor to Libya at that time could witness the unreality of that assessment. The privately owned shops were active, selling goods that had been brought in by private sector importers, and substantial parts of all major cities were given over to informal sector activities. Extensive markets of stall holders selling goods brought in overland in suitcases and in other hastily improvised containers (together with some goods produced by local petty manufacturing) had come into being.

12. Formally, the private commercial sector was left reasonably free to operate through 1996, but after 1996 the government sought through the purification committees to close down businesses that were circumventing price regulations. In practice, however, the latter policy was not consistently applied—not only because the purification committees had often become party to the regulation evasion but also because the authorities had to ensure that measures against the merchants did not result in shortages of consumer goods in the market. It is worth noting that even before sanctions Qaddafi had at times appeared to encourage black market activity. At a gathering of the revolutionary committees on 1 September 1989, held on the twentieth anniversary of the 1969 revolution, he described the black market as based on "spontaneous actions by the people carried out independently of the government and providing a people's market which the masses needed." *Al-Zahaf al-Akhdar*, 2 September 1989.

13. Figures taken from World Bank, *World Development Indicators* (Washington, D.C.: World Bank, 1998), p. 43. It is important to stress that the figures on population growth given here relate to the 1980s and not to the 1990s. Although there are at present no statistics for the later years, there is evidence that population growth fell during the 1990s. The number of pupils starting primary education appears to have been less over the 1996–1999 period than over the first half of the decade. Nonetheless, the number of pupils and students in education as a whole over these years increased, the result of population growth in the 1980s and early 1990s.

14. Dar al-Jamahariya lil-Nashr, *The Revolution in Libya*, p. 529. The figures relate to undergraduate student numbers only.

15. The native Libyan population stood at a little less than 5 million in 1998. There were, in addition, some 1.5 million non-Libyans residing in the country.

16. Mission of the Libyan Jamahariya to the United Nations, "Report on the Impact of UN Sanctions Against Libya," September 1996.

10

The Political Impact
of Sanctions

The political impact of sanctions must be analyzed within the context and characteristics of the political system that exists in Libya. First we outline the general characteristics of the system, then assess whether the dynamics of Libyan politics changed as a result of sanctions.

In the Western world, the Libyan political system has generally been characterized as a personal dictatorship. Qaddafi is seen as holding all the levers of power, manipulating and controlling all aspects of Libyan politics and society. The structure of institutions that exist tends to be discounted, seen as a front to camouflage the realities of power. This characterization holds some truth, but it is also misleading. The dynamics of power and policy cannot be understood solely in terms of Qaddafi's personal whims and wishes.

Formal political authority in Libya, since the Declaration of the Authority of the People on 2 March 1977, has resided in a structure of people's congresses. The roles and powers of the congresses are outlined in Qaddafi's *Green Book*.[1] Basic people's congresses, now constituted in units referred to as *mahallat* (localities),[2] form the foundation of the *jamahiri* structure. At the beginning of 1999 there were 375 such congresses in existence,[3] covering the whole of the country's population. Each locality has a people's committee, responsible to the congress and exercising an administrative role within the commune. Similar congresses and committees, consisting of individuals delegated by the basic people's congresses and committees and by the professional associations and unions, operate at the level of the *sha'abiyat* (provinces/municipalities, of which there were twenty-six in 1999). At the national level, formal authority rests with the General People's Congress. The members of the latter are

82

described as carrying delegated instructions from the lower-level congresses and associations, rather than exercising a wider role of representation. National executive and administrative powers reside with the General People's Committee, which is responsible to the General People's Congress. Some of the functions normally exercised by a head of state, such as the acceptance of ambassadorial credentials, rest with the secretariat of the Congress. Qaddafi has held no position within the formal structure of authority since the end of the 1970s.

The intention that the General People's Committee should be tightly bound by the guidelines of policy laid down by the General People's Congress is given expression by the titles carried by the members of the committee. Although the committee plays the role of a cabinet or council of ministers, its members carry the title of "secretary" rather than "minister," and ministries are referred to as "secretariats."

The formal structure of authority outlined above, however, does not accurately reflect the realities of power and influence. This is made clear in the regime's own political texts. The final sentence in the first part of Qaddafi's *Green Book* reads: "Theoretically, this is genuine democracy. But realistically, the strong always rule, that is, the stronger part in society is the one which rules."[4] To gain a more realistic picture of the actual processes whereby power is exercised, reference must be made to the volumes of commentaries on the *Green Book*;[5] to the speeches of Qaddafi, which are compiled in the *Sijil al-Qawmi* (National Register);[6] and to the account of the political system given in the internally produced account of the regime's achievements over its first thirty years.[7]

In the documents cited above, the popular congresses still constitute the basis of legitimate authority, but the development of policy depends crucially on two other elements: the "leader of the revolution" (Qaddafi), and the revolutionary committees (first formed in 1977 but not publicly announced until 1979). The former is described as shaping the political debate in the congresses and committees through his political speeches (*al-khutab al-siyasi*). This was affirmed in a document on "revolutionary legitimacy" that was adopted by the General People's Congress in March 1990, wherein Qaddafi's inalienable right to lead the revolution was recognized.[8] The revolutionary committees hold responsibility for inciting the masses to exercise authority; practicing revolutionary supervision; agitating the popular congresses; directing the popular committees and the secretariats of congresses to the "right path"; and protecting, defending, and propagating the revolution.[9] In this perspective, the close relationship between the leader and the revolutionary committees provides much of the dynamic of practical politics. No doubt the perspective leaves out some other dimensions of actual political power, such as the role of the military and the security services, but it does represent a broadly realistic picture of the processes of decisionmaking—especially during the late 1970s and 1980s.

Consistent with this outline of power, Qaddafi has clearly been the central figure in framing policy in all spheres. No major decision is likely to be taken unless specifically approved by him. He has also set the operational style of Libyan policymaking. On issues of significance, he makes the main policy pronouncements and statements, determines the form and timing of initiatives, and deals directly with foreign governments and representatives. His individual approach and inclinations determine which national and international causes the Libyan government chooses to support, encompassing such diverse struggles as those involving the rights of African Americans and Native Americans, the republican movement in Northern Ireland, and Kurdish rights to self-determination.[10]

The role played by Qaddafi stems mainly, of course, from his actual control of the levers of power. It would, however, be wrong to discount a charismatic element in his relationship with the Libyan population. Although the charisma is no doubt engendered in part by the manner in which the regime projects his character and leadership, not to mention the propaganda that infuses education and all other aspects of life in the country, it does add another dimension to his power. His relationship with the masses can be used to prevent challenges to his authority from others in the leadership and to suggest that without him at the helm Libya would fall into antagonistic regional, tribal, and political conflict. Qaddafi devotes time to meetings with the population at large,[11] and his speeches are phrased in a way that makes them readily comprehensible to the population. To some degree, therefore, his charisma is built upon an articulation of ideas that have a resonance among elements of the Libyan population. Libya's historical experience may be of relevance here, especially the prolonged war that followed the Italian occupation of Libya in 1911 and, subsequently, Benito Mussolini's policy of Italianizing Libya (through settlement as well as through suppressing and replacing indigenous Libyan Arab culture).[12] This has shaped in Libyan popular consciousness a wariness of the maneuvers of external (especially Western) powers in their dealings with Libya, a suspicion that their objectives are harmful to Libyan interests, a receptiveness to Arab nationalist rhetoric, and a feeling of solidarity with those who are prepared to confront the Western powers in the cause of protecting Libyan interests. Qaddafi portrays himself as the "ordinary Libyan," coming from a humble origin in the desert, who has had the courage to stand up to the oppressive and destructive West.

Despite Qaddafi's centrality in the political system, there are nonetheless other individuals and groupings that can at times affect policy. In order of closeness to the leader, first, we see the inner circle of influential individuals (generally known as the *rijal al-khaimah*) with whom Qaddafi discusses and develops his policy positions. In the early years these were largely members of the free officers' organization, but beginning in the mid-1970s more were drawn from the ranks of the revolutionary youth. The latter were young activists to whom Qaddafi appealed to bring about social and economic transformation and who formed the leadership of the revolutionary committees after 1977. Although the role of the revolutionary committees has been restricted since 1988, the old leadership remains integral to the inner circle. Of increasing importance in recent years are members of Qaddafi's family, especially those occupying senior positions in the security services. The central value around which the inner circle revolves is that of loyalty—a value that binds Qaddafi to others and others to him. Qaddafi has needed, therefore, to ensure that his actions do not run counter to his loyalties to the inner circle. The possibility of his handing over members of the inner circle for trial by foreign governments for alleged crimes, for example, has never been practicable: it would destroy the foundation upon which the system rests. Nonetheless, individuals can drop out of the inner circle, as happened to Abd al-Salaam Jallud in the early 1990s, and it would be clearly wrong to suggest that members of the inner circle are on equal footing with Qaddafi in formulating policy.

Second, the Liaison Committee of the Revolutionary Committees (the central leadership of the revolutionary committees) has played a key role in formulating and, at times, implementing policy. This is possible thanks to its direct links to the inner circle. Although the role of revolutionary committees in guiding and controlling popular opinion was restricted after 1988—when Qaddafi denounced them for having "deviated, harmed, and tortured" and insisted that they operate by persuasion and not violence— they retain a clear role in "agitating" the popular congresses. The latter role involves helping to frame the agendas for discussion and ensuring that the issues discussed are properly understood. Whatever the changes at the base, moreover, the central leadership has remained strong. The Liaison Committee has its own structure for reviewing policymaking in all major spheres of government, and its influence is felt in every domain. Libya's militancy on the international stage during the early and mid-1980s, when Libya supported a range of organizations committed to radical and often violent change in other countries, was carried forward by the revolutionary committees and not by the secretariat for foreign liaison—

except to the extent that the latter was for a time itself used by and controlled by the revolutionary committees.

Third, the security organizations and the army occupy important positions within the power structure. In this case also, it is significant that those in the most influential positions in the military and the security organizations form part of Qaddafi's inner circle. The military element in the inner circle, indeed, constituted the initial basis of the circle. The free officers had formed a tightly organized and secret group as part of the army under the monarchy, and their mutual loyalty enabled them to organize the takeover of power without being discovered by army intelligence. Over the years some of the core members broke with the regime, but others have remained at the center of the system. The chief of staff of the army since the late 1970s has been Abu Bakr Yunis Jabir, a key member of the free officers. Several other senior military personnel were also free officers. The security and intelligence organizations, in contrast, have tended to be under the control of Qaddafi family members (such as Qaddafi's brother-in-law Abdallah al-Sanussi) or have been leading elements in the revolutionary committees (such as Musa Kusa).

Fourth, the popular congresses also play a role. Although the congresses clearly do not constitute a major policy channel, they do affect policymaking thanks to their role in projecting the regime's legitimacy. It would be difficult for the regime to ignore completely opinions expressed within the congresses, because the congresses are projected as the cornerstone of the political system. The congresses also provide the regime with access to popular opinion—a means to learn of popular concerns and discontents that may need to be addressed. Although important matters of policy go to the General People's Congress simply for legitimation rather than for impartial discussion and decision,[13] the material demands made in basic people's congresses cannot always be ignored. For local populations, these congresses are a vehicle to press for local development, and some of the projects proposed at the local level do find their way into national development plans.[14] This has a positive dimension, but it can also frustrate the creation of a coherent planning framework.

Fifth, the administrative machinery, coming under the General People's Committee, has the technical and professional expertise needed to realize policies. Although it is described in the regime's literature as simply an instrument for implementing policies determined in the General People's Congress, in practice the power to implement cannot be separated from the power to decide. Practical considerations are bound to affect policy formulation, and coherent policies will therefore require the involvement of those who have technical and professional expertise. The significance of the administrative machinery in Libyan policymaking has depended to a substantial degree on the importance of the field concerned to the country's economic survival. The efficient operation of the oil industry, for example, has been left largely in the hands of the administrative machinery (whether in the National Oil Company or the energy secretariat), as has the Great Man-Made River project. In foreign affairs, the secretariat for foreign liaison has at times wielded less influence on policy than has the external section of the Liaison Committee. Yet the secretariat played an effective role in galvanizing opinion in other Arab and African governments to oppose measures taken against Libya by Western powers and in pursuing legal and UN channels to challenge the legitimacy of Western actions. When the secretary for foreign liaison has been strong, the secretariat has succeeded in limiting the Liaison Committee's pursuit of independent activities.

The Impact of Sanctions on Policies and Structures

The main structures of political power in Libya have not changed since the imposition of sanctions. There have, nonetheless, been some changes in the political and ideological balance underpinning the regime. Of critical importance is the impact of sanctions on the governing system's central ethos—egalitarianism. The slogans that festooned the streets—"Houses belong to those who live in them"; "Partners not wage-workers"—gave expression to this egalitarian objective. Although some of these slogans remained in the streets at the end of the 1990s (appearing as a hangover from previous times), the inequalities spawned by the sanctions regime removed any reality from the concepts that they projected. Perhaps a gradual shift in this direction would have taken place in any case as the flush of revolutionary fervor waned and measures of economic liberalization were introduced, but the extent and nature of the change was certainly shaped by the sanctions. The regime continued to proclaim egalitarianism, but the ideology gave the appearance of being an empty shell.

The weakness stemming from an ideology losing its relevance, however, was offset by other developments. Some of these were the incidental effects of sanctions, whereas others stemmed from the regime's political strategies to buttress its position. First, the confrontation over sanctions underscored the leadership role that Qaddafi was most suited to playing. At the end of the 1980s, there was reason to doubt whether Qaddafi's leadership could retain credibility and coherence in a New

World Order that emphasized human rights, democratization, economic liberalization, and global integration. Qaddafi clearly realized this danger himself and was quick to adopt new frameworks of human rights (discussed below) and liberalization. The transition from a defiant international militancy, which gave no quarter to the enemies of the regime at home or abroad, to the propounding and defense of human rights, would never have been easy. Sanctions enabled the regime to return to ground upon which it was most secure and effective: projecting the leader as the defender of the Libyan people against an aggressive and ill-intentioned West. A new layer of charismatic legitimacy was laid over Qaddafi by virtue of the determination with which he resisted Western bullying and defended the rights of Libyans to trial within a framework that was acceptable to their own government (in the perception purveyed to the Libyan public by the state media).

Qaddafi's success in countering a strong internal threat to his regime in October 1993 provides some evidence that his political position may have been strengthened by the perceived external threat. Three tribal groupings had, up to this time, been prominent in the leadership of the armed and security forces: the Warfalla, the Magarha, and the Qadadfa (Qaddafi's tribe). The close alliance between these groups was of critical importance in creating a unified army and security service leadership committed to defending the regime. In October 1993, a number of Warfalli officers were arrested on suspicion of having links with the opposition and planning a coup. Their arrest led to demonstrations in Beni Walid, the tribal center of the Warfalla, in which both civilians and army officers participated. The demonstrators sought to take control of an army ammunitions dump in the town. The immediate problem was solved when an air force plane, flying from the air base in Misurata, bombed the ammunitions dump. The more critical problem, however, related to longer-term considerations: how the regime could cope with the possibility of disaffection coming from a group that was so crucial to regime security—the largest tribal grouping in Libya—whose members remained embedded not only in the army and the security services but also in many parts of the administration.[15] Moreover, this came just as doubt was raised as to the future loyalty of the Magarha elements in the armed forces. Major Abd al-Salaam Jallud, a former member of the Revolutionary Command Council that had carried out the 1969 coup and who was widely seen as the second most influential individual in the country, made clear his strong disapproval of the government-orchestrated visit of Libyan pilgrims to Jerusalem in October 1993.[16] It was widely believed that he was then placed under house arrest. He made no further public appearance until June 1998. Jallud came from the Magarha group and clearly played a role as patron of other senior Magrahis within the army. Qaddafi's ability to maintain his leadership despite the uncertainties that now existed over the loyalty of two of the main props to regime security, at a time when external pressures against the country were being intensified, suggests that the latter may have strengthened rather than weakened Qaddafi's position.

Second, the regime created (for the first time since 1969) a role for the country's traditional elite in managing and controlling the population. This was done through the institution of "popular social leadership," announced in September 1993. Popular social leadership involved forming, in every part of the country, groups composed of the "respected natural leaders" of the local communities. These groups were then entrusted with responsibility for countering "corruption, deviation, and attempts at treasonable conspiracy," spreading "revolutionary culture," resolving local conflicts, liaising with the popular congresses and committees, following up the development plans for the area, and agitating local forces to ensure that production was expanded.[17] Although the texts that announced the introduction of the new policy left the concept of "respected natural leaders" unspecific, the principal elements that the authorities were seeking to draw in were the tribal leaders, and the emphasis was on rural rather than urban areas. Tribal and community leaders were in effect being instructed to take over responsibility for maintaining local order. This became more evident in 1994 and 1995, when the regime introduced the notions of communal responsibility and communal punishment in cases where members of tribes had "betrayed the country and the regime." Tribal and community leaders were deemed to carry responsibility for the actions of tribal and community members, and their failure to control disaffection would lead to suffering for the whole tribe or community. The introduction of communal responsibility and communal punishment came in reaction to the activity of Islamist elements in the Green Mountain region and to the regime's belief that these elements had been given protection by local tribes.

Third, the institutions that oversaw public behavior were strengthened. Following Qaddafi's criticism of the revolutionary committees in 1988, the committees had been given a less prominent role within the system—at least in terms of the latitude within which they could act directly in their dealings with the public. The annual meetings that had previously been convened—bringing together committee members from all parts of the country for instruction and inspiration—were not held between 1989 and 1992. In 1993, however, a new emphasis was placed on the role of the committees, and an annual meeting of committee members was convened. The meetings have been continued since. The institution of purification committees in 1996 and, subsequently, volcano committees also constituted a new level of social control. The latter committees were, moreover,

linked into and coordinated by the Liaison Committee of the Revolutionary Committees.

A further dimension of change in the political arena relates to the
opposition. The period following the imposition of sanctions saw a general strengthening of the Islamist movement in the country at two levels. On
one level, there was armed conflict: armed elements established themselves on Green Mountain in eastern Libya and sought to confront the
regime from there. The most prominent group was the Libyan Islamic
Fighting Group, many of whose fighters had fought for the Islamist cause
in Afghanistan. The difficulty of the terrain meant that dislodging them
would be difficult for the army. Sporadic clashes between the army and
the insurgents took place between 1995 and 1997, ultimately involving the
bombing of an escarpment where the insurgents had concentrated. The
leader of the insurgents, al-Ham, appears to have taken his own life when
he was surrounded by the Libyan army. His body was displayed in Benghazi in early 1998. Although the army had succeeded in reestablishing
control over the area, some incidents indicated that individual insurgents
might still have been active: there were at least two assassination attempts
apparently staged by Islamists against Qaddafi in the summer of 1998.

On the second level, there was a general deepening of Islamic sentiment that was capable of being mobilized for Islamist political ends. A
1996 study of attitudes among Libyan students showed that a majority
defined their identity more as Arab-Islamic than as purely Arab or
Libyan.[18] There was a widespread conviction among Libyan university
staffs in the late 1990s that Islamist sentiment in the student body was
growing stronger year by year. The social and economic discontents that
fostered the spread of Islamism in other Islamic countries were given a
unique twist thanks to the sanctions in Libya: the growth of poverty and
the unreality of the egalitarian values around which the regime had framed
its moral purpose created a natural vacuum for a new ideological framework to evolve. Moreover, the attraction of movements calling for liberal
democracy (which had been the focus of the exile opposition movements
prominent throughout the 1980s) was lessened by the sanctions experience. The suffering arising from sanctions was being imposed by the liberal democracies of the West.

Notes

1. M. Qaddafi, *The Green Book (Part One): The Solution to the Problem of
Democracy* (Tripoli: Public Enterprise for Publishing, n.d.).

2. These units were for a time referred to as "communes." This designation appears, however, to have been dropped.

3. Information from interviews carried out by the writer in Tripoli, January 1999.

4. Qaddafi, *The Green Book (Part One)*, p. 40.

5. Some 100 commentaries (*shuruh*) on *The Green Book* have been published by the International Centre for Studies and Research on the Green Book in Tripoli. The first one has a special status, insofar as it was written by Qaddafi (although his authorship is not acknowledged in the published text). The commentaries cover the practical operation of people's power and the ideological perceptions that underpin the system.

6. *Al-Sijil al-Qawmi: Bayanat wa Khutab wa Ahadith Mu'ammar Qaddafi* (The National Register: Pronouncements, Speeches, and Talks by Muammar Qaddafi) (Tripoli: Markaz al-Thaqafiah al-Qawmiyah, annual publication).

7. Dar al-Jamahariya lil-Nashr, *The Revolution in Libya*.

8. *Al-Zahaf al-Akhdar*, 17 March 1990.

9. The most thorough internal account of the operation of revolutionary committees is that given in Dar al-Jamahariya lil-Nashr, *The Revolution in Libya*, pp. 169–179. Also see 'Amer 'Abdalla al-Hamali, *Al-Safwah, al-Talia'a . . . wa Zahirat Istilab Sultat al-Sha'ab* [The Elite, the Vanguard . . . and the Phenomenon of Stealing Away the Power of the People], Commentaries on *The Green Book*, no. 17 (Tripoli: International Centre for Studies and Research on the Green Book, 1984). For an external account, see Mattes, "The Rise and Fall," pp. 89–113.

10. Qaddafi asserted the Kurdish right to self-determination during the visit of Turkish prime minister Necmettin Erbaken in October 1996. He told the prime minister that "the state of Kurdistan should take its place under the Middle Eastern sun." *Guardian*, 7 October 1996.

11. One unusual example was a videoconference arranged at the end of December 1999, enabling Qaddafi to address and answer questions from students and staff in the political science departments in Libyan universities. The event involved a real exchange of views: one participant strongly criticized Qaddafi's apparent abandonment of Arab nationalism, commenting that the population could not be realistically expected to abandon an ideology that the regime itself had instilled in people over a thirty-year period. He accepted the validity of this view but argued that Libya now had to base its policy on real interests and not on feelings.

12. It is important for non-Libyans to bear in mind that by the end of the Italian occupation the Libyan Arab population had declined by one-third.

13. An example of congresses being used to give the stamp of popular legitimacy to a decision that had already been taken can be found in the final stages of the crisis over the handover of the pair accused of the Lockerbie bombing. In December 1998 Qaddafi submitted to the basic people's congresses the decision as to whether Libya should accept the handing over of the two accused, in accordance with the proposals put forward by the British and U.S. governments the previous August. Previous proposals over the handling of the Lockerbie case had not been submitted to the congresses.

14. The sessions of the congresses occur twice a year, with meetings continuing over approximately two weeks (in the evenings). In congresses in city areas, some 200–400 people would usually participate at some stage of the meetings. The March sessions of the congresses are intended to collect the recommendations made by the members of each congress; the September sessions are described as being geared to decisionmaking. By the time of the latter sessions, the General People's Congress will have formulated the demands coming from the March sessions into what it conceives to be a workable program of action.

15. One indication of Qaddafi's sensitive treatment of the Warfalla was the case against nine Warfalli officers arrested for planning a coup in October 1993; it was handled slowly and carefully. Whereas some previous instances of plotting had led to summary executions, the nine officers were not executed until 1998—at the end of a long investigation process.

16. Jallud had also been critical of Qaddafi's reluctance to give explicit support to Iraq when the Coalition forces were bombing Iraq in January 1991, and of Qaddafi's proposal in 1993 that Libyan oil revenues should be distributed directly to the Libyan population—an idea that ultimately involved the distribution of $500 per family. A further significant dimension to the differences was that one of the Libyans accused of the Lockerbie bombing was a Magrahi, and Jallud was said to have been strongly resistant to any discussion of him being extradited for trial abroad.

17. Dar al-Jamahariya lil-Nashr, *The Revolution in Libya*, pp. 149–154.

18. A. Obeidi, "Political Culture in Libya: A Case Study of Political Attitudes of University Students" (Ph.D. diss., University of Durham, 1996), pp. 93–107.

11

Conclusion

The effectiveness of UN sanctions will be judged here, first, according to the expectations that were raised by the United States, Britain, and France when they were first imposed; and, second, according to whether their use has promoted values and conditions that will create a more stable international environment.

The central demand made by the Western powers was for the extradition of the two Libyans accused of the Lockerbie bombing for trial outside of Libya. This was achieved. However, the framework for the trial that the United States and Britain eventually proposed, and whose acceptance by Libya provided the grounds for the suspending of sanctions, was similar to the proposal Libya first advocated in 1992. The Western powers also sought an end to Libyan support for international terrorism. There is ample reason to believe, however, that the Libyan government had itself abandoned such support at the end of the 1980s. The demise of the Soviet Union and the communist regimes in Eastern Europe, from which Libya had received logistic and intelligence support, together with the more limited role of the revolutionary committees after 1989, necessitated such a change. There were no reports of Libyan support for international terrorism during the 1990–1992 period or after.

As for promoting values and conditions that create a more stable international environment, there is no evidence that sanctions did so. The regime has not been significantly weakened, and it has not been pushed toward greater respect for human and democratic rights. Indeed, such moves as were made toward addressing a human rights agenda (however superficial) and introducing a measure of political and economic liberalization were made during the 1988–1991 period. Since the introduction of

sanctions, there has been some tightening of central controls. Deteriorating social and economic conditions have increased the dependence of
Libyans on the state (especially through the rationing system). Such conditions, coupled with the growth of inequality, have laid the basis for long-
term social disruption and interregional antagonism—and a consequent
lessening of the chances for creating a stable democratic system.

PART 2

The Case of Iraq

12

UN Resolutions on Iraq, 1990–1991: The Basis for International Action

Iraq's invasion and occupation of Kuwait on 2 August 1990 was an event of global consequence, as was the response by the external powers and institutions that formed the allied Coalition. The UN Secretary-General of the mid-1990s, Boutros Boutros-Ghali, filled his official account of developments on and after 2 August with terms that reflected the unique character of the Iraqi action, as well as the UN's opportunity to break new ground as peacemaker, peacekeeper, and peacebuilder. This was, he pointed out, the "first instance since the founding of the [United Nations] in which one Member State sought to completely overpower and annex another." No other crisis in the history of the United Nations had "elicited such attention and action from the Security Council in such a compressed span of time." The United Nations had risen to the challenge and, he said, "demonstrated the far-reaching ability of the [United Nations] to act as a powerful instrument for international peace and security."[1]

Boutros-Ghali described Security Council Resolution 687, which was passed at the end of the Gulf War in 1991, as representing "one of the most complex and far-reaching sets of decisions ever taken by the Council."[2] It was, in fact, the longest text ever adopted by the Council; the resolution sought "to involve Iraq cooperatively in post-war measures to build lasting peace and stability in the region." More than ten years after the initial sanctions were imposed on Iraq, it is clear that this objective has not been fulfilled. The success that the United Nations achieved in enforcing Iraq to withdraw from Kuwait has not been followed either by the creation of a stable and peaceful order in the region, or by the successful integration of Iraq into that order. The prospects for such a development appear even farther away than they were in 1991. The reasons for this are examined in Chapters 12–21.

The dynamics of Iraqi foreign policy, during the period since the Ba'thist regime first came to power in 1968 and especially since Saddam Hussein assumed the presidency in 1979, are relevant to any real understanding of Iraq's response to the UN resolutions since 1990. Also relevant are the events that occurred while Iraq occupied Kuwait and during the ensuing Gulf War. Because there has been so much writing on these matters,[3] however, only the directly relevant details will be offered to illuminate the understanding of subsequent developments. A brief comment on the character of Iraq's international posture prior to 1990 is necessary.

The conduct of foreign policy in Iraq since 1979 could be described as combining tactical brilliance with disastrous strategic miscalculation. Central to policymaking has been the focus on power, seen (consistent with the realist school's theory of international relations)[4] as providing the key ingredient to Iraq's ability to influence regional and international politics. The need for Iraq to wield such influence was justified by reference to the existing weakness of the Arab world relative to non-Arab powers in the Middle East (Israel in particular) and to external powers, creating a situation where Arab governments had lost the ability to defend or promote the interests of their own peoples. The establishment of a strong domestic political base for the regime, and the construction of a powerful military infrastructure, were the cornerstones deemed essential if Iraq were to decisively influence regional developments. The determination and technical skill with which the government pursued its military programs, aided during the 1980s by Western powers eager to contain the radicalism of revolutionary Iran, were evident in the military infrastructure that would have to be dismantled after Iraq's defeat. Much of the diplomatic maneuvering necessary to Iraq's aspired regional role was also skillfully implemented.

Yet its ability to play this role was undermined by miscalculation. On the one hand, some of the forceful internal and regional policies pursued by the regime impinged on the willingness of peoples and governments in the eastern Arab world to work with Iraq, thereby weakening its claim to regional Arab leadership. On the other hand, the use of force—in the short term demonstrating the military power at Iraq's disposal—ultimately led to the destruction of much of the military infrastructure. The full consequences following from the use of that military infrastructure, in situations that created far-reaching international reactions, were poorly assessed and inadequately provided for.

UN resolutions on Iraq differ in the nature of their concerns and the means provided for their implementation. Particular attention needs to be given to separating out resolutions that place Iraq under military-backed compulsion (adopted under Chapter 7 of the UN Charter) from those that carry no sanction; and those that seek to remove Iraq's alleged military threat from those that seek to promote human rights in the country. These distinctions will be further clarified in the chapters that follow.

Furthermore, Security Council measures will be analyzed here without further explaining which governments guided their adoption, unless divisions on the Council affected the content of resolutions. However, Security Council action was guided primarily by the United States, with Britain playing a strong supporting role.

The Initial Resolutions Adopted Under Chapter 7 of the UN Charter, August 1990–April 1991

The original basis for UN sanctions against Iraq was Security Council Resolution 661, passed on 6 August 1990—just four days after Iraq's invasion and occupation of Kuwait.[5] It required all UN member states to prevent any trade or financial dealing with Iraq or occupied Kuwait, including any transfer of funds to Iraq or Kuwait "for the purposes of such activities or dealings." An exception was made for "supplies intended strictly for medical purposes, and, in humanitarian circumstances, foodstuffs." The UN Secretary-General was asked to provide reports to the Security Council on the progress made in implementing the resolution, the first report due within thirty days of passage of the resolution. A committee of the Security Council, consisting of all the members of the Council, was established to examine the reports submitted by the Secretary-General and to "seek from all states further information regarding the action taken by them concerning the effective implementation of the provisions laid down in the present resolution." The committee subsequently became known as the Sanctions Committee. The resolution was adopted under Chapter 7 of the UN Charter, which provides that the Security Council can "take such action by air, sea, or land forces" as may be necessary to fulfill the Council's objectives.[6]

Resolution 661 was strengthened by Security Council Resolution 665 of 25 August 1990, which authorized measures to enforce the embargo on Iraq and occupied Kuwait.[7] The resolution called upon all member states that were deploying military forces in the area, in cooperation with the legitimate government of Kuwait, to use such measures as might be necessary "to halt all inward and outward maritime shipping, in order to inspect and verify their cargoes and destinations and ensure strict implementation of the provisions related to such shipping laid down in Resolution 661."

Security Council Resolution 666 of 13 September 1990 further tightened the measures, setting forth the conditions under which medicines could be supplied to Iraq and the "humanitarian circumstances" that would justify the provision of foodstuffs. The former had to be "under the strict supervision of the government of the exporting state or by appropriate humanitarian agencies," and the latter was dependent on the Sanctions Committee determining that a situation of urgent humanitarian need existed. Foodstuffs could be supplied only "through the United Nations in cooperation with the International Committee of the Red Cross or other appropriate humanitarian agencies and distributed by them or under their supervision."[8]

Another potential loophole was closed on 25 September 1990 by Security Council Resolution 670.[9] It confirmed that sanctions applied to all means of transport, including aircraft. States were instructed to "deny permission to any aircraft to take off from their territory if the aircraft would carry any cargo to or from Iraq or Kuwait other than food in humanitarian circumstances . . . or supplies intended strictly for medical purposes or solely for the UN Iran-Iraq Military Observer Group." In the case of foodstuffs, authorization had to be obtained from the Sanctions Committee for any flight.

The end of the Gulf War brought a change to the sanctions regime. Security Council Resolution 687 of 3 April 1991 continued the sanctions but modified both the content and the objectives.[10] Because it created the framework within which Iraq was forced to exist and operate henceforth, the resolution deserves closer analysis. As with the previous resolutions, Resolution 687 was passed under Chapter 7 of the UN Charter. It affirmed the continued validity of the earlier resolutions but stated that the prohibitions on the export to Iraq of foodstuffs and associated financial transactions would be lifted, subject to notification being given to the Sanctions Committee. Some leeway was also given for imports for "essential civilian needs." As for the latter, the Sanctions Committee could give permission under a "no objection" procedure (i.e., provided that no member of the Security Council raised an objection to an Iraqi request for the import of a specific item) and where humanitarian grounds had been established. The latter grounds could be established on the basis of a report on humanitarian needs in Iraq written by UN Undersecretary-General for Management and Administration Martti Ahtisaari on March 20 following a visit to Iraq,[11] or by further findings of humanitarian need by the Sanctions Committee.

The requirements of Resolution 687 were formidable. It demanded that Iraq and Kuwait respect the inviolability of the international boundary agreed on 4 October 1963, as demarcated by a body to be constituted by the UN Secretary-General (what became the Iraq-Kuwait Boundary Demarcation Committee). To forestall Iraqi misconduct on this issue, it created a demilitarized zone along the boundary, extending ten miles inside Iraq and five miles inside Kuwait. The zone would be patrolled by a UN observer unit (UNIKOM). Iraq was invited to reaffirm unconditionally its obligations under the Protocol for the Prohibition of the Use in War of Asphyxiating, Poisonous, or Other Gases and Bacteriological Methods of Warfare, and to ratify the Convention on the Prohibition of the Development, Production, and Stockpiling of Bacteriological (Biological) and Toxin Weapons and Their Destruction.

With regard to disarmament, the resolution "decided that Iraq shall unconditionally accept" the destruction, removal, or rendering harmless, under international supervision of: (1) all chemical and biological weapons and all stocks of agents and "all related subsystems and components and all research, development, support, and manufacturing facilities related thereto;" and (2) all ballistic missiles with a range greater than 150 kilometers and "related major parts and repair and production facilities."

The UN Secretary-General was asked to develop plans for the UN Special Commission (UNSCOM), which would carry out immediate inspection of Iraq's biological, chemical, and missile capabilities; take responsibility for destroying, removing, or rendering harmless all of the chemical and biological weapons; and supervise the destruction by Iraq of all its missile capabilities. Iraq would, furthermore, be required "not to acquire or develop nuclear weapons or nuclear-weapon-usable material or any subsystems or components or any research, development, support or manufacturing facilities related to such." The International Atomic Energy Agency (IAEA) was asked, with the cooperation of UNSCOM, to carry out immediate on-site inspection of Iraq's nuclear capabilities, to destroy, remove, or render harmless all nuclear-related materials and facilities, and to produce a plan for future ongoing monitoring and verification of Iraq's compliance with the resolution in this field.

Resolution 687 held Iraq responsible under international law for all losses and damages—including environmental damage and the depletion of natural resources—or injury that had occurred to non-Iraqis as a result of the invasion and occupation of Kuwait. The UN Secretary-General was instructed to develop recommendations for a fund (the United Nations Compensation Fund), from which payments would be made to those individuals, organizations, and governments that had suffered loss. The monies in the fund would be drawn from a percentage of the revenues from Iraq's oil exports, once those were permitted. Account would be taken of Iraq's payment capacity and of the requirements of the people of Iraq.

Perhaps with a view to widening international acceptance of the measures imposed on Iraq, the resolution sought in some parts to set the action against Iraq within a wider framework for establishing a peaceful order in the Middle East. In the preamble it made reference to the "objective of the establishment of a nuclear-weapon-free zone in the region of the Middle East," the "threat that all weapons of mass destruction pose to peace and security in the area and the need to work towards the establishment in the Middle East of a zone free of such weapons," the need "to achieve balanced and comprehensive control of armaments in the region," and the desirability of attaining such ends through dialogue among the states of the region. In paragraph 14, furthermore, the actions against Iraq were described as "steps towards the goal of establishing in the Middle East a zone free from weapons of mass destruction and all missiles for their delivery." No measures were taken, however, to give effect to this wider vision, and no progress in this direction occurred during the 1990s.

Some of the clauses in Resolution 687 raised the expectation of a rapid relaxation of the economic controls. Paragraph 21 stated that the sanctions arrangements would be reviewed every sixty days in light of the policies and practices of the Iraqi government, "for the purpose of determining whether to reduce or lift the prohibitions." Paragraph 22 stated that once the Compensation Fund had been established, and when Iraq had undertaken all the measures required of it relating to disarmament, the sanctions on nonmilitary commodities "shall have no further force or effect." Progress toward the latter end was to be subject to regular review, "taking into account Iraq's compliance with the resolution and general progress towards the control of armaments in the region" (paragraph 27). Most significant, the possibility was opened for Iraq to obtain permission to export some oil so it could import foodstuffs, medicines, and supplies for essential civilian needs. Paragraph 23 determined that the Sanctions Committee was "empowered to approve, when required to assure adequate financial resources on the part of Iraq . . . , exceptions to the prohibition against the import of commodities and products originating in Iraq."

In practice, however, these review arrangements did not lead to the short-term removal or reduction of sanctions, and the Security Council chose not to allow Iraq to benefit significantly from the provisions of paragraph 23. The only "exception to the prohibition against the import of products . . . originating in Iraq" that was ever approved by the Sanctions Committee was for Jordan to import a small amount of oil by road from Iraq.

No substantial lightening in the impact of sanctions, therefore, followed from Resolution 687. Permitting Iraq to import food, medicines, and some civilian commodities did not actually enable Iraq to import such goods. For as long as Iraq could not sell its oil, it had no means of raising the foreign currency that would be needed for a substantial level of imports. This was the sanctions regime that remained in force until December 1996.

Iraq's reaction to the resolution at the time deserves attention. A letter dated 6 April 1991 from Ahmed Hussein, the Iraqi minister of foreign affairs, to the UN Secretary-General stated that "Iraq has no choice but to accept this resolution."[12] Nonetheless, he stated several objections. The resolution, he said, embodied a fundamental contradiction: it began with a reaffirmation of Iraq's sovereignty but in practice constituted an "unprecedented attack on Iraq's sovereignty." Of particular importance was the border issue, which was being imposed on Iraq by the Security Council rather than achieved through negotiation. In this respect it violated Security Council Resolution 660, which had called upon Iraq and Kuwait to resolve their differences through negotiation. It was being imposed, moreover, on the basis of an agreement (the "Agreed Minutes" of 1973) that had never been ratified by the Iraqi side. The measures taken by the Council to deprive Iraq of "its lawful right to acquire weapons . . . for defence" were described in the letter as facilitating external military intervention in the country's domestic affairs, thereby threatening to destabilize Iraq. This was not only damaging for Iraq but would endanger peace, security, and stability throughout the region.

With regard to sanctions, the minister complained that Iraq had now accepted all previous Security Council resolutions passed following its occupation of Kuwait, yet the sanctions that had been imposed to force Iraqi compliance had largely been kept in effect. The lifting of sanctions under Resolution 687, moreover, left "broad discretionary authority to certain influential members of the Council which have drawn up the Council's recommendations in an arbitrary manner in order to impose them for political purposes which bear no relation to the Charter or to international law." On the issue of compensation, Ahmed Hussein complained that the resolution failed to recognize that Iraq had justifiable claims to compensation of its own. These related to the deliberate destruction of the country's civilian infrastructure: generating stations, water distribution networks, irrigation dams, civilian bridges, telephone exchanges, factories producing powdered milk for infants and medicines, shelters, mosques, churches, commercial centers, residential neighborhoods, and the like.

The letter placed emphasis on the "double standards" of the Security Council. The Council had, in Resolution 487, condemned Israel in 1981 for its attack on Iraqi nuclear installations "which were used for peaceful purposes and were under international safeguards" and had considered that Iraq was entitled to appropriate compensation for the destruction it had suffered. Yet no actions were taken by the Council to implement that resolution. The same resolution had called on Israel to place its own nuclear facilities under international safeguards, yet Israel's failure to do this was ignored. The lip service paid to the elimination of weapons of mass destruction in the region, therefore, was simply a cover for creating an imbalance of power in the region favorable to Israel. Placing Iraq's development of weapons of mass destruction within the context of an attempt to create a regional balance with Israel, the letter contended that Iraq had become "the target of a plot aimed at destroying the potential it had deployed with a view to arriving at a just balance in the region which would pave the way for the institution of justice and of a lasting peace."

The positions adopted in the letter remained the basis of Iraq's stance with regard to Resolution 687 over the years that followed—an acceptance that Iraq had no alternative but to admit, coupled with a deep level of resentment at the resolution's provisions.

Security Council Resolution 688:
The Human Rights Dimension

Two days after the passage of Resolution 687, another resolution was passed. This concerned internal conditions in Iraq. Resolution 688 of 5 April 1991 noted the "repression of the Iraqi civilian population in any parts of Iraq, including most recently in Kurdish-populated areas, the consequences of which threaten international peace and security in the region," and demanded that Iraq "immediately end this repression."[13] The resolution called for open dialogue to ensure that the human and political rights of all Iraqi citizens were respected, and insisted that Iraq allow "immediate access" by international humanitarian organizations "to all those in need of assistance in all parts of Iraq and make available all necessary facilities for their operations." Resolution 688 was not adopted under Chapter 7 of the UN Charter and thus carried no military or economic sanction.

Notwithstanding the lack of any authorized sanction in the resolution, the United States and Britain used Resolution 688 as a basis for creating two no-fly zones in Iraq banning Iraqi military flights. The northern zone, covering territory above the 36th parallel, was established in June 1991; the southern zone, covering territory below the 32nd parallel, was established in August 1992.[14] Iraq objected strongly to the no-fly zones on the grounds that they ran counter to international law. They were, moreover, political in nature: the objective was "to interfere in Iraq's internal affairs and to dismember it on an ethnic and religious basis."[15]

Despite Iraq's failure to accept Resolution 688, and especially its opposition to the manner in which the United States and Britain chose to use the resolution, the Iraqi government acted quickly to give the United Nations a central role in providing humanitarian assistance "to alleviate the suffering of the affected Iraqi civilian population." One major aspect enabled Kurds, who had fled when the Iraqi army entered Kurdish areas at the end of the Gulf War, to return to their homes, but UN involvement was not intended to be restricted to the Kurdish areas. The United Nations was in practice seeking to operate a human rights undertaking under the cover of a humanitarian program.[16] In a memorandum of understanding signed between the Iraqi government and the United Nations on 18 April, the government of Iraq pledged itself

> to cooperate with the United Nations to have a humanitarian presence in Iraq, wherever such presence may be needed, and to facilitate it through the adoption of all necessary measures. This shall be ensured through the establishment of United Nations sub-offices and Humanitarian Centres (UNHUCs), in agreement and cooperation with the Government of Iraq.[17]

The scale of UN involvement that the Iraqi government was prepared to accept was substantial. Every UNHUC would be staffed by UN civilian personnel who, in addition to regular staff members of the relevant UN agencies, could also include staff co-opted from the nongovernmental organizations (NGOs). The UNHUCs, besides providing humanitarian assistance, would also "monitor the overall situation . . . to advise the Iraqi authorities regarding measures needed to enhance their work." The government of Iraq would make available cash contributions in local currency in order to help cover the in-country costs of the program. It was agreed that humanitarian assistance should be impartial and that all civilians in need, wherever they were located, were entitled to receive it. The UN field staff would be given access to all parts of the country requiring relief. The intention of close cooperation between the United Nations, its various agencies, and NGOs was clear from the program's title: the UN Consolidated Inter-Agency Humanitarian Program (UNIAHP).

The preparedness of the Iraqi government to allow such a major international involvement in Iraq, wherein the United Nations and NGOs would be in close contact with the population (providing services upon which the population would be dependent), appeared significant. International bodies would, through this instrument, have a direct impact and influence on Iraqi civil society.[18] In practice, the most active UNHUCs were in the Kurdish areas, reflecting the need to resettle Kurds who had fled, but the United Nations also had a presence in Amara, Mosul, and Basra, as well as Baghdad.[19] The coherence and effectiveness of the program, however, were seriously undermined by insufficient funding. Despite official UN involvement, the program was largely dependent on voluntary contributions paid directly to individual UN agencies and NGOs, in addition to cash contributions made by the government of Iraq. The voluntary contributions covered only a small part of what was needed.[20]

Political confrontations between the government of Iraq and the international coalition aligned against it, however, explain why the UN Inter-Agency Program, as originally envisaged, did not continue. Iraqi suspicions that the United States and other Western powers were actively plotting to dismember Iraq and remove the existing regime—and intent on using the UN structure to achieve those ends—created an uneasy relationship with the Inter-Agency Program. The establishment of the northern no-fly zone in June 1991, as well as moves to create an autonomous government in the Kurdish areas later that year, intensified Iraqi government suspicions. There were frequent complaints from the government that too large a proportion of program resources were going to the north, and too little to the southern and central regions. In November 1991, the Iraqi government withdrew all its civilian and administrative personnel from northern Iraq and imposed an economic blockade on the region, further burdening the program. The scope for cooperation increasingly narrowed.[21]

The imposition of the southern no-fly zone in August 1992 led to the final abandonment of the UNIAHP countrywide humanitarian program. As in the north, the southern no-fly zone was a reaction to the violence the Iraqi government used to stamp out discontent in the region. The confrontations between the government and the Security Council over arms inspections, especially following UNSCOM's attempt to search the ministry of agriculture in June and July 1992, added to U.S.-British-French determination to restrict the regime's room for maneuver. Following U.S. president George Bush's announcement on 26 August 1992 that the United States, Britain, and France would enforce a no-fly zone over southern Iraq (coupled with advice to the Iraqi population to topple their "brutal" leader),[22] the Iraqi government announced it would not renew the memorandum of understanding for the Inter-Agency Program.[23] A new memorandum was in due course signed in October 1992, but there were to be no UNHUCs, and the United Nations was restricted to a more limited and constrained role—especially in the southern and central regions. Two-thirds of the funding provided by the UN Inter-Agency Program between 1991 and 1995 went to northern Iraq.[24]

Accordingly, the central government could neither obtain effective support from outside to bring relief to its population nor use its own oil resources to satisfy the population's humanitarian needs. Sadruddin Aga Khan, the executive delegate of the UN Secretary-General for humanitarian assistance in Iraq, commented:

> At a time when the international community is beset with disasters of daunting dimensions around the globe, we continue to appeal to the same donors to fund emergency programmes in Iraq that the country could pay for itself. With considerable oil reserves in the ground, Iraq should not have to compete for scarce aid funds with a famine-ravaged Horn of Africa, or with a cyclone-hit Bangladesh.[25]

That situation, however, is precisely the one that the Iraqi government faced.

Notes

1. United Nations, *The United Nations and the Iraq-Kuwait Crisis, 1990–96* (New York: United Nations, 1996), p. 3.

2. Ibid., p. 29.

3. See, e.g., A. Baram, *Culture, History and Ideology in the Formation of Ba'thism in Iraq* (London: Macmillan, 1991); F. Hazelton (ed.), *Saddam's Iraq: Revolution or Reaction?* (London: Zed, 1986); K. Matthews, *The Gulf Conflict and International Relations* (London: Routledge, 1993); P. Marr, *The Modern History of Iraq* (Boulder: Westview, 1995); and P. Sluglett and M. Farouk-Sluglett, *Iraq Since 1958: From Revolution to Dictatorship* (London: I. B. Tauris, 1990). This, however, represents only a small selection of the literature available.

4. See the recommendations for foreign policy formulation and conduct put forward in Hans Morgenthau's classic work, *Politics Among Nations: The Struggle for Power and Peace,* 5th ed. (New York: Knopf, 1972).

5. United Nations, S/RES/661 (1990), 6 August 1990.

6. Article 42, Charter of the United Nations.

7. United Nations, S/RES/665, 25 August 1990.

8. United Nations, S/RES/666, 13 September 1990.

9. United Nations, S/RES/670, 25 September 1990.

10. United Nations, S/RES/687, 3 April 1991.

11. United Nations, *Report on Humanitarian Needs in Iraq in the Immediate Post-crisis Environment by a Mission to the Area Led by the Under-Secretary for Administration and Management, 10–17 March 1991,* S/22366, 20 March 1991.

12. United Nations, *Letter from the Minister of Foreign Affairs of Iraq to the President of the Security Council Stating That Iraq Has No Choice but to Accept the Provisions of Security Council Resolution 697 (1991),* S/22456, 6 April 1991.

13. United Nations, S/RES/688, 5 April 1991.

14. United Nations, *The United Nations and the Iraq-Kuwait Conflict, 1990–96* (New York: United Nations, 1996), p. 41.

15. Ibid.

16. S. Graham-Brown, *Sanctioning Saddam: The Politics of Intervention in Iraq* (London: I. B. Tauris, 1999), p. 269.

17. United Nations, *Letter from the Permanent Representative of Iraq to the Secretary-General Transmitting the Memorandum of Understanding Dated 18 April 1991 Between Iraq and the United Nations Concerning Humanitarian Assistance,* S/22513, 22 April 1991.

18. Although Iraqi society is clearly dominated by state institutions and organizations, it would be wrong to conclude that no civil society exists. Even within the party- or state-affiliated professional associations, educational institutions, charitable bodies, and cultural organizations, the individuals involved may be pursuing interests and objectives that are not dependent on party or state direction.

19. See Graham-Brown, *Sanctioning Saddam,* p. 70.

20. For an official UN account of the establishment and operation of the Inter-Agency Humanitarian Program, see United Nations, "United Nations Consolidated Inter-Agency Humanitarian Programme in Iraq for the Period from April 1995 to March 1996," in United Nations, *The United Nations and the Iraq-Kuwait Conflict,* pp. 722–725. Considerable criticism by independent relief groups was directed at the United Nations for failing to operate an effective program. See *Guardian,* "UN's Aid to Kurds Close to Collapse," 27 July 1992. The underfunding of the UNHUCs, however, was such that a better outcome would have been unlikely.

21. These events are covered well in Graham-Brown, *Sanctioning Saddam,* pp. 267–272. Also see A. Cordesman and A. Hashim, *Iraq: Sanctions and Beyond* (Boulder: Westview, 1997), pp. 76–79.

22. *Guardian,* 27 August 1992.

23. United Nations, *Letter Dated 24 August 1992 from the Secretary-General to the President of the Security Council Concerning the Memorandum of*

Understanding Governing the Inter-Agency Humanitarian Programme in Iraq, S/24509, 2 September 1992.

24. United Nations, "United Nations Consolidated Inter-Agency."

25. United Nations, *Report to the Secretary-General Dated 15 July 1991 on Humanitarian Needs in Iraq Prepared by a Mission Led by the Executive Delegate of the Secretary-General for Humanitarian Assistance in Iraq,* S/22799, 17 July 1991, para. 130.

13

The Security Council, Iraq, and Sanctions, 1991–1995

During the years that followed the imposition of the initial sanctions on Iraq, and the consequent requirements for compliance, the Security Council (guided mainly by the United States, with close British involvement) pursued three main lines of policy. First, it pressed hard for fulfillment of the disarmament and monitoring provisions in Resolution 687. This meant continued support for UNSCOM (through the end of 1998) in its pursuit of Iraqi ballistic missiles and chemical and biological weapons and facilities; and support for the IAEA in its pursuit of nuclear capabilities and facilities.[1] When the United States deemed that Iraq was not cooperating with UNSCOM, the United States and Britain took military action against Iraq by bombing Iraqi installations.

Second, the Security Council sought the efficient and effective running of the non–weapons related programs for which it was responsible under Resolution 687: the Compensation Commission, the Boundary Demarcation Committee, and the humanitarian activities (focusing mainly on northern Iraq until the Oil for Food program was initiated in 1996). Linked to the Security Council's activities, but falling under the General Assembly of the UN, was the monitoring of human rights in Iraq, carried out by a special rapporteur appointed for that purpose.[2]

Third, the Council maintained and developed practices for operating the framework of economic sanctions imposed on Iraq, which were to remain in place until Iraq fulfilled its obligations. There was, however, a problem. The UN role in Iraq was intended to be financed from Iraqi money, and unless Iraq was permitted to export some oil, there would be no resources available for UNSCOM, UNIKOM, the Boundary Demarcation Commission, the Compensation Commission, or the humanitarian activities. The suffering of the Iraqi population, moreover, was being documented by highly reputed external bodies, and such publicity tended to undermine international support for the measures imposed on Iraq. The interests of the United Nations itself, therefore, were for sanctions to be loosened and for Iraq to be permitted to export oil.

The objectives pursued by the Iraqi government are not easily documented. This account, therefore, is an interpretation based on the policies pursued and their probable motivation, as well as an analysis of Iraqi policy statements. It is contended here that Iraqi policy was guided by three main objectives. The first objective was the protection of the regime—of immediate relevance given the uprisings following the Gulf War that threatened to destroy the Ba'thist state, as well as statements by Western leaders that they would welcome a change in political power.[3] Once the initial crisis facing the regime had passed, and the regime had reestablished its power base, this objective was perhaps no longer so influential in shaping policy day to day, but it remained of underlying significance.

The second objective was to protect the sovereignty of Iraq. This was made clear in the foreign minister's letter to the UN Secretary-General following the passage of Resolution 687 and was repeated consistently in most subsequent formal communications to the United Nations. The Iraqi government was determined to escape from those elements of Resolution 687 that gave outside bodies direct control of Iraqi resources and capabilities. There was no way Iraq could avoid UNSCOM or the destruction of its weapons of mass destruction and associated facilities, but it sought to safeguard such elements of those programs that it could and ensure that UNSCOM's role was eventually terminated. In practice, these two aims proved to be in mutual conflict: any attempts to retain elements of the weapons programs ensured that UNSCOM remained in place. The Boundary Demarcation Committee was opposed on the grounds that border questions should be determined by agreement between two sovereign governments and not by imposition—especially when Iraq disputed part of the documentary base on which the demarcation was to proceed.[4] Ultimately, however, the Iraqi government had no alternative but to accept what the Security Council decided. The arrangements for the Compensation Fund, and for the funds accruing from any Iraqi oil exports as might be permitted to be placed in the hands of the United Nations—which would then be able to determine how the money was spent—were also viewed as compromising Iraqi sovereignty.[5]

Third, the government sought the lifting of the sanctions imposed on Iraqi exports and imports. Although the ultimate objective may have been to remove all restrictions, there was little expectation as to military equipment and supplies. The government, therefore, concentrated on ensuring that Iraq could export oil and import nonmilitary goods without restriction. It should be noted, however, that this objective could run counter to the second objective. If the Security Council was offering to permit Iraq to export oil and to import larger quantities of food, medicines, and supplies for civilian needs, and if the overall arrangement and expenditures would be closely controlled by the United Nations, then the Iraqi government had to prioritize. In practice, sovereignty prevailed, as Iraq's long-term future could not be assured otherwise.

The dynamics of the struggle between the Security Council and Iraq in the period after April 1991 follow from the struggle over these objectives. Although it was in the interests of both sides to end sanctions, neither would allow progress in that direction if this frustrated the achievement of its other objectives. For the Security Council, granting permission to export oil (and then to increase such exports) depended on Iraq accepting the regulatory framework for disarmament, border demarcation, and financial control. For the Iraqi government, exporting oil was not worthwhile if it ensured Iraq's long-term weakness and turned the loss of sovereignty that was implicit in Resolution 687 into a permanent feature.

The struggle over sanctions was accompanied by continuing military confrontations between Iraq and the United States and Britain. This was, on the one hand, an attempt to force Iraq to accept the requirements of Resolution 687 relating to weapons of mass destruction—mostly in support of UNSCOM. On the other hand, there was direct action to defend the no-fly zones. The military confrontation will not be given emphasis here, although some mention will be needed for context.

Other UN bodies raised the issue of human rights. In addition to the 1991 resolution, the General Assembly passed resolutions condemning the violations of human rights in Iraq on 20 December 1993 and 23 December 1994,[6] and the UN Commission on Human Rights adopted several similar resolutions in the light of annual reports produced by the special rapporteur.[7] None of these resolutions, however, carried enforceable sanctions.

Resolutions to Modify the Sanctions Regime, May 1991–March 1995

To find a basis for financing the UN role in Iraq, and in light of reports on living conditions within Iraq, the Security Council began deliberations in mid-1991 with a view toward permitting Iraq to export petroleum and petroleum products in limited amounts. The UN's financial need for such an arrangement became apparent once Resolution 699 passed on 17 June 1991,[8] calling on UN member states to "provide maximum assistance, in cash and in kind" to ensure that the United Nations could carry out the tasks of weapons inspection, destruction, removal, and monitoring. It stated, however, that in the absence of such assistance Iraq would be liable for the full costs of the operations. In the event, the voluntary contributions made by member states came to no more than $2 million—a small fraction of what was required. Following recommendations prepared by the UN Secretary-General, therefore, a resolution making possible the sale of some Iraqi oil was drawn up.

Security Council Resolution 706, passed on 15 August 1991, authorized Iraq to export up to $1.6 billion in oil over a six-month period beginning on that date.[9] The extent to which proceeds from oil sales would be under UN control was evident from the title: "Resolution Authorising the Import of Oil Products Originating from Iraq for a Six-Month Period in Order to Finance United Nations Operations Mandated by Security Council Resolution 687." All proceeds from oil sales would be placed in an escrow account established by the United Nations and administered by the Secretary-General. Expenditure of the funds would be limited to three purposes: payments into the UN Compensation Fund (30 percent of total proceeds, already decided by the Security Council in Resolution 705[10]); payments to the United Nations for the disarmament and security-related operations envisaged by Resolution 687 and for the UN role in facilitating the return of Kuwaiti property seized by Iraq; and payments for the purchase of food, medicines, and supplies for essential civilian needs under a scheme that would be devised by the Secretary-General.

The government of Iraq, however, was not prepared to implement the resolution, which it described as prejudicial to Iraqi sovereignty. The conditions that were being imposed on Iraq, in the view of the Iraqi government, were "unnecessary and obtrusive." They impaired Iraqi independence and interfered in its internal affairs. Given that Iraq had fulfilled most of the requirements of Resolution 687, it should now be permitted to "export oil in a normal and regular manner, with an understanding between Iraq and the United Nations as to the percentage of the proceeds to be deducted for the benefit of the United Nations . . . with the Security Council, if necessary, obliging states not to export a particular kind of goods to Iraq."[11] Iraq had earlier maintained, moreover, that a grace period of two to five years was needed before Iraq could begin paying reparations: the economy needed to be functioning properly so as to enable these payments to be made.[12]

Despite several attempts to circumvent Iraqi objections to it, the resolution was never put into effect. Four rounds of talks were held between the UN Secretariat and Iraq, wherein the former sought to persuade the latter to accept the resolution through 1992 and 1993—with the last round being held in July 1993. Iraq continued to maintain that the resolution involved "unacceptable encroachments on its sovereignty."[13] Without the implementation of Resolution 706, the regular sixty-day reviews of sanctions (in accordance with Resolution 687) ended inevitably with the Security Council concluding that there was "no agreement that the necessary conditions existed for a modification" of the sanctions regime.[14] Some measures were taken, however, to simplify the procedures whereby Iraq could import the goods covered by Resolution 687.

The Security Council found another means to cover some expenses. Security Council Resolution 661 of 6 August 1991 had ruled out the possibility of the United Nations making use of any of Iraq's frozen assets. Funds and resources resulting from Iraqi petroleum that had left Iraq, but had not been sold, before 6 August were not formally frozen (although Iraq had been prevented from obtaining access to them). The Security Council now turned its attention to these assets and resources. Resolution 778, passed on 2 October 1992, instructed that all states "in which there are funds of the Government of Iraq . . . that represent the proceeds of sale of Iraqi petroleum or petroleum products, paid for, by or on behalf of the purchaser, on or after 6 August 1999" should transfer these funds to the United Nations escrow account provided for in Resolution 706.[15] Furthermore, states in which there were stocks of petroleum or petroleum products owned by Iraq should arrange for their sale, then transfer the proceeds to the escrow account. These measures raised $101.5 million, slightly less than the $106.3 million the UN Secretary-General estimated was needed for the United Nations to conduct the activities envisaged in Resolution 687 through 1993.

There remained, however, the wider needs of UNIAHP, projected at $489 million for one year (1993). The continuation of activities under Resolution 687 beyond the end of 1993, moreover, would need new funding. In 1994, then, the UN Secretary-General proposed raising extra funds by asking oil companies that had received Iraqi oil before 6 August 1990, but had not paid for it due to the sanctions, to transfer those funds to the escrow account. Nothing came of that initiative. There was a strong need for a new resolution that would stand a greater chance of being acceptable to the Iraqi side.

Notes

1. Following his appointment as head of UNSCOM in April 1991, Rolf Ekeus was surprised to learn that no funds had been allocated for the operation of UNSCOM. The only way in which he could acquire the funds to start activities was by personally vouching for a loan from the Secretary-General's cash fund. See A. Cockburn and P. Cockburn, *Out of the Ashes: The Resurrection of Saddam Husain* (New York: HarperCollins, 1999), p. 97.

2. The special rapporteur had been appointed by the UN Commission on Human Rights in March 1991—before Security Council Resolution 687 was adopted. The Commission had instructed the rapporteur to "make a thorough study of the violations of human rights by the Government of Iraq, based on all the information the special rapporteur may deem relevant." Information collected by the special rapporteur led the General Assembly in December 1991 to pass a resolution regretting "the failure of the Government of Iraq to provide satisfactory replies to all the allegations of violations of human rights," and calling on the government of Iraq to "release all persons arrested and detained without ever being informed of charges against them, and without access to legal counsel or due process of law," and to abide by its obligations under the International Covenant on Civil and Political Rights (to which it was a party). See United Nations, A/RES/46/134, 17 December 1991. The first of the substantive reports by the special rapporteur, Max van Stoel, was transmitted to the Security Council by the General Assembly on 9 March 1992. See United Nations, *Report on the Situation of Human Rights in Iraq Prepared by the Special Rapporteur of the Commission of Human Rights on the Situation of Human Rights in Iraq*, S/23685, 9 March 1992.

3. Most of these statements have come from U.S. quarters. In 1991, President George Bush's deputy national security adviser declared that sanctions would remain as long as Saddam Hussein ruled Iraq. In August 1992 Brent Scowcroft, the national security adviser, was reported (*Observer*, 2 August 1992) to have told Iraqi opposition leaders that the United States would not abandon them until Saddam Hussein was removed. This followed the dispatch of 2,500 troops for "exercises" in the Persian Gulf. In March 1997, Secretary of State Madeleine Albright told an audience at Georgetown University that "we do not agree with the nations who argue that if Iraq complies with its obligations concerning weapons of mass destruction, sanctions should be lifted." See A. Cockburn and P. Cockburn, *Out of the Ashes*, pp. 263–264. British statesmen have, especially since the mid-1990s, avoided any implication that sanctions were linked to regime survival.

4. The Iraqi position is laid out in detail in a letter addressed by the foreign minister to the UN Secretary-General in June 1993. See United Nations, *Letter Dated 7 June 1993 from the Permanent Representative of Iraq to the Secretary-General Transmitting a Letter Dated 6 June 1993 from the Minister of Foreign Affairs of Iraq Concerning the Work of the Iraq-Kuwait Boundary Demarcation Commission*, S/25905, 8 June 1993.

5. The Iraqi foreign minister contended that responsibility for reparations under Resolution 687 should be determined "in accordance with the rules and

procedures established by international law," rather than through the offices of a body that could be manipulated in the interests of individual major powers. For the Iraqi position, see United Nations, *Letter from the Permanent Representative of Iraq to the President of the Security Council Transmitting a Letter Dated 27 May 1991 from the Minister for Foreign Affairs of Iraq Commenting on Security Council Resolution 692*, S/22643, 23 May 1991.

6. United Nations General Assembly, A/RES/48/144 of 20 December 1993, and A/RES/49/203 of 23 December 1994.

7. One of the most forthright of these was resolution 1994/74 of 9 March 1994.

8. United Nations, S/RES/699, 17 June 1991.

9. United Nations, S/RES/706, 15 August 1991. The provisions of this resolution were later confirmed by, and strengthened by, Security Council Resolution 712, S/RES/712, passed on 19 September 1991.

10. United Nations, S/RES/705, 15 August 1991.

11. Taken from a letter from the Iraqi foreign minister to the UN Secretary-General, quoted in United Nations, *The United Nations and the Iraq-Kuwait Conflict*, p. 101. Iraq was not opposed in principle to the United Nations monitoring the expenditure of revenues it obtained through the sale of oil but objected to the level and character of the control that was proposed. The acceptance in principle had been expressed to the Secretary-General's delegate for humanitarian assistance to Iraq in July 1991. See United Nations, S/22799, para. 34.

12. This was conveyed to the Security Council in a letter from Iraq's permanent representative in the United Nations. See *Guardian*, 12 June 1991.

13. United Nations, *The United Nations and the Iraq-Kuwait Conflict*, p. 102.

14. The result of the first of these reviews was made public by the president of the Security Council on 5 August 1991. See United Nations, *Letter Dated 6 August 1991 from the President of the Security Council Addressed to the Secretary-General*, S/22904, 7 August 1991. Similar reviews and announcements were made every two months following that.

15. United Nations, S/RES/778, 2 October 1992. Security Council Resolution 661 had ruled out the possibility of the United Nations making use of any of Iraq's frozen assets accrued through financial transactions that occurred unequivocally before the resolution was passed; S/RES/661, 6 August 1990.

14

Easing Sanctions: Oil for Food Resolutions, 1995–1999

Security Council Resolution 986, passed on 14 April 1995, was another attempt to create a framework for selling Iraqi oil, the proceeds of which would finance UN operations in Iraq, make compensation payments, and allow imports of products permitted under Resolution 687. Although the mechanisms for permitting exports were based on those in Resolutions 706 and 712, this resolution was phrased in a manner that took account of Iraqi objections. There was an explicit acknowledgment of Iraqi sovereignty and of the temporary nature of the proposed arrangements. The preamble reaffirmed the "commitment of all member states to the sovereignty and territorial integrity of Iraq," and the penultimate paragraph stated that "nothing in this resolution should be construed as infringing the sovereignty or territorial integrity of Iraq." Mention of the Kurdish areas was placed in the context of the "sovereign territory of Iraq." The resolution referred, moreover, to the Security Council's conviction "of the need as a temporary measure to provide for the humanitarian needs of the Iraqi people."

Iraq was allowed to export up to $2 billion in petroleum and petroleum products over a six-month period.[1] Most exports were to be pipelined through Turkey (the Kirkuk-Yumurtalik pipeline); the remainder would be shipped from the Mina al-Bakr oil terminal on the Persian Gulf. As was envisaged under Resolution 706, the proceeds from oil exports would flow into the escrow account controlled by the UN Secretary-General and would be available for most of the purposes identified in 706. Resolution 986 did specify, however, arrangements and funding that would be available to the three Kurdish governorates in the north. UNIAHP would be provided with $260–$300 million from the escrow account for the distribution of goods in those governorates.

The Iraqi reaction was initially unfavorable. The criticism, however, was no longer based on the principle of sovereignty but on practicalities. On 15 May, the Iraqi minister of foreign affairs informed the UN Secretary-General that Iraq objected to "the proportion of petroleum to be exported via the Kirkuk-Yumurtalik pipeline, and to the modalities for distribution of humanitarian relief in the three northern governorates."[2] At the suggestion of the Secretary-General, the Security Council postponed the implementation of the resolution pending discussions with the UN Secretariat. Informal contacts took place in late 1995, leading to formal talks beginning on 6 February 1996.[3] On 20 May 1996, a memorandum of understanding was signed between the UN Secretariat and the government of Iraq, covering the implementation of the resolution.[4]

The memorandum of understanding, besides clarifying the processes whereby Resolution 986 would be put into effect, illuminates Iraq's objectives at the time. The issue of sovereignty was crucial. The Iraqi side insisted on the restatement of the phrases from Resolution 986 that were crucial to its own acceptance of the resolution.[5] Under the general provisions of the memorandum, it was stressed that "nothing in the present Memorandum should be construed as infringing upon the sovereignty and territorial integrity of Iraq" and that "the provisions of the present Memorandum pertain strictly and exclusively to the implementation of the Resolution and, as such, in no way create a precedent." The arrangement provided for in the memorandum was described as being "an exceptional and temporary measure." Differences over the amount of petroleum and petroleum products to be exported through Turkey rather than by sea through the Gulf were resolved in Iraq's favor: no proportion was fixed for either outlet.[6] All imports into Iraq financed from the escrow account would be at the request of the government of Iraq. They would have to cohere with a distribution plan drawn up by the government.

The memorandum set modalities for the distribution of supplies in the Kurdish governorates of northern Iraq by UNIAHP that were designed to give formal acknowledgment to Iraqi sovereignty over the governorates. Although UNIAHP would "collect and analyze pertinent information on humanitarian needs in the three northern governorates," this information would be discussed with the government of Iraq, and the relevant recommendations would form part of the overall distribution plan drawn up by the Iraqi government.[7] Decisions over which supplies for the northern governorates should be procured by the central government and held in storage centers in Kirkuk and Mosul, and those that should be procured directly by the UNIAHP and held in storage centers in the northern governorates, would depend on discussions between the government and UNIAHP.

Despite the emphasis on Iraqi sovereignty, there was no doubt that the United Nations would closely supervise imports into Iraq under the Oil for Food resolution. The Iraqi government bound itself to "effectively guarantee equitable distribution" of the imports, and the government's distribution plan had to be approved by the UN Secretary-General.[8] States exporting to Iraq would have to gain the approval of the Sanctions Committee for all goods exported, and the goods could only consist of humanitarian supplies: medicine, health goods, foodstuffs, and items for essential civilian needs. The arrival of goods in Iraq would have to be confirmed by independent inspection agents, appointed by the UN Secretary-General, who would check that the goods were consistent with what the Sanctions Committee had authorized.

Once the Secretary-General reported to the Security Council that measures were in place for the implementation of Resolution 986, then Iraq could begin pumping oil for export. This duly began on 10 December 1996, with the proceeds from the sale of oil being deposited in the UN escrow account on 15 January 1997. The first shipment of commodities to Iraq (chick peas and white beans from Turkey) under Resolution 986 crossed the border from Turkey on 20 March. Distribution of goods, under observation by the United Nations, began in April.[9]

Subsequent Oil for Food Resolutions

Because Resolution 986 covered only a six-month period, the continuation of the Oil for Food program since then has depended on a series of reauthorizing Security Council resolutions. All remained within the framework of 986, with some changes in the scale of oil exports permitted and of the scope within which exports could be permitted. Each resolution introduced a new phase of Oil for Food, such that by mid-2000 seven phases had been completed. Resolution 1111, passed on 4 June 1997, approved a six-month extension and authorized another $2 billion in oil sales.[10] The Iraqi government announced that oil would not be exported under phase 2 until the Secretary-General had approved its new distribution plan. Approval of the latter was given on 4 August.[11] Resolution 1143, passed on 4 December 1997, provided for a further $2 billion in oil sales.[12] The government again delayed the implementation of the new phase until the Secretary-General accepted its distribution plan for phase 3.

Resolution 1143 did, however, open the way to Iraq being permitted to export more oil. The Secretary-General was asked to make recommendations with regard to finding "ways of improving the implementation of the humanitarian program" and to taking "such action over additional resources as are needed." The Secretary-General's report, submitted to the Security Council on 1 February 1998, noted that $2 billion in oil exports was not sufficient to provide the Iraqi population with a reasonable level of humanitarian goods:

> Since the start of the implementation of Resolution 986 (1995), it has become increasingly apparent that this sum is inadequate to prevent further deterioration in humanitarian conditions and cannot effect the improvement in the health and nutritional status of the Iraqi population the Council hoped for when it unanimously adopted the measure.[13]

The report recommended that oil exports be raised to a value of $5.2 billion per six-month period. Resolution 1153, passed on 20 February 1998, followed the Secretary-General's recommendations and allowed Iraq to export $5.26 billion in oil over the subsequent six-month period.[14] The resolution also indicated that Iraq might, for the first time, be able to spend some Oil for Food money on equipment for the power-generation and oil sectors. The Secretary-General was asked to present a report on Iraq's needs in the electricity sector and to establish a group of experts to advise on production and capacity in the oil sector. The enhanced distribution plan, made necessary by Resolution 1153 and prepared by the government of Iraq, was approved by the Secretary-General on 29 May 1998, with immediate effect. In phase 4, funding for the humanitarian program doubled.

The decision to allow Iraq to export more oil, and to increase humanitarian spending on the basis of the higher revenues, however, depended on Iraq's ability to produce more oil. The state of the Iraqi oil industry, operating without access to spare parts for seven years, rendered this impossible. The group of oil experts established by the Secretary-General reported in April that the state of the oil industry was lamentable and that Iraq would be unable to produce oil at the level authorized by the Security Council unless it could acquire new equipment and spare parts. Security Council Resolution 1175, passed on 19 June 1998, authorized Iraq to import up to $300 million in spare parts and equipment to increase the production of oil for export.[15] However, the limited quantity of spares and equipment that could be acquired, and the length of time required to obtain them, were such that there was no short-term increase in oil production. In practice, therefore, the plans for increased expenditure on humanitarian goods did not come to fruition. The UN Secretary-General reported: "Regrettably, most of the objectives of the enhanced distribution plan could not be achieved, primarily owing to a substantial shortfall in revenues."[16] The approved plan required funding of $3.1 billion, but only $1.9 billion was available.

Phase 5 (Resolution 1210, 24 November 1998) and phase 6 (Resolution 1242, 21 May 1999) initially brought no major changes to arrangements in force under phase 4.[17] Both permitted Iraq to sell the same value of oil as stipulated in Resolution 1153, and Iraq was allowed to continue to allocate $300 million to spare parts and equipment. One small innovation in Resolution 1210 was a facility allowing Iraq, on the basis of specific requests approved by the Sanctions Committee, to draw from the escrow account "reasonable expenses related to Hajj pilgrimage."

Halfway through phase 6, however, a substantial change occurred. It had become apparent that the rising price of oil in the international market would enable Iraq to exceed the $5.2 billion in oil exports permitted for the six-month period—with no increase in actual oil production. The UN Secretary-General, in his report to the Security Council on 19 August 1999, pointed out that the price fetched by Iraqi oil had increased by $5 per barrel since the beginning of phase 6, with the price now standing at $17 per barrel. At its lowest point, in December 1998, Iraqi oil had been priced at $7 per barrel. The Secretary-General predicted that oil revenues, at the current rate of oil production, could reach $6.3 billion during phase 6. As Iraq had not been able to export as much oil as it was permitted to in previous phases, with severely negative effects on the humanitarian programs, there was clearly a case for increasing the permitted value of exports for phase 6.[18]

Security Council Resolution 1266, passed on 4 October 1999, permitted Iraq to export an additional $3.04 billion worth of oil during phase 6, representing the accumulated deficits carried over from phases 4 and 5.[19] In practice, as phase 6 was due to end some six weeks after the resolution was passed, Iraq could not have obtained the full financial benefit from the new resolution—especially as the state of its oil industry made any substantial increase of production impossible. Nonetheless, Iraq did obtain oil revenues of $7.4 billion during phase 6, taking up $2.2 billion of the additional $3.04 billion that Resolution 1266 had permitted. The high revenue was attributable to the continuing rise in the price of oil (averaging $19 per barrel during phase 6).[20]

Difficulties in the Security Council in agreeing to the text of a new resolution on Iraq led the Council to extend phase 6, initially for two weeks (Resolution 1275, 19 November 1999) and then by one additional week (Resolution 1280, 3 December 1999).[21] The final extension took phase 6 through 11 December.[22] The government of Iraq, however, was not prepared to accept extensions of such short duration. It stopped exporting oil during the three-week period on the grounds that the extensions were insufficient to conclude relevant agreements for oil sales and for purchases of humanitarian goods.[23] The government's real concern was probably more over the political objectives that it believed lay behind the temporary extensions. It saw them as instruments to pressure Iraq to accept the new resolution that the British and Dutch governments were putting together, one that would link the ending of sanctions with Iraqi acceptance of a new weapons monitoring operation (ultimately passed as Resolution 1284).

After a period of uncertainty, the Security Council passed Resolution 1281 on 10 December 1999, extending Oil for Food for a further six months. The terms, and therefore the framework, for phase 7 were the same as those in phase 6. Iraq was permitted to export $5.2 billion in oil, and of the amounts available for humanitarian goods Iraq would be able to import $300 million in spare parts and equipment. The government of Iraq had been seeking $600 million in equipment and spares, maintaining that the proper upkeep of the oilfields and exporting facilities was not possible with only the $300 million allocation. This position was supported by the UN Secretary-General, who, in late 1999, consistently called for the allocation to be raised to $600 million.[24] The Secretary-General pointed out that the continued deterioration of the oil facilities in Iraq may "cause a major breakdown in Iraq's oil production and export capacity, which will have serious repercussions on the implementation of the humanitarian program," and that it was also "adversely affecting the safety of the workers in the oil fields and causing serious environmental damage as well as damaging oil wells—some permanently."[25] Oil experts reported at the end of 1998 that Iraq's production capacity was declining at an estimated rate of 4–8 percent annually and that it was most unlikely that exports could exceed 1.9 million barrels per day in the foreseeable future—even with the allocation for spares that had been agreed.[26] In order to bolster his position, the Secretary-General dispatched a group of experts to Iraq, from 15 January to 31 January 2000, to survey the condition of the oil sector and to "make recommendations on necessary additions to the current allocation for oil spare parts and equipment."[27] The experts reported on 10 March that there had been a massive decline in the condition, effectiveness, and efficiency of the oil infrastructure and that "without prompt action a continued decline in production is strongly indicated."[28] In the light of the information and the pressure coming from the UN Secretariat, the Security Council accepted an increase in the allocation of Oil for Food money for oil equipment and spare parts. Resolution 1293, passed on 31 March 2000, increased the allocation to $600 million—to be used during phase 7.[29]

Moving Beyond 986: Resolution 1284 and the Accompanying Controversy, 1999–2000

The need for a new Security Council resolution on Iraq stemmed mainly from the ongoing confrontation over weapons inspections. On 5 August 1998, Iraq had stopped cooperating with UNSCOM, after the head of UNSCOM (Richard Butler) refused to certify that Iraq had destroyed its banned weapons. In an attempt to reestablish Iraq's cooperation with UNSCOM, the UN Secretary-General promised a comprehensive review of Iraq's compliance with UN resolutions. UNSCOM's activities, however, had to be restarted before such a review could be undertaken. The credibility of UNSCOM was, in the meantime, undermined by revelations that it had since 1994 been liaising closely with Israeli intelligence.[30] On 29 October, the Security Council decided to carry forward the comprehensive review but failed to link this review to the removal of sanctions—which the government of Iraq had demanded. On 31 October, the government cut off all dealings with UNSCOM,[31] insisting that there would be no cooperation until the Security Council "seriously examined the lifting of sanctions."[32] On 11 November, UNSCOM inspectors were withdrawn from Iraq at the insistence of the United States, indicating that military action against Iraq was planned.[33] The action, however, was delayed after Iraq backed down and agreed, on 14 November, to resume cooperation with UNSCOM inspectors. Armed U.S. bombers had already lifted off for Iraq when the mission was called off.[34]

Within a month, however, UNSCOM and Iraq were in renewed confrontation, with UNSCOM alleging that Iraq was blocking some inspections, and Iraq alleging that inspectors were not following the modalities for inspection under the memorandum of June 1996.[35] Four days of intensive U.S.-British air strikes (Operation Desert Fox) were unleashed against Iraq between 16 December and 19 December. Sporadic air attacks were to continue through 1999 and 2000 in response to Iraqi attempts to challenge U.S.-British flights in the no-fly zones. The air strikes did not, however, lead to the resumption of Iraqi cooperation with UNSCOM and, indeed, appeared to reinforce Iraqi determination not to allow the weapons inspectors (who left during the bombing) to re-enter the country. Opinion among some Security Council members, moreover, indicated that a new framework would be needed. The Chinese ambassador to the United Nations told the Security Council that UNSCOM had "concealed information from the Council, deceived and misled the Council and even acted without Council authorisation."[36]

Secondary to this, but nonetheless significant, was the recognition that international criticism over the operation of sanctions, and publicity over the effect that sanctions were having on the Iraqi population, were reducing the preparedness of some states to continue complying with the Security Council resolutions. The Security Council needed to respond, as the Secretary-General acknowledged, to "concerns that the underlying weaknesses in the implementation of resolutions 986 [1995] and 1153 [1998] had not been adequately addressed and that, consequently, improvements in the humanitarian situation have been below expectations."[37]

Consequent to the Security Council's decision in October 1998 to undertake a comprehensive review of its dealings with Iraq, and in the light of the subsequent crisis, the Council established three subpanels at the end of January 1999 to make recommendations as to how to proceed. The subpanels, meeting under the chairmanship of the Brazilian ambassador to the United Nations, covered the three main areas in which there were ongoing problems: disarmament; the humanitarian situation; and prisoners of war and Kuwaiti missing persons and archives.[38] The subpanels delivered their reports by 15 April 1999, and the remainder of the year was taken up with drafting and redrafting a resolution. Given that the British delegation to the United Nations, in close collaboration with the U.S. delegation, was playing the central role in drafting the resolution, and given that some members of the Security Council were highly critical of the British-U.S. air strikes and determined to see an early end to the sanctions regime, the process was difficult and protracted.

Security Council Resolution 1284, finally adopted on 17 December 1999, introduced two major changes to the regulatory framework of Resolution 687 and subsequent resolutions.[39] The first involved the replacement of UNSCOM by the United Nations Monitoring, Verification, and Inspection Commission (UNMOVIC). Its role was similar to that of UNSCOM, with responsibilities for verifying Iraqi compliance with Resolution 687. It would, in addition, operate a reinforced system of ongoing monitoring and verification.

The second change was in the specification of measures that could lead to the suspension of sanctions. If UNMOVIC and the IAEA submitted favorable reports—confirming that Iraq had cooperated fully in completing a work program covering the remaining disarmament and monitoring requirements of Resolution 687—and with the reinforced system of ongoing monitoring and verification having been operational for at least 120 days, then the Security Council intended to suspend "prohibitions against the import of commodities and products originating in Iraq, and prohibitions against the sale, supply and delivery to Iraq of civilian products."[40]

The suspension, however, would be for only 120-day periods (which were renewable) and was subject to "the elaboration of effective financial and other operational measures to ensure that Iraq does not acquire prohibited items." If there were any subsequent reports from UNMOVIC and IAEA suggesting that Iraq was not cooperating with either of those bodies, the sanctions could be reimposed.

There was, however, a lack of clarity as to what suspension of sanctions would involve. The text did not specify whether Iraqi oil revenues would continue to pass through the UN escrow account, with expenditure requiring UN authorization. Paragraph 36 of the resolution appeared to suggest that these procedures, or some similar control over Iraqi finances, would continue. The paragraph expressed the Council's intention "to approve financial and other operational measures, including on the delivery of and payment for authorised civilian commodities and products to be sold or supplied to Iraq, in order to ensure that Iraq does not acquire prohibited items." Given that other means could have been found to prevent weapons-related material from reaching Iraq, the concern with retaining financial control was perhaps motivated primarily by a determination to ensure that Iraq continued to pay reparations through the Compensation Commission. It was openly admitted that in the absence of external financial control there was no means whereby Iraq could be made to continue payments.[41]

The second change involved adaptations in the sanctions regime that could be implemented immediately and would, it was suggested, improve humanitarian conditions in Iraq. The resolution removed all limits to exports of petroleum and petroleum products. The Sanctions Committee was instructed, furthermore, to give general approval to categories of humanitarian items that would no longer need committee approval. These included "foodstuffs, pharmaceutical and medical supplies, as well as basic or standard medical and agricultural equipment and basic or standard educational items."[42] The export of such items to Iraq, however, would still have to be notified to the Secretary-General and financed from the escrow account, as before. Measures were also instituted to speed up the approval of contracts and reduce the number of contracts on hold. These changes were not dependent on Iraqi acceptance of the resolution as a whole.

The impacts of these changes, however, were not likely to be substantial. Given that the state of the Iraqi oil industry left Iraq with little capacity to increase oil production, the removal of the limit was not very significant. The promised changes in the processes for authorizing Iraqi imports could have been implemented within the framework of previous UN resolutions. The UN Secretariat, indeed, had sought over a prolonged period to speed up processes in the manner indicated by the new resolution.

Even within the UN Security Council, support for Resolution 1284 was incomplete. Three of the permanent members of the Council—China, France, and Russia—chose to abstain. The government of Iraq rejected the resolution outright on the grounds that UNMOVIC simply replicated UNSCOM, with no recognition that Iraq had fulfilled almost all of its obligations under Resolution 687; that the procedures for lifting sanctions provided Security Council members antipathetic to Iraq with ample means to delay or block the lifting and to reimpose them once lifted; that accepted international practice required Iraq, as a member of the United Nations, to be consulted before measures were imposed on it; that the text of the resolution, unlike that of Resolution 986, placed insufficient emphasis on Iraqi sovereignty;[43] that some of the conditions now being imposed (e.g., as to ongoing monitoring and financial controls) were unlimited in time, whereas previously imposed conditions were either limited in time or else subject to removal once Iraq had fulfilled its obligations; and that many of the provisions of the resolution were vague, such that individual Security Council members would be able to use the resolution to their own ends.[44] It was pointed out that the continuing U.S.-British military strikes against Iraq, justified on an interpretation of UN resolutions not shared by other members of the Security Council, did not incline the Iraqi government to confidence.

Although Iraq was prepared to accept a continuing monitoring presence, it would do so only if sanctions were first removed.

Notes

1. United Nations, S/RES/986, 14 April 1995.

2. Quoted from the UN Secretary-General's account of the communication, in United Nations, *Letter Dated 1 June 1995 from the Secretary-General to the President of the Security Council Concerning Resolution 986,* S/1995/495, 19 June 1995.

3. United Nations, *The United Nations and the Iraq-Kuwait Conflict, 1990–1996* (New York: United Nations, 1996), pp. 103–104.

4. United Nations, *Memorandum of Understanding Between the Secretariat of the United Nations and the Government of Iraq on the Implementation of Security Council Resolution 986,* S/1996/356, 20 May 1996.

5. This description is taken from interviews conducted by the writer with Iraqi foreign ministry officials in December 1997 in Baghdad. The outcome can be attested by referring to the text of the memorandum. See ibid.

6. In practice, rather more oil has been exported through the Mina al-Bakr facility than through the Turkish pipeline under Resolution 986. In 1999, for example, 1.19 million barrels per day were being exported through the former, 914,768 barrels per day through the latter. See United Nations, *Report of the Secretary-General Pursuant to Paragraph 6 of Security Council Resolution 1242*, S/1999/1162, 12 November 1999, paras. 8 and 10.

7. United Nations, *The United Nations and the Iraq-Kuwait Conflict.*

8. Ibid.

9. The information in this paragraph is taken from United Nations Office of the Iraq Program, *Implementation of Oil-for-Food—a Chronology* <http://www.un.org/Depts/oip/chron.html>.

10. United Nations, S/RES/1111, 4 June 1997.

11. UN Office of the Iraq Program, *Implementation of Oil-for-Food.*

12. United Nations, S/RES/1143, 4 December 1997.

13. United Nations, *Report of the Secretary-General Pursuant to Paragraph 7 of Resolution 1143*, S/1998/90, 1 February 1998, para. 66.

14. United Nations, S/RES/1153, 20 February 1998.

15. United Nations, S/RES/1175, 19 June 1998.

16. United Nations, *Review and Assessment of the Implementation of the Humanitarian Programme Established Pursuant to Security Council Resolution 986*, S/199, 28 April 1999, para. 20.

17. United Nations, S/RES/1210, 24 November 1998, and S/RES/1242, 21 May 1999.

18. United Nations, *Report of the Secretary-General Pursuant to Paragraph 6 of Security Council Resolution 1242*, S/1999/896, 19 August 1999, paras. 3–8 and 91–95.

19. United Nations, S/RES/1266, 4 October 1999.

20. United Nations Office of the Iraq Program, *Basic Figures as 11 January 2000* <http://www.un.org/Depts/oip/latest/basicfigures.html>.

21. United Nations, S/RES/1275, 19 November 1999, and S/RES/1280, 3 December 1999.

22. As the renewal of the Oil for Food arrangement was due, members of the Security Council were considering a new resolution that would substantially change the Oil for Food framework—what became Security Council Resolution 1284. Russia was initially unwilling to support a simple rollover of the Oil for Food arrangement, believing that the time had come to lift sanctions. Ultimately, the rollover of the existing arrangement was deemed by the Iraqi side preferable to the new resolution that the British and Dutch governments were putting together.

23. The halt to Iraqi oil exports led to the price of oil rising to $27 per barrel. The Iraqi government may have wanted to use this experience as an indication to the West of Iraq's ability to inflict economic damage on the Western economies. If the cutoff of Iraqi oil exports had continued, however, it would have been possible for other OPEC states to make up the shortfall in production. For a discussion of this, see the article by Jihad Khazen in *Al-Hayat*, 24 November 1999.

24. This was initially put forward by him in a letter to the Security Council, dated 12 October 1999, S/1999/1053. It was then repeated in his subsequent

reports to the Council. See United Nations, S/1999/1162 *(Report of the Secretary-General on Resolution 1242)*.

25. See United Nations, *Letter Dated 14 January from the Secretary-General Addressed to the President of the Security Council*, S/2000/26. Most of the points made here had also been put forward in the Secretary-General's reports on Iraq from mid-1998. See United Nations, S/1998/330, 15 April 1998; S/1998/1233, 29 December 1998; S/1999/746, 2 July 1999; S/1999/1053, 12 October 1999; and S/1999/1162 *(Report of the Secretary-General on Resolution 1242)*.

26. United Nations, S/199 *(Review and Assessment of the Humanitarian Programme)*.

27. Ibid.

28. Quoted from the UN press release that covered the Security Council's discussion on this issue, as part of its general debate on the humanitarian program in Iraq, on 24 March 2000. See *Security Council Meets to Consider Humanitarian Situation in Iraq; Secretary-General Describes "Moral Dilemma" for United Nations*, United Nations Press Release, SC/6833, 24 March 2000.

29. United Nations, S/RES/1293, 31 March 2000.

30. *Guardian*, 30 September 1998. Scott Ritter, a former inspector with UNSCOM, told a press conference that he had visited Israel many times between 1994 and 1998 and that UNSCOM would not have been able to carry out its work without Israel's help.

31. *Observer*, 1 November 1998.

32. *Guardian*, 7 November 1998.

33. *Guardian*, 12 November 1998.

34. *Observer*, 15 November 1998.

35. *Guardian*, 16 December 1998.

36. United Nations Press Release, *Security Council Establishes New Monitoring Commission on Iraq Adopting Resolution 1284 (1999) by Vote of 11–0–4*, SC/6775, 17 December 1999.

37. United Nations Press Release, *Humanitarian Situation in Iraq*, SC/6833, 24 March 2000.

38. Office of the Iraq Program, *Implementation of Oil-for-Food*.

39. United Nations, S/RES/1284, 17 December 1999.

40. Ibid., para. 33.

41. A spokesman for the British Foreign and Commonwealth Office confirmed this to a *Guardian* journalist. See *Guardian*, 16 June 2000.

42. United Nations, S/RES/1284, para. 36.

43. The reference here is to the manner in which Iraqi sovereignty was referred to in the two resolutions. Whereas recognition of Iraqi sovereignty was given specific and separate emphasis in Resolution 986, Resolution 1284 put the commitment to Iraqi sovereignty together with that of Kuwait and other neighboring states.

44. This list of Iraqi objections is taken from statements of Iraqi spokesmen after the resolution was passed and from the writer's interviews with Iraqi officials in Baghdad in March 2000.

15

Oil Sales, Revenues, and Expenditures, 1996–2000

The UN humanitarian program in Iraq has been subject to criticism. The most critical stated objective of Resolution 986, namely, "to provide for the humanitarian needs of the Iraqi population," has been pursued, but the benefits to the Iraqi population have been less than anticipated.

There are conflicting claims as to who or what has been responsible for such program failure as occurred. To some observers, the structure of the resolution is flawed in that the funding available to meet Iraq's needs is insufficient, and the mechanisms whereby funding becomes available are too cumbersome. To others (primarily Western observers), the problems stem from Iraqi governmental attempts to frustrate the effective operation of the program. It is said that Iraq's strategy in doing so is to retain an important political weapon: the ability to rally international support against the whole sanctions regime on the grounds of its impact on the Iraqi population. In the view of the Iraqi government, the restrictions placed on the program by certain members of the Security Council have limited its utility in improving living conditions in Iraq.

The content and operation of the program from 1996 up to the end of 1999 (the end of phase 4—the last period for which full figures are available) must be examined in order to evaluate the validity of these differing claims. The section immediately following looks at the generation of oil revenues under Oil for Food, examining the extent to which they fell short of expectations, as well as the reasons for the shortfall. The next section outlines the record of expenditures in different sectors and assesses the impact that delays and holds had on overall expenditures within each sector. Chapter 16 will then examine the record of achievement and of regression in different sectors of social provision and social and economic infra-

129

Table 15.1   Volume and Value of Iraqi Oil Production, 1996–1999

Phases 1–6	Volume of oil (in millions of barrels)	Value of oil exported (in millions of dollars)	Average price per barrel ($)
1	120	2,150	18.0
2	127	2,125	16.7
3	182	2,085	11.5
4	308	3,027	9.8
5	361	3,947	10.9
6	390	7,402	19.0
Totals/average	1,497	20,742	13.9

Source: United Nations Office of the Iraq Program, *Basic Figures as of 11 January 2000*, <http://www.un.org/Depts/oip/latest/basicfigures.html>.

structure, placing developments under Oil for Food within the context of the situation prior to Oil for Food and the sanctions.

The Generation of Oil Revenues Under Oil for Food

During the first six phases of the Oil for Food program, the value of oil that Iraq would have been permitted to sell under the various Security Council resolutions was some $21.6 billion (excluding the extra $3 billion made available for phase 6, as that stemmed from underproduction in phases 4 and 5). The value of its actual oil exports came to $20.7 billion. Table 15.1 shows that Iraq's attainment of the latter total was in fact a result of the sudden rise in oil prices during the second half of 1999. Oil revenues in phases 3 and 4 were substantially less than what had been agreed to, with substantial effects on the humanitarian program. The failure of Iraq to export up to the limit was almost entirely due to the "lamentable state of its oil industry" (in the words of the UN Secretary-General). Although Iraq had of its own volition halted oil exports at the beginning of phases 2 and 3, until the UN Secretary-General had approved the distribution plans, this did not prevent it from reaching its exporting limit in either of those phases. Neither would the brief interruption of exports in late 1999 have made any appreciable difference.

As noted in Chapter 14, the Security Council was slow to act on the concerns expressed by the UN Secretary-General and the government of Iraq over the state of the oil industry. Allocations of Oil for Food money for spare parts and equipment took time, and it was generally less than what Iraq and independent oil experts believed was necessary.[1] Of greater importance than the allocation of money, however, were the delays in effecting expenditure. Security Council authorization for imports in a particular field, it should be recalled, did not mean that Iraqi import orders could automatically proceed. It was still necessary for every individual order to be approved by the Sanctions Committee. By the end of phase 6, the government of Iraq had issued contracts for $1.24 billion in spare parts and equipment in the oil sector, but only $581 million of it had been approved.[2] Of the remainder, $207 million was "on hold,"[3] meaning that a member of the Security Council had raised an objection to the contract in question; sale could not proceed until the contract had been further investigated—usually to establish whether the equipment had so-called dual use potential (i.e., it could be used for military as well as civilian purposes). In practice, all such objections came from either the United States or Britain (mainly the former). The remaining contracts were under consideration by the Sanctions Committee, or by the UN office of the Iraq program, prior to being submitted to the committee.[4] The impact of these holds and delays was considerable. Some of the equipment that had been approved could be used only in conjunction with equipment that had not yet been approved.

The UN Secretariat left the Security Council with little doubt about the effects of the delays and holds—directly on the oil industry and indirectly on the whole humanitarian program. All of the reports on the humanitarian program presented by the Secretary-General to the Security Council from early 1998 through March 2000 were explicit about the poor condition of the Iraqi oil industry and of the impact it was having on the humanitarian program. The Secretary-General's report to the Security Council on 4 September 1998 estimated that the sums available for the humanitarian programs in phase 4 would come to $1 billion less than had been envisaged ($2.1 billion rather than $3.3 billion).[5] On 4 November of that year, the Secretary-General reported to the Security Council that the $300 million for the oil sector that had been made available was "sufficient only for the most essential and urgent needs," and that "the delays in the pace of approvals for spare parts and equipment for the oil industry are regrettable."[6] The Secretary-General's next report to the Security Council, dated 22 February 1999, invited the Sanctions Committee to "expedite the approval" of contracts in the oil sector and noted that "the most serious issue facing the implementation of the [humanitarian] program at present is the growing shortfall in revenues required to implement the approved distribution plan."[7] Three days later the executive director of the program called for "bold, imaginative and pragmatic" approaches to investment in Iraq's oil industry to increase revenues.[8]

Despite concerns of this nature, the delays and holds continued. Problems with the applications process can be seen in a letter that the Secretary-General addressed to the president of the Security Council on 14 January 2000. The Office of the Iraq Program, he said, had received a total of 1,991 applications for spare parts and equipment with a total value of $1.1 million; 1,392 had been circulated to the Sanctions Committee, and fifty had been declared null and void. Nine hundred applications, with a total value of $447 million, had been approved by the committee, 438 applications with a total value of $217.8 million had been placed on hold, and fifty-four applications with a total value of $56.2 million were pending the committee's decision. One hundred thirty-three applications, with a total value of $120.5 million, had been evaluated by the Office of the Iraq Program but had not been circulated to the Sanctions Committee due to lack of information. Finally, there were 416 applications, with a total value of $263 million, that were "under review" by the Office of the Iraq Program.[9] The figures indicate that delays to applications could be the result of several factors, among them the fact that applications had to pass through the overstretched Office of the Iraq Program, as well as through the Sanctions Committee.

When the executive director of the program briefed the Security Council in February 2000 about the needs of the oil sector, he noted that to date only about $250 million in spare parts and equipment had reached Iraq since imports were authorized, whereas about $288 million remained on hold.[10] The Secretary-General's report to the Security Council at the end of March 2000 was still asking for a special effort to be made so as to "approve most expeditiously the applications for oil spare parts and equipment," pointing out that the total value of such applications placed on hold as of 31 January 2000 was $291 million—more than half of the $506 million approved since Resolution 1153 had first permitted purchases in this field.[11] In addressing the Security Council, the Secretary-General said that Iraq's oil industry was "seriously hampered by lack of spare parts and equipment, and this threatens to undermine the program's income in the long term." This, he said, was why he had "repeatedly recommended a significant increase in the allocation of resources under the program for the purchase of spare parts for the oil industry." He stressed that "many of the 'holds' on contract applications, imposed by members of the [Sanctions] Committee, do have a direct negative impact on the humanitarian program, and on efforts to rehabilitate Iraq's infrastructure, most of which is in appalling disrepair."[12]

Expenditures and the Impact of
Holds and Other Delays

We now turn to the purposes to which revenues from oil sales were put. Details of disbursements from the UN Iraq escrow account are provided in the Secretary-General's reports to the Security Council on the implementation of the Oil for Food resolutions. The Secretary-General's report, presented on 10 March 2000, indicates that up to 31 January 2000 (over the period since Oil for Food was initiated) a total of $21.48 billion had been deposited in the escrow account from oil sales and that the money had been allocated as follows:

- Humanitarian supplies, central and southern Iraq: $10.98 billion. These were for supplies administered directly by the government of Iraq. There was an additional $211.4 million in the escrow account constituted by interest earned on the account, and $192.0 million was due for reimbursement for purchases made by the government of Iraq for supplies destined for northern Iraq. Actual expenditure had come to $8.32 billion.
- Humanitarian supplies, northern Iraq: $2.67 billion. These were for supplies administered by the United Nations in the Kurdish governorates. Actual expenditure had come to $1.56 billion.
- United Nations Compensation Fund: $6.42 billion. This represented Iraq's obligation under Resolution 687 to pay 30 percent of its oil revenues in compensation for losses incurred by its occupation of Kuwait. Actual expenditure had come to $5.81 billion, of which $5.63 billion was allocated to actual compensation payments and $175 million was to cover the operating costs of the Compensation Commission.
- UN allocation for operating Resolution 986: $454 million. This was to cover the UN costs involved in paying inspection agents, certified public accountants and other activities associated with implementing Resolution 986. Actual expenditure had come to $241.8 million.
- UN allocation for the expenses of UNSCOM: $154 million. Actual expenditure had come to $74 million.
- Oil transportation costs through the Kirkuk-Yumurtalik pipeline: $681 million. Payment of funds in this category were made to the government of Turkey. Actual expenditure had come to $567 million.
- Repayments to states for monies drawn from Iraqi funds held in their territories: $119 million. This stemmed from provisions made in Resolution 986 relating to the implementation of Resolution 778. Actual expenditure had come to $119 million.

Table 15.2   Allocated Funding and Actual Expenditures Stemming from Iraqi Oil Sales Under Oil for Food, up to 31 January 2000 (in thousands of U.S. dollars)

Recipient area	Allocation (in thousands of U.S. dollars)	Percentage of allocation	Actual expenditure (in thousands of U.S. dollars)	Percentage of expenditure
Humanitarian, central and southern Iraq	10,982,000	51.1	8,322,100	49.8
Humanitarian, northern Iraq	2,666,300	12.4	1,562,700	9.4
Compensation Fund	6,418,900	29.9	5,807,600	34.8
UN: operation of Res. 986	454,300	2.1	241,800	1.4
UN: operation of UNSCOM	154,000	0.7	74,400	0.5
Oil transport by pipeline	680,700	3.2	566,000	3.4
Repayments to states (Res. 788)	119,500	0.6	119,500	0.7

Source: United Nations, *Report of the Secretary-General Pursuant to Paragraph 28 and 30 of Resolution 1284 and Paragraph 5 of Resolution 1281*, S/2000/208, 10 March 2000.

Table 15.2 summarizes the above information, indicating the percentages of allocated and actual expenditures for each category. The actual expenditure relates to money drawn from the escrow account once a contract was approved by the Sanctions Committee and does not indicate that the goods concerned actually reached Iraq (see Table 15.3). It should be noted that the basis of comparison between funding for central/southern Iraq and that for northern Iraq is skewed by costs associated with the oil industry. All of the Oil for Food funding was dependent on the oil industry, yet the costs of operating the industry were borne entirely by the central government (either from domestic resources or Oil for Food money).

Table 15.3 compares (as of 11 January 2000) the value of contracts received by the Sanctions Committee in different sectors with (on the one hand) that of the contracts which were approved by the committee and (on the other hand) that of contracts placed on hold. All of the contracts had been submitted by the government of Iraq. The difference between the total of contracts received, and the combined total of contracts approved and on hold, is accounted for by contracts under consideration by the Office of the Iraq Program or the Sanctions Committee. The final column shows the value of goods that had actually reached Iraq by 1 December 1999. The figures show that somewhat less than half of the goods that Iraq had requested since Iraqi oil sales were restarted in December 1996 had arrived by 1 December 1999. Of the shortfall, 10.9 percent of the goods

Table 15.3   Contracts Received, Approved, and On Hold, up to 11 January 2000 (in millions of U.S. dollars)

Phases 1–6	Contracts received		Contracts approved		Contracts on hold		Arrived[a]
Sector	Number	$ value	Number	$ value	Number	$ value	$ value
Food	1,495	5,482	1,331	5,418	10	6	4,051[b]
Food handling	429	604	256	301	56	157	168
Health	1,854	1,277	1,475	1,016	94	130	746
Oil spare parts	1,969	1,240	890	581	430	207	179
Electricity	745	1,309	455	508	135	435	209
Water/sanitation	358	569	203	288	34	86	80
Agriculture	732	701	470	441	91	171	227
Education	304	274	114	128	39	43	47
Infrastructure	67	215	5	4	18	107	0
Northern governorates	2,355	660	2,122	638	8	0.5	268[c]
Total	10,308	12,331	7,321	9,323	915	1,343	5,975

Source: United Nations Office of the Iraq Program, *Basic Figures as 11 January 2000,* <http://www.un.org/Depts/oip/latest/basicfigures.html>.

Notes: a. As of 1 December 1999.

b. Includes food and health supplies bulk purchased by the government of Iraq for the three northern governorates.

c. Excludes food and health sector supplies purchased by the government of Iraq for the northern governorates.

requested were covered by contracts that the Sanctions Committee had placed on hold; 13.5 percent were in contracts that were under consideration; and 27.2 percent were in contracts that had been approved, but the goods had not yet reached the country.

The figures may exaggerate slightly the delays, shortcomings, and problems in the supply of goods to Iraq, once contracts from the government of Iraq had been submitted. Given that the number of contracts submitted by Iraq in phase 6 was higher than that in earlier phases (as a result of the rise in oil prices), and that the transport of goods to Iraq was itself difficult, the nonarrival of goods covered by such contracts approved in phase 6 was perhaps not surprising. Nonetheless, in some other ways the figures understate the scale of the delays. Even for a contract to reach the Sanctions Committee, the item concerned had to figure in Iraq's distribution plan forwarded to the UN Secretary-General, and the implementation of the plan had in turn to await the approval of the Secretary-General. Intended contracts often had to be the subject of discussion between government departments and the UN Office of the Iraq Program before being submitted. Clearly, the overall record of the supply of goods to Iraq was not impressive.[13]

Not all of the delays that occurred were the outcome of failings on the part of the Sanctions Committee or the approval processes within the UN structure. The government of Iraq on occasions failed to submit contracts for some essential goods, was tardy in putting contracts forward, and provided faulty documentation in support of contracts.[14] UN reports, however, do not seek to suggest that these factors were of key importance in frustrating effective expenditure.[15] There was rather more UN criticism of delays in the delivery of goods once they had arrived in Iraq; this is discussed in Chapter 16.

Notes

1. By the time the Security Council had agreed to one request for an increase in the allocation for spares and equipment, the situation had usually deteriorated to such an extent that an even larger sum was required. One example of this occurred at the end of March 2000. On the same day as the Security Council adopted Resolution 1293, increasing Iraq's allocation for purchases in the oil sector to $600 million, the Secretary-General reported that a further $300 million was now needed for phase 7. See United Nations Press Release, *Security Council Adopting Resolution 1293 (2000) Unanimously Doubles Amount Iraq May Spend for Oil Spare Parts, Equipment*, SC/6838, 31 March 2000.

2. Office of the Iraq Program, *Basic Figures as 11 January 2000*.

3. Ibid.

4. The Office of the Iraq Program had the role of checking all applications for contracts before they were sent on to the Sanctions Committee. They would be sent on to the committee only if they contained all of the information required. Some delays in approval were on the grounds that Iraq had provided insufficient information. The contract was then held up until the information was provided.

5. Office of the Iraq Program, *Implementation of Oil-for-Food*.

6. United Nations, *Report of the Secretary-General Pursuant to Paragraph 10 of Security Council Resolution 1153*, S/1998/1100, 19 November 1998.

7. United Nations, *Report of the Secretary-General Pursuant to Paragraph 6 of Security Council Resolution 1210*, S/1998/187, 22 February 1999.

8. Office of the Iraq Program, *Implementation of Oil-for-Food*.

9. United Nations, S/2000/26.

10. United Nations Office of the Iraq Program, *Briefing by Benon V. Sevan, Executive Director of the Iraq Programme, of the Security Council at its Informal Consultations Held on 7 February 2000* <http://www.un.org/Depts/oip/reports/feb7bvscouncil.html>.

11. United Nations Press Release, *Security Council Adopting Resolution 1293*, SC/6838. The figure of $506 million, representing the value of contracts approved, is less than that given by the Office of the Iraq Program on 11 January. No explanation is given for this discrepancy.

12. United Nations Press Release, SG/SM/7338, 24 March 2000.

13. The figures help explain why the public sector was making purchases from the private sector for goods that could have been obtained more cheaply through Oil for Food. Computers for the University of Baghdad, for example, were bought in 1998–1999 from the private sector, as they were urgently needed and the university could not wait for Oil for Food arrangements to be made. The cost of the computers was some 50 percent more than would have been paid through Oil for Food, with considerable benefit accruing to the merchants who had smuggled the computers into the country. Information from University of Baghdad, March 2000.

14. These are the main criticisms to which reference is made in the UN Secretary-General's report to the Security Council early in 2000. See United Nations, *Report of the Secretary-General to Paragraphs 28 and 30 of Resolution 1284 and Paragraph 5 of Resolution 1281*, S/2000/208, 10 March 2000, para. 94.

15. The review and assessment of the humanitarian program that the UN Secretary-General presented to the Security Council two years into the program devoted only two sentences to delays caused by the Iraqi government. See United Nations, S/199 *(Review and Assessment of the Humanitarian Programme)*.

16

Humanitarian Goods and Economic Infrastructure: Central and Southern Iraq

The record of satisfying Iraq's stated needs in humanitarian goods has, not surprisingly, varied according to the sector concerned. Problems faced within each category will be reviewed here, based primarily on reports drawn up by UN personnel. Consistent with the UN reports, the programs in the northern governorates are all taken together as one category, covered in Chapter 17. The topics covered here, therefore, relate exclusively to southern and central Iraq.[1]

The dilemma the UN Secretariat faced in Iraq is worth emphasizing. UN reports have monitored in detail, and with considerable honesty, the effects that UN sanctions have had on Iraq. Many of these reports have documented the weaknesses and failings in the sanctions regime, as well as the harm being inflicted on large parts of the Iraqi population. During 1999 and early 2000, indeed, some of the pressure on the UN Security Council to change its policies was coming from within the UN Secretariat and from former UN officials who had resigned in protest at the policies being pursued.[2] The dilemma for the United Nations was put frankly by the Secretary-General in his address to the Security Council on 24 March 2000, at a session convened to consider the humanitarian situation in Iraq:

> The humanitarian situation in Iraq poses a serious moral dilemma for this [organization]. The United Nations has always been on the side of the vulnerable and the weak, and has always sought to relieve suffering, yet here we are accused of causing suffering to an entire population. We are in danger of losing the argument, or the propaganda war if we haven't already lost it—about who is responsible for this situation in Iraq—President Saddam Hussein or the United Nations.

I am particularly concerned about the situation of Iraqi children, whose suffering and, in all too many cases, untimely death has been documented in the report prepared by UNICEF and the Iraqi health ministry last year. That report, which has been echoed by many other observers, showed that, in [central and southern] Iraq, infant mortality and morbidity have increased dramatically and reached unacceptable levels.

We cannot in all conscience ignore such reports, or assume that they are wrong.[3]

It is telling—and of considerable value to the wider international community—that the Secretariat of the United Nations provides such excruciating detail on the damaging effects of the UN policy being pursued under its auspices.

Food and Nutrition

Food supplies for central and southern Iraq were subject to few holds under the Oil for Food program, and the delivery was in general effective.

All of the food supplies, together with some other supplies for household use, were distributed through the rationing system that the Iraqi government had instituted after Security Council Resolution 661 was passed in 1990. The foodstuffs that became available under Resolution 986 were kept in specific warehouses designated for this purpose, under the control of the Iraqi ministry of trade but subject to inspection by UN bodies.[4] Under the rationing system, the ministry distributed foodstuffs every month to a network of 45,864 ration agents. Every Iraqi citizen and foreigner residing in the country was entitled by law to obtain a ration card from registration centers established by local people's councils for the purpose, where the name, age, and number of consumers in every household were listed. Householders had an obligation to inform the centers immediately if there was any change in the makeup of the household (e.g., if a member was away for an extended period, or if there was a death in the family). Random checks were made to ensure that the information was correct. On the basis of the registration lists, food distribution centers were instructed to dispatch a specified quantity of goods to the ration agents, and ration agents could supply the goods to households within their designated area—in exchange for coupons on the ration card. Coupons were collected monthly.

Prior to the Gulf War, the average Iraqi diet was drawn from a variety of foods. The most basic diet items were subsidized by the government—an arrangement that covered nineteen categories of food, together with six

Table 16.1   Pre–Oil for Food Consumption Patterns of Iraqi Citizens: Supplies of the Most Basic Commodities, 1989 and 1996 (per individual)

Food	Subsidized supplies per person, 1989 (kg)	Minimum human need, per person monthly (kg)[a]	Monthly ration per person, 1996 (kg)	Percentage of minimum need covered by ration
Wheat flour	15.0	7.38	7.0	95%
Rice	3.28	3.0	1.2	42%
Sugar	3.4	2.7	0.5	19%
Tea	0.25	0.15	0.10	66%
Cooking oil	1.28	0.9	0.75	84%
Infant milk	3.06	–	1.7	–

Source: Republic of Iraq, *Athar al-Hisar al Iqtisadi al-Shamil ala al-Iraq* [The Effects of Comprehensive Economic Sanctions on Iraq] (Baghdad: Ministry of Foreign Affairs, 2000).
Note: a. As estimated by the Iraqi Institute for Nutritional Research, Baghdad.

categories of household commodities (e.g., washing powder, soaps, toothpaste, etc.). The subsidized foods included some red meat, chicken, fish, cheese, and vegetables, as well as basic commodities that tend to attract subsidies under centralized economic systems: sugar, tea, rice, flour, and cooking oil.[5] The rationing system, which was introduced in 1990 and continued until the beginning of Oil for Food deliveries in 1997, covered only the six most basic foods: wheat flour, rice, sugar, tea, cooking oil, and children's powdered milk. Soap and washing powder were also supplied.[6] Still, the quantities of these foods and commodities made available were substantially less than had been consumed previously. Table 16.1 details the supply of such goods, before and after rationing, relating the level of individual consumption to the "minimum basic requirement" regarded as essential for human beings, as assessed by the Iraqi Institute for Nutritional Research. Prior to the introduction of the Oil for Food program, the Iraqi government had been distributing rations with a calorific value of 1,300 kilocalories per person per day.[7] Dietary intake in the late 1980s had averaged 3,120 kilocalories per day.[8]

Under Oil for Food, the range of foods being supplied expanded slightly, with the addition of dried whole milk/or cheese, pulses, fortified weaning material, and iodized salt. Quantities also increased. When the program was first introduced, the target was to increase the calorific value of rations from 1,300 to 2,030. The target was increased to 2,300 under the enhanced distribution plan of June 1998. Under phase 7 the target was increased to 2,463 kilocalories. In practice, the nutritional value of the dis-

Table 16.2   Monthly Per Capita Rations, and Total Value of Rations for All Iraq, Under Phase 7 of Oil for Food

Items	Monthly ration per capita (kg)	Total value of rations for all Iraq (in millions of U.S. dollars) for six months
Wheat flour	9.0	264.0
Rice	3.0	120.0
Sugar	2.0	80.0
Tea	0.15	42.0
Cooking oil	1.5	147.0
Milk powder	3.6	42.0
Dried whole milk and/or cheese	0.5	180.0
Fortified weaning cereal	0.8	7.0
Pulses	1.0	88.0
Iodized salt	0.15	3.0
Soap	0.25	34.0
Detergents	0.35	43.0
Total		1,050.0

Source: Republic of Iraq, *Distribution Plan Submitted by the Government of Iraq to the UN Secretary-General in Accordance with . . . Resolution 1281 (1999)* (Baghdad: Ministry of Foreign Affairs, 1999).

tributed basket did not exceed 1,993 kilocalories under phases 4–6. Shortfalls were due to spending cutbacks when oil revenues did not achieve projected levels, as well as to delivery delays.[9] Table 16.2 details the monthly rations that every Iraqi was expected to receive under phase 7 of Oil for Food, starting in December 1999. The figures are those given in the distribution plan drawn up by the Iraqi government and approved by the UN Secretary-General. With a total rations expenditure of $1,050 million to cover a six-month period for a population of about 24 million, the value of the monthly rations per capita under phase 7 came to about $7. It should be noted that there was no meat, fish, vegetables, or fruit in the rations, which still covered only basic foods and commodities. For most Iraqi families, the flour ration was sufficient for the month, but the other rations did not last more than ten to fifteen days.[10]

Oil for Food also had an indirect effect that brought some benefit to the standard of living. The increased quantities of food available depressed prices for similar goods purchased on the open market. Commercial prices for these goods still remained much higher (mostly several hundred times the pre-1990 prices), but they were nonetheless lower in December 1998 compared to December 1995. Table 16.3 details this

Table 16.3   Prices of Basic Foods on the Open Market, 1990, 1995, and 1998 (in dinar)

Food	1990 price, per kg	1995 price, per kg	1998 price, per kg (to nearest dinar)
Wheat flour	0.06	713.31	275.0
Rice	0.24	1,184.21	350.0
Sugar	0.20	1,375.65	450.0
Tea	2.00	4,502.02	3,000.0
Cooking oil	0.60	2,566.73	1,300.0
Infants' milk	1.60	3,010.48	1,000.0

Source: Republic of Iraq, *Athar al-Hisar al-Iqtisadi al-Shamil ala al-Iraq* (Baghdad: Ministry of Foreign Affairs, 2000), pp. 19–20.

movement in prices. Prices for other goods were not affected and continued to rise; chances for most of the population to achieve a more balanced diet did not significantly improve.

Despite the increase in the food basket available to Iraqis following the introduction of Oil for Food, UN reports simply reported that the extent of malnutrition seemed to have stabilized.[11] A nutritional survey in October 1998 showed little change in the nutritional status of children since Oil for Food had begun. General malnutrition was found to occur in 14.1 percent of infants in 1996, 14.7 percent in 1997, and 14.7 percent in 1998. The percentage of babies born underweight (less than 2.5 kilograms), which stood at 4.5 percent in 1989, rose from 22 percent in 1995 to just over 24 percent in 1999.[12] Malnutrition among children under five was found to occur in 23.4 percent of children in 1996, 24.7 percent in 1997, and 22.8 percent in 1998.[13] A report by the UN Food and Agriculture Organization, based on a survey carried out in 1998, suggested that in fact infant feeding patterns were still deteriorating.[14] In practice, for most Iraqis a balanced diet was as difficult to achieve as before, especially given that such a diet was dependent on goods that were outside of the ration and that prices for nonrationed goods like meat and eggs remained prohibitive.

The increased food supplies under Resolution 986 might have had more impact if performance in another related sector had been better—food-handling equipment. Here, only about 25 percent of goods the Iraqi government sought to import since phase 1 had reached the country by January 2000. Of the remaining goods, one-third was covered by contracts that the Sanctions Committee had placed on hold, and the remainder was delayed by the length of the procedures and the difficulties experienced in dispatching the goods to Iraq (see Table 15.3). The role of this sector in helping to satisfy food needs is clear from the objectives for expenditures, which the Iraqi government had set forth in its distribution plans: repairing and rehabilitating the equipment in grain silos so as to ensure the speedy handling of imported grains, and the supply of these to the mills; ensuring the minimum needs of mills so as to keep them operating; financing new means of transportation to enhance the ability to transport foodstuffs around the country; and covering the minimum needs for cold storage and warehousing for foodstuffs.[15]

Health

The acquisition and delivery of health goods were more difficult than food supply and distribution. In the words of a UN report, "The overall health situation has not improved, in part because of inefficiency in the ordering, processing and delivery of medical supplies."[16] As can be seen from Table 15.3, the position on 11 January 2000 was that contracts worth $1,277 million had been issued, and $1,016 million had been approved, but the delivery was slow: the value of the goods that had arrived came only to $746 million. Contracts valued at a total of $130 million (about 10 percent of the total applied for) were on hold.[17] Delivery within Iraq was also slow: figures at the end of January 2000 showed that of the $803 million that had by then reached Iraq, $567 million had actually been distributed to end users. The UN Secretary-General reported in March 2000 that the remaining medical supplies and equipment were either undergoing quality control procedures or were in warehouses.[18] Given that the government had been importing $500 million in health goods annually in the late 1980s,[19] and had found the resources to import $50 million in 1996,[20] the year before it gained access to Oil for Food revenues, the improvement in the availability of health goods was clearly not as substantial as might have been expected.

Controversy over the supply of medicines in Iraq has been fueled by allegations that they were deliberately withheld by the government to increase the suffering of the population and thereby strengthen the case for removing sanctions. George Robertson, addressing the British House of Commons on 25 January 1999, told the House that Saddam Hussein "has in warehouses $275 million-worth of medicines and medical supplies which he refuses to distribute" and asked "what kind of leader watches his children die and his hospitals operate without drugs, but keeps $275 million-worth of medicines and medical supplies locked up in a warehouse?"[21]

UN reports have attached some blame to the government for failing to order the most appropriate health goods, for "poor procurement planning and stock management," and for "inefficiency of processing and delivery."[22] The criticism on ordering and procurement was, on the one hand, that the process was not carried out quickly enough; and, on the other, that medical equipment represented a disproportionate share of the health goods for which contracts were issued, leading to a continuing shortage of pharmaceuticals (and the consequent need to continue rationing medicines). Generally, however, such reports did not attribute malicious intent to government actions (e.g., an intent to aggravate suffering). The poor record on ordering and procurement was in part blamed on the attempt by Kimadia, the Iraqi state company for drug imports, to computerize the ordering process—in a situation where there was insufficient expertise to operate the system.[23] As for the level of stocks held in warehouses, the UN Secretary-General reported:

> The delays in distributing medical supplies, resulting in accumulations in warehouses, are due in part to the lack of modern managerial tools, poor working conditions within the warehouses and the lack of transport for moving the supplies to health centers. They are also due, in part, to the rigid hierarchy in the Ministry of Health administration which makes it difficult for functionaries to approve deliveries without approval of superiors, and this takes time. A variety of sources, including WHO, suggest that stockpiling seems to have increased following September 1998, when tensions mounted, and superiors may have deliberately withheld supplies in anticipation of emergency needs.[24]

The panel established by the UN Secretary-General to assess the humanitarian situation in Iraq suggested that "mismanagement, funding shortages (absence of the so-called 'cash component') and a general lack of motivation" could explain such delays as occurred.[25] A later report identified the "key reason" for the distribution bottlenecks in the health sector as "the decline in professional competence and motivation." Given the general difficulties under which Iraqi officials conducted their professional work, the lack of competence and motivation is hardly surprising.[26]

There have been other reports, moreover, suggesting that the level of medical stocks held in Iraqi warehouses is not unusually high. The UN Secretary-General's report to the Security Council in February 1998 asserted that the level of stocks was inadequate and needed to be built up.[27] Similarly, Hans von Sponeck, in a press briefing upon resigning as UN humanitarian coordinator for Iraq, acknowledged that the distribution of medicines was proceeding more slowly compared to other goods, but he pointed out that this reflected World Health Organization recommendations on standard medical stockpiling practices and the extra time required for quality control. His opinion was that "the situation was not that bad."[28]

Although UN reports spoke of increased supplies leading to an expansion of the range of medical treatment, drugs becoming more available at all health facilities, patient attendance in health facilities increasing by 46 percent, and some 90 percent of the essential drug needs of hospital inpatients being met, the Secretary-General's report to the Security Council in March 2000 stressed the continuing (and perhaps worsening) problems:

> I remain seriously concerned at key aspects in the provision of health care; improvements in neither the distribution of health care nor in the health infrastructure envisaged in my supplementary report have materialised. Erratic, the uncoordinated arrival of drugs to treat chronic disease has prevented the monthly requirements of all patients from being met, which may have contributed to the increase in deaths attributable to cardiac, diabetic, renal and liver disease.[29]

Reports from other quarters confirm the realism of the Secretary-General's overall perspective. Although some aspects of the health situation may have improved marginally since Oil for Food was initiated, medical services were operating at a much lower level compared to the late 1980s. Tables 16.4–16.6, providing information on deaths from serious health conditions, indicate the scale of change in the incidence of life-threatening conditions between 1989 and 2000; Table 16.6 indicates that the situation continued to deteriorate after the introduction of Oil for Food. Other statistics from the Iraqi ministry of health reveal that the number of major surgical operations carried out in Iraqi hospitals had fallen in 1996 to about 28

Table 16.4 Monthly Deaths of Under-Five-Year-Old Children from Specified Health Conditions, February 1989 and February 2000 Compared (monthly figures)

Health condition	Number of deaths February 1989	Number of deaths February 2000	Rate of increase
Diarrhea	104	1,377	1,224.04%
Pneumonia and respiratory infections	158	3,002	1,800.00%
Malnutrition	94	2,560	2,623.40%

Source: Statistics provided by the Ministry of Health, Baghdad, March 2000.

Table 16.5   Monthly Deaths of Over-Fifty-Year-Old Adults from Specified Health Conditions, February 1989 and February 2000 Compared (monthly figures)

Health condition	Number of deaths February 1989	Number of deaths February 2000	Rate of increase
Heart diseases and hypertension	71	593	735.21%
Diabetes	90	589	554.44%
Malignant neoplasms	318	1,868	487.42%

Source: Statistics provided by the Ministry of Health, Baghdad, March 2000.

percent of those in 1989 and remained at approximately the same level into 2000.[30] The number of people suffering psychological and mental disorders grew steadily throughout the 1990s. Although accurate figures for the latter are not available, the UN estimates that the number rose from some 200,000 at the time of the Gulf War to some 510,000 in 1998.[31]

Part of the blame for deteriorating health conditions rests in the inadequacy of the support systems within the medical sector. The distribution plan for phase 7 pointed out that "there is no full benefit from medicines and medical supplies without medical apparatuses, equipment and other support systems necessary for the rehabilitation of hospitals." It estimated

Table 16.6   Total Deaths from Specified Health Conditions,[a] 1989–1999

Year	Children below 5	Population above 5	Total
1989	7,110	20,224	27,334
1990	8,904	23,561	32,464
1991	27,473	58,469	85,924
1992	46,933	76,530	123,463
1993	49,762	78,261	127,023
1994	52,905	80,774	133,681
1995	55,823	82,961	138,784
1996	56,997	83,284	140,281
1997	58,845	85,942	144,878
1998	71,279	88,760	160,039
1999 (to August)	53,579	64,057	117,236
Total	482,499	722,601	1,205,100

Source: Republic of Iraq, *Athar al-Hisar al-Iqtisadi al-Shamil ala al-Iraq* (Baghdad: Ministry of Foreign Affairs, 2000), p. 39.

Note: a. The "specified health conditions" are those constituting the major causes of death. For children under five years of age, the conditions are those covered in Table 16.4. For the population over five, the conditions are heart disease, high blood pressure, diabetes, liver disease, kidney disease, and malignant neoplasms.

that some 50 percent of medical equipment was obsolete and/or unrepairable. Many Iraqis were of the view that sanitary conditions in the hospitals created a health risk to patients, such that public hospitals tended not to be used by middle-class patients unless there was no alternative.[32] UN reports also indicated that the absence of adequate training for health workers was seriously affecting health care: according to surveys in 1999, only one child in ten with respiratory infection was being correctly treated, and only 10 percent of pneumonia cases were being correctly treated. Eighty-three percent of health workers were described as not having adequate training.[33]

It is also important to note that the health condition of the Iraqi population was greatly affected by developments in other sectors. Clearly there was a strong link between illness and inadequate food supplies, but health conditions were also linked to unclean water supply and poor sanitation. As illustrated by Table 16.4, many of the deaths of children under five were from diarrhea, contracted as a result of poor water and sanitary systems. The considerable number of holds and delays in the water and sanitation sector were thus highly detrimental to health conditions in Iraq.

Water and Sanitation

This sector was among those most adversely affected by holds and delays in Oil for Food expenditures. As illustrated by Table 15.3, only $80 million of the $569 million in goods for which Iraq had submitted contracts since the beginning of Oil for Food had reached the country by January 2000. Of the shortfall, $86 million was on hold, $208 million had been approved but had not reached the country, and the remainder was awaiting approval.

Not surprisingly, in light of the relatively limited quantities of goods that reached Iraq in this sector, the state of water and sanitation did not improve substantially after the introduction of Oil for Food. The UN Secretary-General's report to the Security Council in March 2000 states that "the overall situation in the water and sanitation sector has seen very little improvement over the past two years"; two factors played a role—the insufficiency of funds available, and the high value of contracts on hold.[34] Other constraints mentioned were "the absence of effective planning, delayed and uncoordinated arrival of supplies, insufficient skilled labor and inadequate local implementation budgets." Reference was also made to problems stemming from the erratic electricity supply and drought. As a result, program "inputs have been able neither to increase the availabil-

ity of drinking water nor to prevent continued leakage and associated contamination of the network. The water authorities were unable to provide
service to some seven million inhabitants, mainly in rural areas."[35]

The state of water and sewerage facilities through the 1990s is best
understood when compared to the prewar situation. Until 1990, the water
grid in southern and central Iraq was able to supply 90 percent of the population with ample safe drinking water, based on a network of 200 water
treatment plants for urban areas and some 1,200 small treatment plants in
rural areas.[36] All of the main population centers, as well as most of the
rural areas, had modern systems of sanitary disposal. The situation deteriorated quickly after the Gulf War as a result of the destruction of some of
the treatment plants, the inability to obtain spare parts and chemicals, and
the disruption to the power supply. By 1996, the quantity of water available per person had declined by 40 percent, and approximately one-quar-
ter of the water was contaminated.

Although the quantities available did not increase after the introduction of Oil for Food, there was some reduction in the contamination of
water (down to 5 percent by the end of 1998, according to UN figures).
The latter development, however, did not lead to a reduction in the incidence of water-borne diseases such as diarrhea and typhoid fever.[37] The
distribution plan for phase 7 reported that at the end of 1999 the water-
supply systems were working at less than 30 percent efficiency, and
breaks and leakages in the water network were leading to a reduction in
water pressure, water quality, and the amount available for consumption.
None of the thirteen sewage treatment plants were working properly, and
raw sewage was still being dispersed directly into rivers.[38] Due to the
insufficient state of domestic water supplies, the rural population made
increasing use of river water for domestic use.

Electricity

Although total allocations for electricity as provided for in the distribution
plans for phases 1–6 of Oil for Food were greater than those in every other
sector except food,[39] and despite the speed with which Iraqi authorities
installed equipment once it arrived,[40] the record in this sector was poor.
The electricity sector was more severely affected by holds than any other
sector. In early 2000, the value of contracts approved only marginally
exceeded that of contracts placed on hold (see Table 15.3), and less than
one-sixth of the equipment for which the Iraqi government had submitted

contracts had reached the country. The practical significance of the holds, as explained by the executive director of the program in November 1999, was that Iraq could have increased its electricity production by 50 percent if the holds had not been in place.[41]

The gap between equipment ordered and equipment delivered, however, explains only a part of the problem. In view of the destruction of much of the power-generating sector during the Gulf War, the need for spare parts and equipment was immense—well beyond the capacity of the Oil for Food revenues and therefore outside what the government could request through distribution plans. The Iraqi authorities had, with an effectiveness and skill that surprised observers, successfully brought most of Iraq's power stations back into service after the war and had also repaired the main transmission lines, but this was achieved by using up existing spares and by cannibalizing some plants. By the second half of the 1990s, however, spares were exhausted, and further cannibalization would result in the loss of critical power-generating capacity.[42] A UN report in early 1998 estimated that a total of $7 billion was needed if the electricity sector, on which so much of the humanitarian program depended, was to function effectively.[43] Compared to the $1.3 billion that was actually ordered, and the $508 million that was approved, the scale of the unmet needs can be appreciated.

Thus, by the early part of 2000 large parts of the population were without electricity for much of the day. Electricity supplies in Baghdad were being cut for two three-hour periods per day. In most other cities, electricity supplies were available for only about three hours per day.[44] In some of the rural areas, houses received electricity for little more than one hour per day. Most of the equipment necessary to improve the situation had been ordered from France but was covered by contracts that were on hold. With summer temperatures in Iraq often exceedingly hot, living conditions were made extremely difficult.

The failure of this sector to benefit from Oil for Food did not reflect a lack of UN awareness that electricity was critical to the living standards and health conditions of the population. The seriousness of the situation was made explicit by the UN Secretary-General in February 1998, when he told the Security Council that "under present circumstances the rate of deterioration will continue to increase and, with it, the threat of a complete breakdown of the network. The humanitarian consequences of such a development could potentially dwarf all other difficulties endured by the Iraqi population."[45] In his review of the humanitarian program, presented to the Security Council in April 1999, he returned to the same theme:

The gap between supply and demand increased by 21 percent between 1997 and 1998. Power outages have increased from four to six hours per day, in mid-summer 1998, to 12 hours per day in January 1999. The progressive decline in power availability directly affects the range of essential services in health, agriculture, and water and sanitation. The continuing deterioration of the power stations has reduced the safety of the system itself. The deterioration of the equipment and the declining safety level have combined to produce a sharp increase in the number of deaths and injuries at generation and transformer sites.[46]

Education

Expenditures available for education were limited, and supplies to the sector were, furthermore, affected by delays in contracts awaiting approval, as well as some holds. Of the $274 million in materials for which the Iraqi government had issued contracts since the beginning of Oil for Food, only $47 million had reached the country by January 2000.[47] Some $43 million in contracts had been placed on hold.

Education had been given emphasis by the Iraqi regime prior to 1990, as its education strategy was a critical element in the attempt to develop skills and reshape the thinking of the Iraqi population. This included reforming the curriculum, legislating compulsory education, and reducing adult illiteracy. By the mid-1980s, there was a well-resourced and uniform educational system; enrollment rates, teacher-pupil ratios, and physical environment were among the best (if not the best) in the Arab world. Despite the damaging impact that the Iran-Iraq War had on the school system (e.g., large numbers of teachers drafted into the armed forces, dropping standards of teacher qualifications, and a sharp fall in government resources), illiteracy was rapidly being reduced. Adult illiteracy fell from 50 percent in 1977 to 20 percent in 1987.[48] Over 5 percent of the state budget was still being spent on education at the end of the 1980s.[49]

The change after 1990 was substantial, and conditions did not improve with Oil for Food. Only 1.2 percent of the total value of Oil for Food contracts approved over the period up to January 2000 were for education. Thus, at least in phases 1–5, expenditures had to be concentrated on supplies and furniture for schools and universities rather than on rehabilitating facilities and infrastructure (not to mention the training and material welfare of teachers). The result was that "the majority of school facilities do not provide an appropriate teaching and learning environment."[50] A UN report in 1999 admitted that "the impact of these inputs has been minimal."[51] Even the materials that arrived were underutilized, as neither the resources nor the infrastructure to deliver them really existed.[52] The same report states:

> Clearly, materials have not been delivered efficiently. Of the quantities which have arrived in the country, 56 percent remains in storage. There is very little transport available for moving commodities from warehouses to schools and once they reach schools there are no resources to provide for labor and ancillary inputs to complete the installation.[53]

The report stresses, however, that even if all of the goods had arrived, the education system would not have benefited greatly:

> Even if the inputs had been processed and delivered efficiently . . . the quantities procured would have been too small to have made much difference. In [central and southern] Iraq, it is unlikely that the [humanitarian program] will have any substantial impact on school attendance, or on the quality of education, without significant changes to the types of input and the efficiency of their implementation.[54]

Elements of the information presented in the Iraqi government's distribution plans present an education system in crisis: 1,000 damaged school buildings still in use; pupils having to share desks, and sometimes being taught in rooms without doors and windows; a large number of schools lacking potable water and sanitation; a severe shortage of school textbooks, with the system needing 50 million books annually but the ministry of education unable to print any due to its inability to obtain the necessary printing materials; and universities unable to obtain new books and laboratory equipment.[55] In November 1999, the UN Secretary-General reported that 38 percent of Iraqi schools "had improved their physical environment to fairly acceptable standards," leaving observers to conclude that 62 percent of schools did not have even "fairly acceptable" standards.[56]

The effects of the material shortages faced by schools and universities are described accurately in an account produced by the Iraqi ministry of foreign affairs: low teacher performance due to low morale, illness, and lack of appropriate teaching materials; falling pupil enrollment in schools despite the rising population; intellectual isolation in universities, where members of staff lacked the human and material means to maintain contact with the development of their subject disciplines; loss of staff in schools and universities, either through personnel leaving the country to work abroad or to pursue more profitable occupations; increased absenteeism; and falling academic standards in all educational institutions.[57] A

UN report in 1997 suggested that adult illiteracy had risen from 20 percent in 1989 to 40 percent in 1998.[58] Hans von Sponeck, when he resigned as UN humanitarian coordinator for Iraq, described the impact of sanctions on the education system as constituting an "intellectual embargo" imposed on Iraq, creating an "educational situation which was not suitable to train the next generation of Iraqis in responsible leadership."[59]

Agriculture

Despite the crucial role of agriculture in the supply of nonrationed foods, Oil for Food funding was limited: the value of contracts approved came to $441 million in January 2000 (out of $701 million ordered), making up less than 5 percent of the total value of Oil for Food contracts approved (see Table 15.3). Some $171 million in goods for which contracts had been issued had been placed on hold. The goods that had reached Iraq, valued at some $227 million, came to a little less than one-third of the total ordered.

The overall impact of Oil for Food in this sector was summed up in the Secretary-General's report to the Security Council in March 2000: "The program's inputs have helped to slow down the rate of deterioration of local food production, but were not sufficient to increase production at the national level."[60] Even the Iraqi government's own projections, in late 1999, talked only of "halting, as much as possible, the sector's deterioration."[61] The acute need for imported inputs in this sector was created by the character of agricultural production in southern and central Iraq. Production was highly mechanized, even at the small farmer level, and almost half of the area under crop production was watered by irrigation. Agriculture was very dependent, therefore, on imported spare parts and equipment.

The dependence on spares and equipment was given added significance by the agricultural strategy pursued by the Iraqi government after 1991. Facing sanctions, and with the loss of the revenues that had enabled the country to rely on imports for some 70 percent of food consumed, the government sought to achieve self-sufficiency in the production of basic foods. To boost production, the government sought to expand the area of land under cultivation, from 4–5 million hectares that had been under cultivation in 1989 to some 8 million hectares.[62] Although the full scale of this expansion was not achieved, cultivated land increased some 18 percent during the 1991–1995 period compared to the 1980s.[63] Naturally, needs for spares and equipment increased. The Iraqi government's distribution plans under the Oil for Food program gave primary emphasis to the import of equipment rather than inputs.[64]

Yet the amount that could be ordered and the amount that arrived fell far short of what was needed.[65] Lack of spares and equipment, not surprisingly, had a critical effect on production. With the breakdown of existing harvesting equipment and without any new equipment arriving, 20–25 percent of the potential crop yield was being lost by the end of the 1990s.[66] Crop yields were similarly affected by the breakdown of pumping systems, the inability of the fertilizer plants (some damaged in the Gulf War) to meet more than a fraction of need,[67] the inadequacy of crop-spraying equipment available, and the incapacitation of cold-storage facilities and seed production units.

Insufficiency of imported seeds, herbicides, pesticides, fertilizers, veterinary medicines, and other agricultural inputs also constrained agricultural production. Several fertilizer plants had been destroyed during the war, such that production had dropped from 2.3 million tons in 1990 to 0.59 million in 1992 to 0.30 million in 1994 due to the breakdown of some plants due to lack of spares.[68] The need for imported fertilizers, therefore, was acute. Similar conditions affected herbicide and pesticide production. A Food and Agriculture Organization report in 1999 estimated that the provision of pesticides and herbicides through Oil for Food came to less than 10 percent of actual needs.[69] A UN report noted that "the lack of inputs, high levels of pest infestation, inappropriate farming techniques, and an alarming increase in salination due to poor irrigation techniques had a negative effect on crop production."[70]

The impact of sanctions on Iraqi agriculture was severe especially when environmental conditions were adverse. The ability of the sector to recover from environmental disaster, with no easy access to emergency supplies, was limited. This became clear during the winter cropping seasons of 1998–1999 and 1999–2000, when Iraq was struck by a drought that led to a complete failure of crop germination in 70 percent of the rain-fed areas of south-central Iraq and low yields in the remaining 30 percent. Irrigated agriculture was also affected by the drought, insofar as flows in the Tigris and Euphrates rivers in early 2000 reached their lowest levels since 1930. Some of the pumps drawing water from the rivers were unable to operate (or were able to extract only smaller quantities); and the lowering of the water table led to the drying up of some wells used for summer irrigation.[71]

Despite the priority given to increasing production of basic commodities, and despite the increase in land under cultivation, these conditions ensured that agricultural production fell after 1993. Table 16.7 details the production of wheat and barley, the two most basic commodities on which the government's self-sufficiency strategy depended, between 1990 and 1997. The table perhaps understates the achievement

Table 16.7   Production of Wheat and Barley, 1990–1997 (millions of tons)

	1990	1991	1992	1993	1994	1995	1996	1997
Wheat	1.2	1.5	1.0	1.2	1.3	1.2	1.3	1.1
Barley	1.9	1.2	1.5	1.6	1.0	0.9	1.3	0.8

Source: Economist Intelligence Unit, *Iraq: Country Profile, 1995/96* (London: EIU, 1996), p. 20; and *Iraq: Country Profile, 1998/99* (London: EIU, 1999), p. 34.

over the first three years after the imposition of sanctions, insofar as the 1990 harvest of wheat and barley (combined) constituted the largest up to that date.[72] Although detailed figures for 1998 and 1999 were not available at the time of writing, it is clear that the drought conditions in those years would have ensured that production fell farther.

Oil

The development of the oil sector, and the factors affecting it, are covered in Chapter 15. Here we wish to refer exclusively to the impact that Iraqi attempts at boosting production, in the absence of sufficient spares and equipment, have had on the long-term value of Iraq's oil producing potential. Several studies conducted by experts found evidence of damage to oilfields.[73] In a letter to the president of the Security Council on 2 July 1999, the UN Secretary-General reported:

> Iraq has been continuing the practice of over-production of crude oil from wells without sufficient well pressure maintenance. Consequently, there have been high levels of production decline from a significant number of producing wells. As reported previously (S/1999/1233), owing to the lack of water removal facilities, a significant number of wells have ceased production, both in the north and in the south. . . approximately 20 percent of those wells are irreparably damaged.[74]

These comments were based on the findings of a group of oil experts who visited Iraq in June 1999. In the early part of phase 7, UN oil experts reported that oil production had peaked and that exports had declined from 2.2 million barrels per day attained in phase 6 to 1.9 million barrels per day despite the government's stated target of increasing production by 500,000 barrels per day over the course of 2000.[75]

The Basic Failings: Inadequate Resources and an Unworkable Administrative Framework

Overall, the delays in the effective implementation of Resolution 986 are incidental to a more fundamental problem in the resolution, namely, that the resources made available for humanitarian goods were simply insufficient to meet the needs of the Iraqi population. Although at the outset UN sources tended to stress the significance of the program in meeting the needs of the population, the focus of later reports was on the limits within which improvement of conditions was possible. A UN panel established to assess the humanitarian situation in Iraq reported the following in early 1999:

> Even if all humanitarian supplies were provided in a timely manner, the [humanitarian program] implemented pursuant to resolution 986 (1995) can admittedly only meet but a small fraction of the priority needs of the Iraqi people. Regardless of the improvements that might be brought about in the implementation of the current [humanitarian program]—in terms of approval procedures, better performance by the Iraqi government, or funding levels—the magnitude of the humanitarian needs is such that they cannot be met within the context of the parameters set forth in resolution 986 (1995) and succeeding resolutions.[76]

A report by the UN Secretary-General to the Security Council, written in the light of the analysis of the above-mentioned panel, was sympathetically explicit about the difficulties faced by the Iraqi government in trying to cope with the inadequate funding:

> The government of Iraq has faced difficult choices in allocating the limited resources available under the [program] across different sectors. Within each sector, decisions had to be made between meeting immediate needs, carrying out urgent repairs, supplying basic inputs to keep systems functioning and consumers supplied, and measures which might slow the deterioration of the infrastructure.[77]

These difficulties led directly to the breakdown of different sectors of services, production, and infrastructure in Iraq, and thence to an all-around deterioration of living conditions. The same report by the Secretary-General makes this clear. Focusing on the manner in which problems in the electricity sector lead to losses in many other sectors, the Secretary-General reported:

The complexity of the humanitarian situation in Iraq poses major challenges, as there is little experience with the type of problems encountered when the whole spectrum of services starts to fail, as is happening in Iraq. The slow collapse of the electricity infrastructure has consequences which are rippling through every aspect of life in Iraq, and provides a good example of how weaknesses in one sector can affect all other sectors. Almost all power stations, distribution networks, automatic control, protection and safety systems are malfunctioning. This has caused damage, in varying degrees, to every type of equipment in the electricity network. The erratic quality of supply and increasingly frequent, unscheduled power outages damage industrial and domestic appliances. The loss of power leads to the spoilage and waste of medicines and vaccines. Refrigerated food suffers similar spoilage, creating dangerous health risks. There have been losses in rice and other crops requiring continuous irrigation where farmers were dependent on electrical pumps. Water treatment plants are unable to maintain output of treated water, and the reduction in pressure of water mains brings greater risk of cross-contamination to water in the distribution network. The use of oil lamps increases the risk of domestic accidents. More importantly, hospitals dependent on inadequate emergency generators cannot operate life-saving equipment. Similar interlinkages could be detailed for all other sectors.[78]

Any attempt on the part of the Iraqi government to plan effectively or to make best use of incoming supplies, moreover, was undercut by the sporadic and unpredictable arrival of goods. The government was given neither the ability nor the inclination to operate within a long-term planning framework:

Government officials were, in many instances, overwhelmed by the mismatch between the speed and the scale of deterioration and the limited resources available to them to respond. They have repeatedly emphasized that the most that can be achieved with inputs provided under the [program] is an ad hoc response to emergencies as they arise. The unpredictable manner in which applications were submitted, approved and delivered has made many ministries understandably reluctant to devise detailed allocation plans until materials actually reach their warehouses.[79]

Even if materials had arrived on a more regular basis, the overall state of the country was such that coherent planning would have been difficult. The systems of data-gathering and monitoring that had been in existence prior to 1990 (at quite a developed and sophisticated level) had broken down. The resources to maintain data-gathering and monitoring were not available. The UN Secretary-General reported:

Effective planning is critically dependent on accurate data. Yet, with the exception of the food rationing system, this rarely appears to be available. . . . In general . . . the relevant Iraqi authorities are operating systems without adequate information, monitoring procedures, expertise or diagnostic equipment to assess the nature and extent of deterioration. In such a situation it is difficult for either the Iraqi authorities or the United Nations observation system to judge implementation against authoritative criteria. Many of the Iraqi authorities' engineering responses appear reasonable given the limited amount of information available to them but, in many sectors, plant, machinery and networks are being operated in conditions which are unprecedented, and the outcome of many interventions is genuinely unpredictable.[80]

Given that planning within a sector was often impossible, planning between and among sectors was almost invariably impossible—with negative implications for the framing and implementation of the distribution plans upon which expenditure of Oil for Food revenues depended. Two years after Oil for Food started, it was still the case that "despite the government's efforts to establish clear priorities for the use of the funds available under the program, it has not yet been possible to achieve a coherent implementation of the distribution plan."[81]

Therein lies the paradox. The Iraqi economy was expected to operate under the framework of Resolution 986. At a time when the Western powers were emphasizing, at an international level, the inefficiency of forms of economic organization that involved close control and supervision, and the benefits that could be drawn from reliance on the free market, the economic procedures that they imposed on Iraq represented an extreme form of systematic bureaucratic control. It should have come as no surprise that the controls severely inhibited the Iraqi economy and its ability to provide for the needs of the Iraqi population.

Notes

1. It should be noted that the definition of the areas follows the pattern adopted in UN reports. Mosul province, therefore, comes under "central and southern Iraq," despite being in the northern part of the country. The "northern governorates" are exclusively those in the Kurdish areas.

2. At the end of 1998, the UN humanitarian coordinator for Iraq, Denis Halliday, resigned his post. He told journalists: "The fact is that Oil for Food is a failure. Anything that sustains malnutrition at 30 percent and leads to the death of so many thousands is a failure." His successor, Hans von Sponeck, lasted in the job for a little more than a year before resigning. Upon his resignation, he told a press

conference that the central reason why Oil for Food was flawed was because the "resources were inadequate." Significantly, the United Nations chose to publicize his grounds for resignation in a press release. United Nations, *Press Briefing by Outgoing UN Humanitarian Coordinator*, 1 March 2000 <http://www.un.org/ News/briefings/socs/2000/20000301.vonsponeck.doc.html>. Immediately after von Sponeck's resignation, the head of the World Food Program's Iraqi office also resigned.

3. United Nations Press Release, SC/6834, 24 March 2000.

4. This account of the rationing system is taken from the distribution plans. See, e.g., Republic of Iraq, *Distribution Plan* [Phase 7] (Baghdad: Ministry of Foreign Affairs, 1999).

5. Republic of Iraq, *Athar al-Hisar al-Iqtisadi al-Shamil ala al-Iraq* [The Effects of Comprehensive Economic Sanctions on Iraq] (Baghdad: Ministry of Foreign Affairs, 2000), p. 12.

6. Ibid.

7. All of the information given here on the calorific values (targets and actual) is taken from United Nations, S/2000/208 *(Report of the Secretary-General on Resolution 1281)*.

8. United Nations, *Report of the Second Panel Established Pursuant to the Note by the President of the Security Council of 30 January 1999 (S/1999/100) Concerning the Current Humanitarian Situation in Iraq*, S/1999/356, 30 March 1999.

9. Republic of Iraq, *Distribution Plan Submitted by the Government of Iraq to the UN Secretary-General in Accordance with ... Resolution 1281 (1999)* (Baghdad: Ministry of Foreign Affairs, 1999).

10. Interviews, Baghdad, December 1997 and March 2000.

11. United Nations, S/1999/356 *(Report of the Second Panel Concerning the Current Humanitarian Situation in Iraq)*, para. 29.

12. Republic of Iraq, *Athar al-Hisar,* p. 44.

13. United Nations, S/1998/187, para. 33.

14. Reference to the survey mentioned here is made in United Nations, S/1999/356 *(Report of the Second Panel Concerning the Current Humanitarian Situation in Iraq)*, para. 30.

15. Republic of Iraq, *Distribution Plan* [Phase 7].

16. United Nations, S/199 *(Review and Assessment of the Humanitarian Programme)*, para. 80.

17. Iraqi doctors pointed out to this writer that the impact of the holds on 10 percent of the goods requested went beyond a 10 percent reduction of medicines that might have been available. In many cases, equipment that was allowed in could not be used without one of the items that had been withheld. Interviews, March 2000.

18. United Nations, S/2000/208 *(Report of the Secretary-General on Resolution 1281)*, para. 140.

19. Republic of Iraq, *Distribution Plan* [Phase 7].

20. Ibid.

21. *Hansard*, 25 January 1999, cols. 1217, 1218, 1222. Quoted in E. Herring, "Between Iraq and a Hard Place: A Critique of the British Government's Narra-

tive on UN Economic Sanctions," unpublished paper delivered to the IR Workshop, University of Exeter, 26 October 1999.

22. See, e.g., United Nations, S/1998/1100, para. 80.

23. United Nations, S/1998/187, para. 29.

24. Ibid., para. 31. The building up of supplies "in anticipation of emergency needs" is a characteristic of the Iraqi governmental ethos. The expectation that the situation will become worse—an expectation that is not devoid of realism—creates a natural tendency to hoard.

25. United Nations, S/1999/356 *(Report of the Second Panel Concerning the Current Humanitarian Situation in Iraq)*, para.37.

26. United Nations, *Report of the Secretary-General Pursuant to Paragraph 6 of Security Council Resolution 1210,* S/1999/573, 18 May 1999, para. 137.

27. United Nations, S/1998/90 *(Report of the Secretary-General Pursuant to Paragraph 7 of Resolution 1143)*, para 35.

28. United Nations, *Press Briefing by Outgoing UN Humanitarian Coordinator.*

29. United Nations, S/2000/208 *(Report of the Secretary-General on Resolution 1281)*, para. 137.

30. Republic of Iraq, *Athar al-Hisar*, p. 46.

31. United Nations, *Press Briefing by Outgoing Humanitarian Coordinator.* The figures given by von Sponeck are based on UNICEF estimates.

32. This view was frequently expressed to the writer during his visit to Iraq in March 2000. The spread of private medical facilities in the late 1990s enabled the wealthiest people to obtain private treatment. The mass of the population, however, simply remained at home, seeking such treatment as was available. The director of the pediatric teaching hospital in Baghdad, which was once among the leading medical institutions in the Middle East, told a group of visiting U.S. congressional staffers that "we have a problem with disposal of dirty water and sewage; and the cooling system is bad, it creates an unhealthy environment in the hospital." *Congressional Staff Report: Iraq Trip*, September 1999 <http://www.geocities...aqinfo/sanctions/sarticles3/report.html>, p. 7.

33. United Nations, S/2000/208 *(Report of the Secretary-General on Resolution 1281)*, para. 138.

34. Ibid., paras. 47–49.

35. Ibid.

36. United Nations, S/1999/356 *(Report of the Second Panel Concerning the Current Humanitarian Situation in Iraq)*, para. 14.

37. United Nations, S/199 *(Review and Assessment of the Humanitarian Programme)*, para. 84.

38. Republic of Iraq, *Distribution Plan* [Phase 7], paras. 42–43.

39. Evidence for this is found in the distribution plans, but it can also be seen from the value of contracts submitted to the Sanctions Committee by the Iraqi government.

40. UN sources reported the installation rate of equipment at 96 percent of deliveries in March 2000, which represents the highest rate of implementation for any sector.

41. United Nations, *Introductory Statement by Benon Sevan to the Report of the Secretary-General Pursuant to Paragraph 6 of Resolution 1242, S/1999/1162*, 17 November 1999 <http://www.un.org/Depts/oip/reports/bvsnov17.html>, p. 4.

42. Interviews with officials in the power sector, Baghdad, November 1997.

43. United Nations, S/1998/90 *(Report of the Secretary-General Pursuant to Paragraph 7 of Resolution 1143)*, para. 26.

44. Personal observation, March 2000.

45. United Nations, S/1998/90 *(Report of the Secretary-General Pursuant to Paragraph 7 of Resolution 1143)*, para.27.

46. United Nations, S/199 *(Review and Assessment of the Humanitarian Programme)*, para. 100.

47. An example of delays in this sector was the contract for school computers issued by the Iraqi government in 1997 under phase 1 of Oil for Food. The consignment eventually reached the country in July 1999. In November of that year, the consignment was still undergoing quality testing by the Iraqi authorities, a process that was lengthened by the inadequacy of qualified personnel to undertake the work. See United Nations, S/1999/1162 *(Report of the Secretary-General on Resolution 1242)*, para. 67.

48. These figures are drawn from a comparison of the 1977 and 1987 census figures.

49. United Nations, S/1999/356 *(Report of the Second Panel Concerning the Current Humanitarian Situation in Iraq)*, para. 15.

50. United Nations, S/2000/208 *(Report of the Secretary-General on Resolution 1281)*, para. 152.

51. United Nations, S/199 *(Review and Assessment of the Humanitarian Programme)*, para. 105.

52. Clearly this is one field in which the redirection of Iraqi domestic resources away from prestige projects would have brought some benefit to the population.

53. United Nations, S/199 *(Review and Assessment of the Humanitarian Programme)*, para. 107.

54. Ibid.

55. These items are mentioned in most of the distribution plans. See, e.g., Republic of Iraq, *Distribution Plan* [Phase 7], paras. 8 and 62.

56. United Nations, S/1999/1162 *(Report of the Secretary-General on Resolution 1242)*, para. 69.

57. Republic of Iraq, *Athar al-Hisar*, pp. 52–60.

58. UNICEF, "Situation Analysis of Children and Women in Iraq—1997," mimeograph, UNICEF/IRAQ, 30 April 1998.

59. United Nations, *Press Briefing by Outgoing Humanitarian Coordinator for Iraq*.

60. United Nations, S/2000/208 *(Report of the Secretary-General on Resolution 1281)*, para. 144.

61. Republic of Iraq, *Distribution Plan* [Phase 7], para. 50.

62. Economist Intelligence Unit, *Iraq: Country Profile, 1995/96* (London: EIU, 1996), p. 16.

63. Abd al-Ghaffur Ibrahim Ahmad, *Al-Amn al-Ghiza'i fi al-Iraq* [Food Security in Iraq] (Baghdad: Bait al-Hikmah, 1999).

64. This was particularly true under the first three phases, when agro-machinery made up 60 percent of the goods ordered, chemicals and spraying equipment 24 percent, and veterinary supplies 16 percent.

65. UN reports criticized the priority given to equipment orders over orders for other agricultural inputs such as fertilizers, pesticides, and the like. The justice of this criticism, however, can be questioned. The mechanized character of Iraqi agriculture meant that spares and equipment were of critical importance to production. Moreover, the agricultural goods placed on hold by the Sanctions Committee were mainly the "other agricultural inputs": fertilizers, pesticides, and the like. For the UN argument, see United Nations, S/199 *(Review and Assessment of the Humanitarian Programme)*, paras. 91–93.

66. Ibid., paras. 51–53.

67. Prior to the Gulf War, Iraq had been producing 1.5 million metric tons of compound fertilizer annually, and 1 million metric tons of nitrogenous fertilizer. This covered the country's needs. By 1999, production had fallen to 130,000 metric tons of phosphate fertilizer and 400,000 metric tons of urea. Ibid., para. 53.

68. Ahmad, *Al-Amn al-Ghiza'i*, p. 106.

69. Quoted in United Nations, S/1999/356 *(Report of the Second Panel Concerning the Current Humanitarian Situation in Iraq)*, para. 31.

70. United Nations, S/199 *(Review and Assessment of the Humanitarian Programme)*, para. 91.

71. Ibid., para. 7. In addition to the problem of pumps being unable to draw water from the rivers, there were also the wider problems stemming from power cuts. Most of the pumps were driven by electricity, and in some of the country areas electricity was available for only one hour a day in 1999 and 2000.

72. For more details of cereals production, see Ahmad, *Al-Amn al-Ghiza'i*, pp. 130–142.

73. The Iraqi ministry of oil itself acknowledged the potential damage. It described its oil production as being carried out "under a regime of severe risk management" rather than under a "planned programme of good reservoir management." See United Nations, *Report Pursuant to Paragraph 9 of Security Council Resolution 1281*, S/2000/26, 14 January 2000. The UN Secretary-General reported to the Security Council that Iraq had increased its oil production "without the technical resources to apply 'good oilfield practice.'" The result had been "a massive decline in the condition, effectiveness and efficiency of the infrastructure, coupled with appalling safety conditions and significant environmental damage." See United Nations, S/2000/208 *(Report of the Secretary-General on Resolution 1281)*, para. 25.

74. United Nations, accompanying letter from the Secretary-General, in *Report of the Group of Experts Established Pursuant to Paragraph 9 of Security Council Resolution 1242* <http://www.un.org/Depts/oip/reports/sgoil6.html>.

75. Ibid.

76. United Nations, S/1999/356 *(Report of the Second Panel Concerning the Current Humanitarian Situation in Iraq)*, para. 46.

77. United Nations, S/199 *(Review and Assessment of the Humanitarian Programme)*, para. 55.

78. Ibid., para. 55.

79. Ibid., para. 60.

80. Ibid., para. 62.

81. Ibid., para. 63.

17

Humanitarian Goods and Economic Infrastructure: Northern Iraq

The impact of sanctions on Oil for Food in northern Iraq will not be covered in as much detail. Given that the focus of this book is on the relationship between sanctions and the dynamics of the polities on which they are imposed, developments outside of the territories controlled by the central government are less critical to the analysis. The main concern here is to outline developments following the introduction of Oil for Food, comparing the conditions in the north of the country with those in the center and south. Thus, we explain the discrepancies in the impact of Oil for Food revenues in order to assess whether they shed light on the factors responsible for adverse economic and social conditions.

Security Council Resolution 986 had a more positive effect on northern Iraq than on central and southern Iraq, in part due to the situation prior to the resolution's approval. Whereas a rationing system had been in force in southern and central Iraq since the later part of 1990, no such system existed in the north between March/April 1991, when the central government lost control over the area, and the initiation of Oil for Food.[1] When rationing was introduced, therefore, conditions improved dramatically, reflected in changing attitudes among the population as to future reintegration into the Iraqi state.[2]

The situation in northern Iraq after 1996, however, also became more positive in real terms compared to southern and central Iraq. The differences should not be exaggerated, however, for conditions in the Kurdish areas remained severe. Nonetheless, facilities and infrastructure were marginally better in most sectors. In education, there was an increase in school enrollment in the north.[3] The morale of teachers in northern schools was generally better, in part because salaries were higher.[4] Five different UN agencies were involved in implementing activities in the education sector, and the support provided was governed by a holistic approach. Help was given, therefore, not only for basic supplies and materials but also for the construction and rehabilitation of schools, teaching aids, teacher training, teacher salaries, and printing equipment.[5] The physical environment of schools improved.

Medicine was more widely available and was not rationed. Prices for medicine were more affordable. A UN panel reported that in the northern governorates "the availability of equipment, trained staff as well as drugs and supplies have contributed to substantially increased patient attendance."[6] The existence of continuing problems, however, was evident from the Iraqi government's distribution plan covering phase 6,[7] which stated that "the health situation in the three northern governorates has not improved substantially. The primary health centers do not provide comprehensive services."[8]

Food and nutrition improved in the north, with a significant drop in acute and chronic malnutrition. The number of families, groups, and social institutions receiving supplementary food from the World Food Program decreased between phases 4 and 6, from 258,995 to 80,575, reflecting a decreasing need.[9] One reason for improvement was the progress made in plant and animal production locally, making food more affordable. Wheat production, however, was adversely affected by the quantities of subsidized wheat flour that were available to the population through the rationing system.

Water and sanitation also fared better. Access to safe drinking water increased from 63 percent of the population in 1996 to 72 percent in 1999, and the share of water for rural consumers increased from twenty to thirty liters per day per person to forty to fifty liters.[10] (In central and southern Iraq the access to water and the quantities available had simply stabilized.) By the end of 1999, expenditures for water and sanitation in the northern governorates were in fact higher than in the rest of the country combined ($35.79 million versus $23.22 million). A noticeable decline in the number of cases of water- and sewage-related diseases was reported.

Nonetheless, some sectors in the northern governorates fared worse. The power generation and distribution installations and networks had been severely damaged in 1991, and for some time the central grid stopped supplying any electricity to the northern governorates. In 1993, the Dohuk governorate was reconnected to the central grid, but Erbil and Suleimaniyyah governorates had to rely on power generation from two hydroelectric plants installed at dams that were originally meant for irrigation.[11] Thus, power shortages were more severe in the northern governorates, at least up to mid-1999, when the deteriorating power supplies elsewhere created parity.

Assessment of the Factors Creating Better Conditions in the Kurdish Areas

The comparably favorable situation in the north allowed Western politicians to blame poor conditions in south-central Iraq on the Iraqi government. Although some blame can be placed on the government for conditions in areas under its control, the causes for the better conditions in the northern governorates are more complex. Five main factors are responsible. First, the administration of the humanitarian program in the northern governorates by the United Nations was an advantage. There was close coordination between the program and the process whereby projects and contracts were agreed. Not surprisingly, northern governorates suffered from the fewest holds on contracts (see Table 15.3). The distribution of food and medicines, once they had reached the Kurdish areas, was more effective. Effective distribution (and, to some extent, procurement) reflected the differences between a well-funded operation run by trained professionals, where the financing was drawn from the UN humanitarian program itself, and a program dependent on hard-pressed local authorities and staff whose morale was low, where the administrative costs were borne by the Iraqi government and local authorities.

Second, the per capita allocation of funds under Oil for Food was higher for the northern governorates than for the rest of the country. Although the percentage of Oil for Food money allocated to the north (13 percent) was proportional to the percentage of the Iraqi population resident in that area, the percentage of Oil for Food money that needed to go to the Compensation Fund (about 30 percent of the total) and to support UN operations in Iraq was taken from the remainder of the funds. Accordingly, the proportion that could be devoted to central and southern Iraq was reduced. Of the actual allocations for humanitarian goods, the northern governorates gained 19.5 percent of the total for the country, whereas southern and central Iraq (with 87 percent of the country's population) obtained 80.5 percent.[12] Moreover, the operation of the oil industry (with all the costs of spares, transport through Turkey, etc.), upon which the whole Oil for Food program depended, had to be covered by central government expenditures. The imported elements in these expenditures came from the central government's allocation for humanitarian goods under Oil for Food, whereas local costs had to come from domestically generated revenue.

Third, Oil for Food funding for the northern governorates included a cash component. In southern and central Iraq, the funding could not be used either for local labor or for local purchases. Inevitably, this made it more difficult in those areas for imported goods to be transported, installed, and serviced. Some of the uses to which the Iraqi government put local resources at its disposal, however, did not encourage sympathy. Spending on presidential palaces and prestige projects, although dependent almost entirely on local labor and materials, undercut complaints about the lack of a cash component for central government expenditure.[13]

Fourth, economic conditions were affected positively by the geographic location of the Kurdish areas. The long borders with neighboring countries, as well as the inability (and perhaps unwillingness) of those countries to prevent goods from crossing into Kurdish areas, meant substantial trade was conducted. Much of the informal trade between central Iraq and the outside world, indeed, came across the border with Turkey through Kurdish areas, and the Kurdish leadership took "informal taxes" on this trade, as well as trade destined for areas under its own control. Although it would be difficult to give an accurate figure for the income received from such taxes, the United Nations estimated that the Kurdish Democratic Party was obtaining $1–2 million daily from this source.[14] General economic activity was stimulated both by the additional funding reaching the area, as well as by the economic stimulation that the commerce itself provided.[15]

Fifth, the resource base in the north was also more suited to coping with sanctions. A significant proportion of Iraq's arable land was situated in the three northern governorates, such that locally grown food was more abundant. The agricultural sector in northern Iraq, moreover, was more dependent on rainfall and, therefore, was less liable to be adversely affected by power shortages that disrupted irrigation systems. The benefit of this situation to farmers was at times reduced by the downward pressure on prices for agricultural goods resulting from Oil for Food imports (especially wheat flour) and the severe drought that struck the country in 1998–1999. Nonetheless, it did enable northern farmers to draw greater gain from agricultural production, and it led to agricultural goods being available to the population at lower prices.

Notes

1. The northern governorates did, however, benefit more from external aid, especially between 1991 and 1993, when many NGOs and aid agencies were active in the region.

2. Aid workers in northern Iraq in 1995 and 1996 were reporting that most Kurds were eager to see the reestablishment of central government control in the north. Although this stemmed in part from disillusionment at the conflicts that had broken out among Kurdish factions, bringing unsettled conditions to many areas, it also reflected the harsh conditions and the feeling that insufficient help had come from outside. By 1998, however, aid workers were reporting that Kurdish opinion was turning against reintegration. The greater stability of political conditions in the north contributed to this change, but it was also conditioned by fears that living standards would drop if reintegration occurred.

3. UN reports indicated, however, that UN funding for new school buildings and equipment was often undermined by the lack of support services to maintain the buildings and equipment. United Nations, S/199, para. 108.

4. This stemmed in part from the availability of a "cash component" in Oil for Food funds available for northern Iraq, whereas the funds for southern and central Iraq were limited to covering the costs of goods and equipment.

5. United Nations, S/199 *(Review and Assessment of the Humanitarian Programme)*, para.108.

6. United Nations, S/1999/356 *(Report of the Second Panel Concerning the Current Humanitarian Situation in Iraq)*, para. 33.

7. The parts of the distribution plans relating to the northern governorates, although put together by the government of Iraq, were based on information provided by UN agencies in the north.

8. Republic of Iraq, *Distribution Plan Submitted by the Government of Iraq to the UN Secretary-General in Accordance with the MOU of 20 May 1996 and Resolution 1242 (1999)* (Baghdad: Ministry of Foreign Affairs, 1999).

9. United Nations, S/2000/208 *(Report of the Secretary-General on Resolution 1281)*, para. 164.

10. United Nations, S/199 *(Review and Assessment of the Humanitarian Programme)*, para. 90.

11. Ibid., para. 101.

12. The population of the northern governorates was put at 3,438,763 in 2000, compared to a total national population of 24,739,300. See Republic of Iraq, *Distribution Plan* [Phase 7]. Reference to the imbalance in funding was made in the press briefing given by Hans von Sponeck following the announcement of his resignation as humanitarian coordinator for Iraq. United Nations, *Press Briefing by Outgoing Humanitarian Coordinator.*

13. Among the prestige projects were a new double-decker bridge over the Tigris River in the southern part of the capital (Saddam Bridge) and the new communications tower, with a revolving restaurant at the top (Saddam Tower). There were also substantial expenditures on new mosques, such as the Shaikh Ma'ruf mosque in the Haifa district of Baghdad. The ability to carry out these projects was impressive (artistically, as well as technically, in the case of the mosques), and presumably part of the intent was to show both the population and the outside world that the state still had the ability to undertake and complete substantial projects. Nonetheless, outside observers were able to point to the waste of resources— which could have been put into ensuring that the distribution system for food and medicines was operating effectively. In practice, it may have been easier for the

regime to see major projects through to completion than to change the ethos of low motivation and morale that was hampering the effectiveness of wider governmental programs.

14. As reported by members of the delegation of U.S. congressional staff who visited Iraq in late August 1999. See *Congressional Staff Report: Iraq Trip.*

15. This point was acknowledged by Hans von Sponeck in *Press Briefing by Outgoing Humanitarian Coordinator.*

18

Disarmament and Security

In this chapter we do not detail the prolonged confrontation between the Security Council and Iraq on issues of disarmament and security; rather we will focus on the aspect most relevant to this book, namely, whether sanctions resulted in Iraqi compliance with the disarmament- and security-related provisions of Resolution 687. Such provisions include the destruction or rendering harmless of all chemical and biological weapons, ballistic missiles with a range of more than 150 kilometers, and nuclear facilities, as well as the recognition of Kuwaiti sovereignty, the acceptance of the border as demarcated by the Boundary Commission, and payment of compensation.

Over the decade that followed the imposition of sanctions, the government of Iraq sought to prevaricate and to prevent the full disclosure of information. Nonetheless, it was brought slowly to comply with most of the requirements mentioned above. The government of Iraq confirmed its "irrevocable and unqualified recognition of the sovereignty, territorial integrity and political independence of the State of Kuwait," as well as of the boundary as demarcated by the UN Boundary Commission; guaranteed that Iraq would not commit or support any act of international terrorism; returned to Kuwait a substantial amount of the property that had been removed during the occupation; and (step by step) revealed most of the required information on its nuclear program, its holdings of ballistic missiles, and its holdings of and facilities for chemical and biological weapons.

It does not follow, however, that sanctions themselves brought about this compliance. Sanctions, in fact, appear to have merely exerted a positive influence on Iraqi compliance in the first few months that followed the adoption of the resolution. The government clearly hoped at the outset that compliance with some of the requirements of Resolution 687 would lead to the removal of the entire sanctions regime. The phrasing of the resolution suggested such removal was possible. Despite Iraq's initial failure to disclose a major part of its past weapons programs and existing weapons stocks, the government did move toward a posture of compliance: agreeing to the modalities of UNSCOM and IAEA operations; accepting the presence of UN guards to protect UN assets and personnel; responding positively to some of the initial requests for information; and agreeing on inspection procedures.

From the second half of 1991, however, no clear relationship between sanctions and Iraqi compliance is apparent. All of the major turning-points—where the Iraqi government was brought to reveal more information on weaponry than it had made available before, to accept the continued presence of UNSCOM, or to accept the outcome of the Boundary Commission's findings—were the result of other pressures. The latter were constituted by the insistent requests for information by UNSCOM (backed up by the Security Council), the diplomatic intervention of the UN Secretary-General and occasionally of national governments (especially Russia), the accidental leak of information (as when Hussein Kamil fled to Jordan in August 1995), and the bombing and missile raids conducted by the United States and Britain.

There was a simple reason for this apparently surprising development. The most critical objective of the government of Iraq, besides ensuring regime survival, was the reestablishment of Iraqi sovereignty. There was no indication, however, that compliance with Security Council demands would lead to that end. The lightening of sanctions, offered by the Security Council following the passage of Resolution 706 in August 1991, would have imposed new restrictions on Iraq's control of its own resources—with no time limit on their termination. Iraq would be able to sell some oil, but at the cost of it ceding sovereignty and losing control over how the proceeds were spent. The resolution established procedures expected to remain for the long term, even though the amount of oil that Iraq was allowed to export might rise. Resolution 986 (1995) was slightly more attractive, but only because it was described as being temporary. There was, therefore, little incentive for Iraq to trade information on its weapons programs for the lightening of sanctions, given that both the disarmament requirements and the proposed arrangements for the lightening of sanctions negated the government's most critical objective.

Iraq maintained that it had done enough to warrant the lifting of sanctions and pressed the international community to bring the sanctions regime to an end. It was, however, interested in the removal of the whole framework of restrictions that had been imposed, not in ameliorative measures that enshrined the long-term loss of sovereignty. The maintenance of the sanctions regime may even have deterred the government from a readiness to disclose its full weapons program. In the power-oriented perceptions of Iraqi policymaking, the retention of some military capabilities may have been deemed necessary as a bargaining counter to obtain the removal of restrictions on national sovereignty.

19

Economy
and Society

The realities of Iraqi economy and society since the imposition of sanctions have already been covered in some detail. This chapter is intended to fill out the picture. First, we analyze some overall statistics on the Iraqi economy; second, we provide an impression of life in Iraq in November 1997 and March 2000, based on visits by this writer to Baghdad.[1] The personal observations are written in the present tense to convey the feeling of conditions at the time. Although the first visit (November 1997) came six months after Oil for Food provisions had started to arrive in Iraq, the quantities that had arrived and been distributed were small. Apart from a rise in the food ration, therefore, conditions remained much as they had been prior to Resolution 986. The second visit (March 2000) came some three years after Oil for Food had been in operation, when conditions might be expected to have changed.

Perspectives on the Overall Economy

The most critical transformation in the Iraqi economy was, of course, that which followed immediately after the occupation of Kuwait and the imposition of sanctions. The figures in Table 19.1 trace the changes to overall GDP, and to the main elements of GDP, between 1989 and 1993. As can be seen, the dramatic fall in GDP in 1991 was followed by a small rally in 1992, then by another drop in 1993. The mining sector was, naturally, in continual decline over this period, as also was manufacturing, banking and insurance, and social and personal services. Agriculture and other sectors made occasional recoveries, reflecting environmental factors and the

Table 19.1   **Gross Domestic Product by Sector, 1989–1993 (in millions of Iraqi dinar at constant 1980 prices; percentage change on year in brackets)**

Sector	1989	1990	1991	1992	1993
Agriculture, forestry, and fishing	982	1,073	801	982	965
	(n/a)	(9.3)	(–25.3)	(22.6)	(–1.7)
Mining	7,760	7,137	155	–22	–562
	(n/a)	(–8.0)	(–97.7)	(–)	(–)
Manufacturing	861	720	452	406	375
	(n/a)	(–8.0)	(–37.2)	(–10.2)	(–7.6)
Construction	686	695	143	151	100
	(n/a)	(1.3)	(–79.4)	(5.6)	(–33.8)
Electricity and water	151	125	65	109	128
	(n/a)	(–17.2)	(–48.0)	(67.7)	(17.4)
Transport, communications, and storage	559	692	304	372	390
	(n/a)	(23.8)	(–56.1)	(22.4)	(4.8)
Commerce and hotels	866	1,136	414	949	686
	(n/a)	(31.2)	(–63.6)	(129.2)	(–27.7)
Banking and insurance	584	575	243	183	108
	(n/a)	(–1.5)	(–57.7)	(–24.7)	(–41.0)
Social and personal services	1,423	1,353	612	450	250
	(n/a)	(–4.9)	(–54.8)	(–27.2)	(–53.3)
GDP at factor cost, including other sectors	14,178	13,863	3,548	4,073	2,982
	(n/a)	(–2.2)	(–74.4)	(14.8)	(–26.8)

Source: Central Statistical Organization, Baghdad. Taken here from Economist Intelligence Unit, *Iraq: Country Profile, 1998/99* (London: EIU, 1999), p. 32.

efforts made by the government to resurrect basic infrastructure. Reliable figures for the sectoral growth of GDP since 1993 are not easy to obtain, but overall GDP estimates indicate that the economy underwent another small retraction between 1993 and 1996. As a result of population growth, the per capita decline in GDP since 1989 was more substantial than the global figure. Estimates for 1995 put annual per capita GDP at no more than some $200 per annum, whereas the World Bank had put it at $2,840 per annum in 1989.[2]

The restarting of oil exports in 1997 led to 25 percent growth in GDP for that year.[3] There does, not, however, seem to have been any increase in other sectors. Industrial production in 1997 was running at about 80 percent compared to 1989. Agricultural production was less severely affected, some 20 percent less than in 1989.[4] The low oil prices in 1998 prevented any further rise in GDP in that year, but the higher prices in 1999 led to renewed GDP growth. Such growth as occurred, however, had little impact on annual per capita income, which remained a fraction of pre-1991 levels.

The fall in the purchasing power of the Iraqi dinar (ID) is indicated by the currency's fall in value against the U.S. dollar. The unofficial market rate fell from about $1 = ID4 in early 1990 to $1 = ID50 in 1993, $1 = ID500 in 1994, and $1 = ID1,000 in the early part of 1996. When Oil for Food was initiated, it rose briefly to $1 = ID450, then quickly declined again to $1 = ID1,000 before declining further to $1 = ID1,500 at the end of 1997 and $1 = ID1,850 in early 2000.[5]

Personal Observations, Baghdad, November 1997

Economic conditions have clearly affected the fabric of society in Iraq. The critical factor that now shapes social conduct is the penury of those living on public-sector incomes (perhaps 40 percent of the employed population).[6] Starting salaries within the public sector begin at ID3,000 ($2) per month, about the cost of one kilogram of meat. Most monthly salaries within the sector come to less than ID10,000 ($7) per month. University lecturers, one of the better-paid occupations in the government sector, earn salaries of about ID12,000 ($8) per month, although if they undertake substantial overtime teaching in the evenings they can raise their income to some ID30,000 ($20) per month. Neither are army officers in a particularly favorable position: a captain's salary would not exceed ID12,000 per month. The highest incomes in the public sector are those of judges, who can earn up to ID80,000 ($53) per month. Estimates made by members of staff of the University of Baghdad are that the cost of maintaining a family of four per month, at a fairly basic level, comes to some ID250,000.

Even the highest-paid officials in the public sector, therefore, do not earn even one-half of what would be needed to maintain a family. Survival depends on four main sources of support: the purchase of subsidized goods through the government's rationing system; the sale of household goods; income in hard currency from relatives abroad (bearing in mind that the receipt of $100 per month from this source will bring in ID150,000); and the use of the individual's public position to gain reward through corruption and the acceptance of bribes.

The acute need to find the means for survival has changed the ethic of the population fundamentally. Before 1990, there was relatively little corruption in Iraq: honesty and straight-dealing (besides being enforced by strong governmental sanctions) were associated with family and individ-

ual honor, and personal generosity was deeply ingrained in popular culture. Today, most aspects of life in Iraq are governed by the payment and
taking of bribes. This has become so routine that it no longer causes surprise or disapproval. Soldiers at roadblocks expect to be given packets of
cigarettes, apples, and the like—and motorists always carry stocks of
these goods for that purpose. The police steal cars and then take bribes
from the owners when the car is "found" (often without its tires). University lecturers take money from students for "private lessons," which then
affect their marks in examinations. Hospital doctors and nurses sell to the
private pharmacies the subsidized medicines that the state makes available, leaving the hospitals even more depleted than before. Public services, such as telephone and electricity, are available only when a bribe is
paid to the individual responsible for the connection.

Some other negative phenomena come from the deep social division
that has opened up between a tiny commercial elite and the mass of the
population. Those merchants (many, but not all, with links to the inner
core of Saddam Hussein's family) who have been able to gain a share of
the import-export trade with Turkey, Iran, Syria, and Jordan have grown
very wealthy. Sanctions have effectively put them in a monopolistic position in the supply of some goods. The reality of wealth among poverty is
clear from the street scenes in central Baghdad. The shops display luxury
and everyday goods, but very few customers enter. The crowds in the
streets walk determinedly past the windows without glancing in, knowing
there is nothing they could afford. The only commercial enterprises that
are crowded are the *mazad*s (auction houses), where carpets, furniture,
and household goods of those desperate to acquire income are sold off. In
the Karrada area of the city, people have laid their possessions out for sale
on the pavement. Small children weave among the traffic, even late at
night, selling matches, cigarettes, and other low-cost items. Prostitution is
common, as are theft and violence. Iraqis refer frequently to the "rough-
ness" that now characterizes interpersonal relations, even within families,
as every individual seeks to ensure personal survival.

The basis upon which a sophisticated cultural life can exist is slowly
being eroded. Crucial to this process has been the damage done to the educational system. Iraq's educational system has, under Ba'thist rule, always
suffered from the ideological straightjacket that the state has imposed.
Nonetheless, until 1990 there was a positive side: schools and universities
were well funded and well organized, with ample resources devoted to
libraries and educational materials. Especially on the science side, the
educational system produced some well-trained and highly qualified grad-
uates. Since 1990, schools and universities have been deprived of new

learning materials. Relying on a steadily deteriorating stock of books and facilities, and with no means to retain contact with outside developments, pupils and students have been shunted into stultifying isolation. University libraries have received virtually no new books. Even when resources are available, books cannot be acquired, for the International Postal Union upholds the sanctions regulations and seeks to prevent the dispatch of parcels containing books (and other materials) to Iraq. Textbooks are passed down from year to year, becoming less usable. Teachers and lecturers have steadily become more isolated from new developments in their subjects of specialization, not having the resources to travel abroad, the books and journals that could inform them of new developments, or the ability to obtain a visa to enter most other countries.

Some Iraqi intellectuals see the world in which they live as being bounded by a double blockade: a combination of the regime's policies and the effects of sanctions, which ensure that their intellectual life is stunted and remove their ability to make independent judgments about developments inside or outside Iraq. The usual channels employed in most of the rest of the world to maintain contact with national and international developments are absent or difficult in Iraq: computers and photocopying facilities are largely unavailable; e-mail and the Internet are totally unavailable; telephone contact with the rest of the world is difficult; satellite dishes are banned by the government, limiting Iraqis to watching the dreary and propagandistic programs on Iraqi television; virtually no foreign publications reach Iraq, and Iraqi newspapers have become steadily smaller (due to the shortage of paper) and less informative. In the past, many Iraqi intellectuals maintained substantial private libraries as a foundation for their individual intellectual formation; now the contents of many of these libraries are spread out for sale in the Suq al-Saraya market to pay for subsistence needs. Even the desire to engage in intellectual development is frustrated: intellectual effort leads to no reward (in terms of a job earning a living wage) and constitutes a distraction from the immediate and urgent need to find the means to survive. There is no basis or dynamic left in society whereby the views purveyed by government sources can be independently analyzed or questioned.

Personal Observations, Baghdad, March 2000

Relative to the situation in November 1997, Iraq gives a greater appearance of normality and of being a going concern. The surface appearance

is of a city dogged more by traffic congestion than by material depriva-
tion, where a small but significant number of new cars mix with those kept
on the roads by deft repair.[7] The shops and markets are adequately
stocked, with modern electrical goods, furniture, and office equipment, as
well as more basic consumer goods, especially in the richer quarters of al-
Mansur, al-Amiriya, al-Qadissiyah, al-Jadiriyyah, and Hindiyyah. New
restaurants have opened in the same areas, geared to the tastes of an elite
accustomed to Western-style requirements. Although the shops and restaurants are clearly not heavily patronized, their ability to remain open (given
that they are privately owned) indicates that a market for their goods and
services exists. The occasional computer can be seen in universities and
research institutes, and some restricted access to the Internet is available.
A limited number of large-scale construction projects create an impression
of some regeneration: reconstruction of sites damaged in the Gulf War,
new projects undertaken since the war such as the Saddam communications tower, some new mosques, the double-decker bridge over the Tigris
River, and the embankment being built along both sides of the river. The
universities are functioning and are providing at least the basic requirements of a university education. A flourishing art scene exists, centered on
or close to Abu Nawas Street.

Yet two realizations soon impinge on this surface impression. The first
is that little of the apparent normality stems from any coherent development
or needs satisfaction undertaken on the basis of the Oil for Food revenues.
Indeed, to some extent the opposite is the case. The high-value goods available on the market have entered the country in breach of the UN sanctions
regime, and the wealth of the merchants who have brought them in (and
who also provide much of the demand for the more expensive goods and
services) is built on their critical role in filling the shortages created by sanctions.[8] Most of the computers in the University of Baghdad have been
acquired from the private commercial sector, not from Oil for Food funding.
The university authorities had ordered computers through Oil for Food, but
the length of the process made it necessary for them to acquire the machines
from local commercial sources. The prestige construction projects act as
symbols of defiance rather than meeting immediate needs: an assertion to
the outside world and to the population that the regime can build in the face
of externally imposed adversity. Outside the capital, prestige projects are not
needed and are not undertaken. The flourishing art scene, stemming from a
rich artistic tradition, is encouraged by the commercial reality that it provides access to foreign currency.

The second realization is that behind the façade the lives of most
Iraqis are marked, perhaps even more than before, by quiet desperation.

The presence of sophisticated goods in the market, and of conspicuous well-being on a limited scale, illuminate the day-to-day privation of the mass of the population. Although the incomes of some public-sector workers have been marginally improved, they remain drastically short of what would be needed to maintain a family. The increase in incomes, moreover, has come not through the raising of overall salaries but through devices aimed at benefiting specific categories. Teachers and civil servants with long service records receive ex gratia payments, payable on specific national or party days (commemorating the 1968 revolution, the foundation of the Bath Party, etc.); those who have fought in the Iran-Iraq and Gulf Wars receive special grants; university lecturers have more access to overtime payments and payments for examination correction.

Even those whose incomes have marginally increased are no better off than before. The market value of the Iraqi dinar against the U.S. dollar has fallen further, from 1,500 in 1997 to 1,850 in 2000, and inflation has increased the prices of nonrationed consumer goods. The state and municipal authorities, moreover, now find it necessary to charge for services that were previously free to shift the burden of some services to the private sector, and to charge realistic prices for electricity (previously highly subsidized). Electricity supply to the kind of houses in which middle-class families reside usually exceeds the average public-sector salary. The inability of the police to cope with crime has led the government to introduce a scheme that enables groups of householders to hire guards to protect their property. Municipal authorities have introduced charges for the collection of rubbish. Parents of schoolchildren have to pay ID500 per year for pencils and paper, although the use of textbooks (mostly handed down from year to year) remains free. Every transaction with government or municipal authorities requires a payment, in addition to the customary bribes. Those who cannot pay for services are denied use of them.

The incomes of those at the bottom of the scale remain derisory. Former public servants receive pension payments of ID550 every three months—only slightly more than is needed for the purchase of a bottle of mineral water. For most of the population, the trade in goods other than basic commodities is restricted to their visits to the ever-active *mazad*s to sell items of furniture, or to the Suq al-Saraya to sell books. The intellectual isolation of students and staff in universities is as complete as before: the universities may be functioning, but there is no new infusion of ideas or books, and there is a steady loss of qualified staff to posts abroad. Desperation expresses itself at all levels in the frequently articulated desire to emigrate.

Coping with disease continues to dominate the lives of most Iraqis. The poor physical condition of much of the population, through a diet that is both inadequate and insufficiently varied, and the risks stemming from use of the public water supply and the leaks in the sanitation system, leave most Iraqis with the sense of living under the shadow of impending disaster—the likelihood of suffering a disease or infection for which no medicine is available at an affordable price. This perception is well justified by reality. The reemergence of diseases that had previously been under control, such as malaria and tuberculosis, and the spread of a wide variety of types of malignancy and goiter, constitute an important element in the popular consciousness. Medicine can in theory be obtained free from hospital pharmacies, on a doctor's prescription, and in exchange for monthly ration coupons, but in practice this is dependent on the medicines having been acquired in sufficient quantities through the framework of Oil for Food—assuming they have not already been sold to private pharmacies by hospital personnel. Painkillers are generally in ample supply, but the more specialized and expensive medicines are often available only in private pharmacies for very high prices. The sanitary conditions in hospitals are generally regarded as constituting a health risk, such that treatment there is a last resort.

The problems in the health sector stem, of course, from the wider conditions in the country. The salaries paid to doctors in the public hospitals are such that they would be unable to live off their salaries alone. Other means of supplementing incomes have to be found, whether through selling medicine to the private sector or leaving work early to earn money elsewhere. One doctor admitted to this writer that his main concern at work was to ensure that he did not miss the free lunch that the hospital provided. There is a drain of medical expertise not only outside of the country but also to the new private clinics that have been established to cater to those who can pay for treatment and medicines. Surprisingly, perhaps, the private health sector is attracting clients not just from wealthy Iraqis but also from some of the poorer Arab countries (especially Yemen). Such clients come because major operations can be carried out more cheaply than elsewhere. The cost of a kidney transplant operation in Baghdad, for example, stands at $6,000, compared to $25,000 in Jordan and perhaps $100,000 in a European country.

The shortage of electricity saps morale and the ability to cope with adversity. The occasional power cuts that had occurred before now occupy a major part of the day. With temperatures rising in central and southern Iraq during the summer, the ability of individuals to lead a normal life—with no means of cooling themselves, and with the loss of any electrically driven aids (from lighting to cooking)—is effectively taken away. The richest parts of society have been able to protect themselves against discomfort through the purchase of diesel generators, but these are out of reach for most of the population. The cost of even the cheapest generator (capable of providing enough power for lighting, but not sufficient for air-conditioning) comes to some $500—approximately 100 times the monthly salary of the average public servant.

Much of Iraqi society has shown a marked willingness for hard work and an inventiveness in seeking economic opportunities despite the difficulties in living conditions. There is probably no other regional state where so large a proportion of the population is working, or one where such inventiveness has been used in keeping unserviceable equipment in use, repairing systems of production and service, and fashioning spares for broken machinery.[9] Individuals are involved in a continuing quest to develop a marketable service. Yet these characteristics stem from desperation: a family's survival often depends on all able members (men, women, and older children) working, and on individuals finding some niche where they can offer a service. In some respects, moreover, damaging effects follow from these characteristics. Given the utter inadequacy of public-sector salaries, employees put their primary efforts into obtaining illicit gain from their positions, or in private work outside formal employment. Despite the greater religiosity apparent in outward forms, furthermore, the loosening of traditional moral standards—driven by the economic dynamic—is even more evident than in 1997. The struggle for sustenance is waged individually, or possibly on the basis of the nuclear family. Nothing but rivalry and competition can be expected from wider society, creating a drive toward social disintegration, social antagonism, and social conflict.

The desperation of the mass of the population is covered over by the ordered and controlled structure of life in Iraq, as well as by some residual feelings of shame in asking others for alms. When the ordered structure is disturbed, however, intense and violent feelings are expressed quickly. Begging is mostly left to children, but the act of bringing out a wallet creates a threatening rush of insistent adults pleading for help.[10] The edge of violence present in such situations (directed both toward the giver and to such recipients who are favored) provides some indication of how social relations in Iraq might develop if there were a widespread breakdown of centralized control and, consequently, of law and order.

There is a widely acknowledged trend toward greater Islamic religiosity. External expression is found in women's dress. In those parts of society where women used to appear publicly in Western dress (predominantly in middle-class circles), it has become more common for women at least to wear scarves covering their heads. Where women had previously worn scarves (mainly in communities that had recently moved to the towns from the countryside), it has become more common for them to wear the full black *abaya*. At present the trend toward stronger Islamic assertion is at one with government policy, which since the Gulf War has emphasized Islamic identity: adding *Allahu Akbar* (God Is Great) to the Iraqi flag, banning the sale or consumption of alcohol in public places, publicizing photographs of the president at prayer, and spending resources on the careful and artistically accomplished restoration of mosques and the construction of new mosques. Although this use of scarce resources at a time of acute privation may attract some criticism, some parts of the Iraqi population welcome it. Such mutuality in governmental and popular feelings in the future, however, is questionable given that the stronger religious identification is accompanied also by the deepening of sectarian identifications: Sunni and Shi'i. Random instances of conflict and killings, and not just within the context of confrontations between the regime and Islamist opposition, bear witness to the growing embitterment engendered by this division.

Notes

1. On both visits, this writer remained within the Baghdad region. He spoke, however, to a wide range of people in many parts of the city and its environs. No attempt was made to restrict or supervise these contacts, and no restriction was placed on the writer's movements.

2. These figures have been taken from the excellent analysis of the Iraqi economy today given by Haris Gazdar in "The Economy Under Sanctions," unpublished paper presented at the conference on Frustrated Development: The Iraqi Economy in War and Peace, Centre for Arab Gulf Studies, University of Exeter, 9–11 July 1997.

3. Economist Intelligence Unit, *Iraq: Country Profile, 1998/99* (London: EIU, 1999), p. 31.

4. The figures for industrial and agricultural production are estimates that were given to this writer by official sources in Iraq in November 1997 and are broadly accepted by international observers in the country.

5. Figures provided to this writer by Bait al-Hikmah Research Centre, Baghdad, March 2000.

6. The concentration here on public-sector employees is justified by the size and critical importance to Iraqi society of this group of employees. Information on public-sector incomes, moreover, is much easier to obtain than information on

incomes of other parts of the population. The information available suggests that the incomes of those working in agriculture have held up in real terms, largely because the sanctions have increased the prices paid for agricultural products. Living conditions in the countryside, however, tend to be worse than in the cities, as repairs to the infrastructure have not been carried out as effectively and consumer goods are frequently unavailable.

7. In addition to privately imported cars, the government imported a substantial contingent of South Korean cars in 1999, selling them at subsidized prices to senior officials in the state sector.

8. There are effectively two distinct types of smuggling in contemporary Iraq. The first is officially sponsored smuggling (i.e., where the regime encourages the evasion of UN controls and benefits from the resulting commerce). This is financed either through the smuggling of Iraqi oil abroad, mostly through Iran, or through the expenditure of such foreign currency as the authorities have been able to retain. The second is unofficial smuggling carried out by private individuals with no benefit going to the state or regime. Unofficial smuggling usually involves illicit exporting as well as illicit importing (the former being necessary to finance the latter). The second type of smuggling can be highly damaging to Iraqi living standards, as the items exported are often food and subsidized goods—which are inevitably cheaper in Iraq than in neighboring countries. Smugglers taking sheep across the border into Saudi Arabia, for example, are able to buy sheep for $15 in Iraq and sell them for $100 in Saudi Arabia. Unofficial smugglers are subject to severe punishment by the authorities when discovered, but the payment of bribes to border guards has enabled many to avoid detection.

9. It would be impossible to provide any realistic figures to back up this contention. Much of the work referred to here is occasional and informal. It would not be registered in formal employment statistics, were these to exist.

10. This is based on the personal experiences of this writer at the Shaikh Ma'ruf and Shaikh Abd al-Qadir mosques.

20

The Domestic Political Dimension

The changes in the Iraqi political system since the Gulf War have been minor. The focus of this chapter, therefore, is on the reasons why the immense challenge that the regime has faced has not led to substantive domestic political change. To understand such change as has occurred, however, it is first necessary to outline the dynamics and institutions that have underpinned the regime since Saddam Hussein became president in 1979. Figure 20.1 seeks to convey the key elements in this underpinning.

The most prominent feature of the Iraqi political system has, of course, been the centrality of Saddam Hussein. His role, however, cannot be fully appreciated without reference to the web of groups and institutional structures upon which he depends for support, for the protection of the regime, for assistance in the formulation of policy, and for the implementation of policy. Figure 20.1 identifies five groups and institutional structures that are of key importance in the maintenance of the regime. First, there are the president's close associates, comprising close family members (in particular his sons Udai and Qusai) and those members of the inner political elite who have been closely involved in the formulation and implementation of domestic and foreign policies since the inception of the Ba'thist regime (such as Taha Yasin Ramadan and Tariq Aziz, who have both served as deputy prime ministers). Second, there is the military leadership, especially that of the elite Republican Guard responsible for the military protection of the regime, subdivided into the capital protection forces, the special protection forces, and the fighting forces.[1] Third, there are two state security services, the general directorate of public security and the general directorate of intelligence, whose activities are coordinated by the presidential intelligence office; they also liaise with the private

**Figure 20.1   The Dynamics and Institutions Underpinning the
Regime**

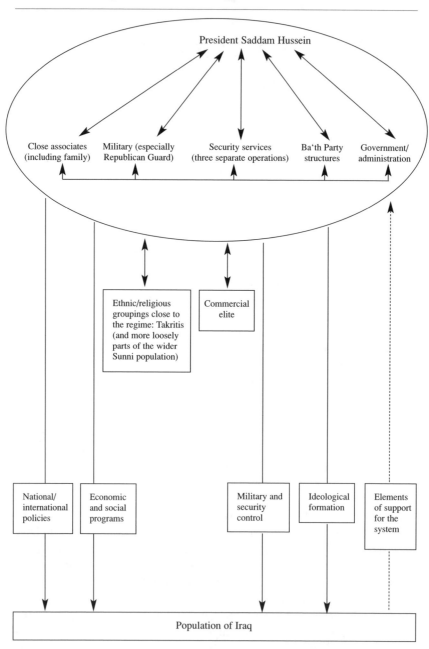

protection organization (for the protection of the presidential palaces).[2] Fourth, the structures of the Ba'th Party comprise not only the civil organization (with an estimated 400,000 members) but also a security and investigations office and a paramilitary organization (with some 22,000 activists involved). Fifth, the governmental and administrative structure provides the technical and administrative backup for formulating and implementing policies and programs. Although the five key groups and institutions have been listed separately above, close links exist between the leading members of each. The close associates hold many of the senior positions in the military, the security services, the Ba'th Party, and the government.

The relationship between the core groups and institutional structures and the rest of the population should not be considered purely in terms of domination and control. There are two reasons for this. First, some social groups benefit from a close relationship with the core of the regime. Members of the Takriti clan, from which Saddam Hussein comes, play a prominent role in many of the security-military institutions, and members of the wider Sunni community are at least more likely to hold positions of trust than are Shi'is. The interests of the commercial elite are closely interwoven with those of core elements in the regime. Second, the impact that regime programs and policies have on the popular consciousness should not be ignored. The intense effort that the Ba'th Party has put into the ideological formation of the Iraqi population over a thirty-year period, using all the educational and informational channels at the disposal of the state, has inevitably had some effect. The impact is deepened when perceptions of social and economic benefit, and of the protection and promotion of Iraqi nationhood and Arab nationalism, are seen as cohering with the Ba'thist message. Some secondary support may also stem from perceptions of a worse alternative: the collapse of the regime being followed by an internecine struggle among all the different elements of the population, or Iraq's dismemberment at the hands of its neighbors.

Explaining the Regime's Survival and Strength

The critical dynamics that characterized the regime before 1991 have changed little since then. The strength and coherence of the core elements have not been substantially weakened. Even the disaffection in 1995 of Hussein Kamil and his brother, two key close associates, failed to trigger any wider crumbling of the power structure.[3] The ability of the regime to buttress the Ba'thist message with evidence of social and economic advancement, or with a vision of Iraq playing a leading and coordinative role in the Arab world, has clearly been severely damaged. Yet there are other respects in which sanctions, and the continuing confrontation with the Security Council over weapons inspections, have buttressed the hold that the core elements of the regime have had over the Iraqi population; this helps to explain why the regime remains in power. Four dimensions are discussed below.

First, sanctions have shifted the balance between civil society and the state, weakening civil society and emphasizing state power. One aspect of the weakening of civil society is straightforward. Conditions are such that Iraqis are forced to concentrate on the mundane needs of day-to-day survival rather than devote time to social organization of any kind. The daily struggle to satisfy needs for food and medicine, and to withstand the other difficulties of life under sanctions, leaves very little energy or enthusiasm for other activities. A population suffering from such fundamental mental and physical debilitation, moreover, is not in a position to focus on political reform. Most of the families this writer visited in Iraq in 1997 and 2000 had at least one member who was seriously ill, and that was their primary concern. It would be wrong to state that those in the core groups and institutions are living in comfort, but they are more likely to have access to goods and basic needs. The coherence of the core, therefore, is not so greatly compromised.

The rationing system reinforces the strength of state power. The population is dependent for survival on the government-run rationing system, a new and powerful instrument of control. The authorities can obtain through this means detailed knowledge of the makeup and needs of every family in the country and of the movement of family members. Whether the rationing system is actually used to deprive potential opponents of the regime of supplies is not the crucial factor.[4] The population's knowledge that the authorities hold the information, and have the practical means to withhold ration cards, can be sufficient to discourage any action that might jeopardize access to rations. Whereas in the past it was the Ba'th Party and the intelligence services that had penetrated all parts of Iraqi society, since 1990 the primary instrument of penetration has been the rationing system.

Second, sanctions have reinforced among the population an image that the government has itself long projected: that of external powers scheming to pursue their own interests to the detriment of the Iraqi people. A strong perception exists among Iraqis that sanctions are part of a long-standing campaign to weaken and divide the Iraqi population and to prevent Iraq from playing its rightful role in the region. This is reinforced by reference to the imbalance in Western-enforced implementation of different Security Council resolutions. Those resolutions critical of Israel are not followed up, save to the extent that the Israeli government wishes to comply with them,[5] whereas those that concern Iraq are implemented in detail. Such perceptions are further reinforced by the manner in which sanctions affect all Iraqi citizens, whether or not they are linked to the present regime. Opponents of the regime living outside the country have the same difficulty as supporters of the regime in gaining access to funds frozen in Western banks.

Sanctions deepen popular acceptance, therefore, of some of the central tenets of regime ideology. The achievement of the Iraqi government in repairing and reconstructing the country's infrastructure after the Gulf War, and in ensuring that all Iraqis have access to the basic ration, is contrasted with the damage to Iraqis inflicted by external powers through sanctions. Without access to opinion and information coming from other quarters, significant parts of the population can easily come to accept the regime's own mind-set.

Third, the strength of the regime is enhanced by fears that abrupt political change would lead to intense social conflict, perhaps even to the country's dismemberment. There is a widespread belief, even among some individuals antipathetic to the regime, that a change of regime in contemporary conditions would lead to bloody conflict. The social conditions spawned by sanctions are, in this perception, undermining the prospects for peaceful and ordered political change, creating instead fertile ground for savage and extreme beliefs and behavior. The regime inevitably draws some strength from such perceptions.

Fourth, the international community has provided no positive encouragement for the Iraqi regime to adopt political practices that cohere more with acceptable standards of human rights. Iraq's acceptance of the establishment of UNHUCs on its territory in 1991 constituted a major concession. UN and NGO personnel would deal directly with the humanitarian needs of Iraqis and would be able to monitor how the government treated its citizens. The government had always sought to avoid international involvement of this nature. The imposition of the no-fly zones in June 1991 and August 1992, however, effectively ensured that the initiative was terminated. There had also been indications of possible change in the domestic political order. On 17 July 1991, Saddam Hussein, in an address to the Iraqi people, stated that "pluralism will be the main pillar of the next new phase" and urged Iraqis "from all intellectual and political trends who are concerned with Iraq's sovereignty, unity and independence to turn a new page and forget the differences and contradictions of the past."[6] He announced that the national assembly had passed a political parties law providing for a limited form of democracy. Given that talks were taking place at this time with Kurdish leaders on autonomy, there was good cause for a new political framework to develop. The record provides no grounds for optimism that the new framework would in fact have been democratic. Nonetheless, some international support for the pronounced belief in pluralism might have encouraged a more circumspect governmental approach to political diversity.

Notes

1. The Republican Guard is divided into six divisions and sixteen brigades. Its numerical strength is believed to be between 240,000 and 270,000. See M. Alani, "Saddam's Support Structure," in M. McKnight, N. Partrick, and F. Toase (eds), *Gulf Security: Opportunities and Challenges for the New Generation* (London: RUSI/Sandhurst, 2000).

2. The security and intelligence organizations are believed to have some 100,000–150,000 employees. See ibid.

3. Lieutenant-General Hussein Kamil al-Majid was married to Saddam Hussein's second daughter, Raghad. He was minister of military industry and as such had been in charge of Iraq's nuclear, chemical, and biological weapons programs. His brother, Lieutenant-Colonel Saddam Kamil al-Majid, was married to Saddam Hussein's third daughter, Rana, and had been in charge of the presidential bodyguard. The flight of the two to Jordan in August 1995, and their subsequent contacts with UN weapons inspectors and Western intelligence organizations, was a severe blow to the regime. In February 1996, having been denied asylum in the West and under pressure to leave Jordan, they returned to Iraq, apparently with a promise of protection from the president. Shortly after their return, however, they were killed—ostensibly by their own al-Majid family, cousins of the president.

4. In practice, there have been surprisingly few allegations that the regime has used the rationing system for political purposes. The Iraqi government's distribution plans, approved by the UN Secretary-General, stress that all citizens are entitled to rations and that distribution will not be affected by any other considerations besides size of family and similar material considerations.

5, As has often been pointed out, Israel did not comply with Security Council Resolution 425 of 1982, which called on Israel to withdraw from Lebanon, until 2000—and then did so primarily to safeguard its own security interests.

6. *Guardian*, 18 July 1991.

21

Conclusion

An assessment of the positive and negative aspects of the UN sanctions against Iraq must cover two dimensions. The first concerns the extent to which sanctions have helped attain the objectives laid out in the Security Council resolutions. The second relates to the impact sanctions have had on the Iraqi polity. Have they created social, economic, and political dynamics that have enabled (or will enable) the transformation of the Iraqi state? The transformation sought is one wherein the Iraqi state adopts and upholds values and policies that cohere with international order and stability. Such transformation covers aspects of domestic as well as foreign policy, insofar as human rights violations have regional reverberations.

The specific objectives, covering the period since 1991, are found in Security Council Resolution 687: the destruction or removal of all Iraq's chemical and biological weapons and facilities; the disabling of any nuclear potential; acceptance by Iraq of Kuwaiti sovereignty and of the demarcation of the border determined by the Boundary Commission; the payment of war reparations; and the return to Kuwait of all Kuwaitis detained in Iraq and of all Kuwaiti property taken during the occupation of Kuwait. During the 1990s, while sanctions were in place, the government of Iraq slowly but steadily fulfilled most of the requirements of Resolution 687. It is also clear, however, that sanctions have not played a prominent part in bringing about compliance. Sanctions appear only to have exerted a positive influence in this regard over the first few months that followed the adoption of the resolution.

Turning to the second dimension, the evidence suggests strongly that the dynamics underlying the Iraqi polity have not been changed positively by sanctions and that the potential for the Iraqi state to interact effectively with neighbors has not been enhanced. The power of the regime compared to civil society has been strengthened; the economic conditions and the intellectual isolation facing the population have engendered emotions and attitudes ill-suited to democratic transformation; there has been no significant improvement in the respect accorded to human rights; and Iraq has not found a stable role for itself in the wider setting of the Gulf and the eastern Arab world.

Recognition that sanctions have been both ineffective and damaging leads to the question of whether there was any alternative. Was there an alternative line of action toward Iraq after the Gulf War that could realistically have contributed more to international stability? The description of the policy pursued as both ineffective and damaging suggests that the simple absence of sanctions would have been preferable. This is the contention here, yet by itself that would not necessarily have helped resolve the wider issues of how Iraq could be brought to play a positive role in a stable regional and international order.

The conditions imposed on Iraq under Resolution 687 were in some respects too extensive and onerous, such that Iraq had no incentive to assist their fulfillment. In other respects, however, they were too limited. Having taken the decision not to support the uprisings against Saddam in the Kurdish areas and in southern Iraq, there were three objectives that the international community could reasonably have sought to attain. The first was to deprive Iraq of its weapons of mass destruction (as well as the potential to develop such weapons); the second was to ensure that Iraq respected Kuwaiti sovereignty within borders that were defined; and the third was to create structures and processes that would lead the Iraqi state to show more respect for human and political rights.

In practice, Resolution 687 omitted the third objective. The absence of any requirements with regard to the human and political rights of the Iraqi population, and the relegation of human rights concerns to another resolution (688), which had no provision for enforcement or implementation, meant that the people of Iraq had nothing to gain from the difficulties faced by the regime. The UN system was not promising to help protect them in this new situation.

The human and political rights of the Iraqi population were of direct relevance to the Security Council's concerns over international peace and stability. It would be simplistic to assume that a government's respect for human and political rights necessarily correlates with respect for the rights and sovereignty of other states,[1] but it is clear that the violation of human rights can add to interstate tensions—especially in situations where ethnic and religious identities straddle borders. Governments that have to cope with a free press and established and protected avenues for criticism of the government, moreover, are inevitably more circumspect with regard to the range of policies they pursue. The Security Council could have established a monitoring organization, with similar means of implementation and enforcement as those enjoyed by UNSCOM, to cover Iraq's compliance with international covenants related to human rights—most of which Iraq had signed. Compliance with the UN Convention Against Torture and Other Cruel, Inhuman, or Degrading Treatment or Punishment, for example, could have been made a requirement for Iraq, in the same way as the destruction of chemical and biological weapons was.

An emphasis on human and political rights would not necessarily have involved any intensification of the confrontation between Iraq and the Security Council. Paradoxically, the Iraqi government in mid-1991 was seeking to find a new political basis for the regime, had opened talks with the Kurdish leaders, and had announced that Iraq was moving toward democratization. It had also accepted the establishment of UNHUCs on its territory, knowing this opened the way to wider international involvement with humanitarian issues in the country. No doubt there were tactical reasons why the Iraqi government adopted this approach at the time, and (given the past record) it is hardly surprising that the government's sincerity was questioned. It would clearly be misleading to suggest that the government was indeed set on democracy. Yet a positive reaction to these developments, within a framework where the United Nations was specifically empowered to work with the Iraqi government in promoting human and political rights, could have enabled some progress to be made. In the event, the Kurdish leaders were discouraged from pursuing their contacts with the government, the democratization statements were derided, and the UNHUCs fell victim to the confrontation on weapons inspection and the establishment of no-fly zones.

The effectiveness of the United Nations in achieving its disarmament objectives in the specified fields, Iraqi respect for Kuwaiti sovereignty, and the protection of human and political rights required sanctions that were clearly defined and directed at the government rather than the people. The sanctions needed, moreover, to contain provisions that made clear the gains that Iraq would enjoy by complying with the Security Council's objectives. The sanctions that were imposed did not possess these attributes. Given that the Iraqi government's main concern in the economic field was to reestablish Iraq's economic sovereignty, UN supervision of the revenues from oil exports constituted the one major sanction that had the power to influence Iraqi policies on disarmament, Kuwait, and human rights. Neither Resolution 687 nor the Oil for Food resolutions (from 706 to 986) promised an end to this limitation on Iraqi sovereignty or indicated how Iraq could free itself of UN supervision. They promised Iraq more resources but no prospect of regaining control of its oil revenues: the United Nations would hold control of these, determining how much should go in payments for reparations, and for the finance of its own activities.

The imposition of reparations (diplomatically termed "compensation") on Iraq, moreover, further reduced the likelihood that Iraq would comply with UN requirements. With 30 percent of oil revenues deducted for this purpose into the indefinite future, the Iraqi government was placed in an equivocal position. The lifting of sanctions would enable Iraq to gain revenue but would also entrench and normalize arrangements whereby a major portion of Iraq's oil wealth was lost to the country. It was a rational strategy for the Iraqi government to seek to discredit the whole regime of regulations that had been imposed, with a view to securing their removal. The lifting of sanctions alone was, therefore, not necessarily in the interest of the Iraqi regime.

The decision of the Security Council to impose reparations was itself anomalous. The experience of Germany after World War I led to a widespread consensus that such reparations measures were ill-judged, fueling the conditions that led to the rise of Hitler. The priority after a war should be to ensure that the conditions for continuing conflict are removed. After World War II the United States, far from favoring the imposition of reparations on Germany, put substantial funding into the reconstruction of West Germany. Even under the disguise of "compensation," the United Nations has wisely refrained from imposing reparations on any other state (besides Iraq) that has waged an aggressive war. The reparations imposed on Iraq bear witness to the realism of the conclusions that were drawn after World War I: reparations make the reestablishment of a stable international order more difficult. According to a recent report from the UN Compensation Commission in Geneva, Iraq has so far paid $7 billion in compensation, and the remaining claims come to $276 billion. Even if the oil price retains its present high level, it would take Iraq fifty-eight years to pay off its debt. It would then be required to pay interest, at a rate still to be decided, for the delays in compensation since 1990.[2] If this were charged at the modest rate of 3 percent per annum, a further $320 billion would then have to be paid. Payment would continue well into the twenty-second century. A more reliable way to guarantee continued Iraqi recalcitrance in the international order would be difficult to imagine.

The most effective sanctions that could have been imposed on Iraq, therefore, would have been limited to ensuring that all revenues from Iraqi oil passed through the United Nations, with no restrictions on the level of exports and no deductions for reparations. The use of revenues should still have required general clearance to ensure that it was not used on weaponry,[3] and the removal of sanctions should have been specifically tied (and limited) to Iraqi compliance with the requirements on disarmament, Kuwaiti sovereignty, and human rights. The choice before the Iraqi government would have been clear-cut, giving it the strongest motivation to comply. Whether or not it complied, living conditions in Iraq would have been unaffected, so the government would not have benefited from the extra control that fell into its hands through rationing and the mobilization of popular opinion against external aggression and intervention. Civil society would have been strengthened, not weakened. Any failure to comply with the UN requirements would have resulted in losses to the state, not to the people. This primary sanction could have been accompanied by more limited diplomatic sanctions directed at the top leadership (e.g., making it impossible for them to travel outside of Iraq, or hold resources outside Iraq, until the objectives of the international community had been attained).

Under this alternative framework, Iraqi compliance with UN resolutions would have been followed by the United Nations abandoning its supervision of Iraqi oil revenues and expenditure. There could, however, have been ongoing requirements for monitoring, both with regard to weaponry and to human rights, to ensure that the requirements of relevant UN resolutions continued to be respected. If such monitoring were refused, or if monitoring revealed that the resolutions were not being respected, then the requirement for UN clearance for the expenditure of oil revenues would be reinstituted. Even the propensity for this arrangement, however, should not have been left unlimited. The perception that Iraq was subject to unique restrictions—whatever regime was in power and whatever the regime did—would not encourage Iraqis to adopt a cooperative and supportive approach to the international order. Issues related to weaponry and human rights in Iraq, therefore, would need to be placed within a wider regional framework. The concern should be to ensure that the Middle East as a whole is free of weapons of mass destruction and has structures through which human and political rights can be protected. This would not involve breaking new ground: UN resolutions, even Security Council Resolution 687, already commit the United Nations to working toward freeing the region from weapons of mass destruction. The UN covenants relating to human rights that regional powers have signed, moreover, provide a basis for regional monitoring structures. There already exists, therefore, a framework of international law that could underpin a new regional order.[4]

Discussion of alternative policies is of direct relevance to what should happen next. Future policy toward Iraq needs to be shaped not only by a recognition that existing policies have failed but also by an understanding of the damage done by those policies. The hubris that the Western governments have shown in their dealings with Iraq—where all the blame for the devastation of contemporary Iraq is placed on a demonized Iraqi regime—should be abandoned. Some of the blame lies with those powers themselves for their imposition of an ill-conceived policy. The most recent Western initiative to resolve the impasse over Iraq (at the time of this writing), Security Council Resolution 1284, may provide a framework through which Iraq could secure the removal of sanctions, but it provides no basis for Iraq to play a cooperative role in the regional and international systems. Direct talks are needed between leading members of the Security Council and the Iraqi government to establish whether such a basis can be found. From the Security Council side, both incentives and limitations need to be made explicit. The central incentive can be to offer to abandon the requirement for continuing compensation payments; the limitations should be that some form of monitoring of weaponry be continued and a form of human rights monitoring be instituted.

Iraqi acceptance of the latter limitations, however, is likely to be contingent on such arrangements being carried out within the wider region—not just in Iraq. The peace and stability of the area would be enhanced by UN acceptance of this. The success of measures in this field, moreover, depend on the Gulf states and the eastern Arab states regaining some of the initiative in determining the security needs of their own region. Regional cooperation and organization would be a necessity.

Beyond the practical considerations of policy formulation, there is also a cardinal moral issue. Can it be acceptable for the international community to pursue its objectives by inflicting severe and lasting damage on a civilian population? This concern was ably expressed by Prince Sadruddin Aga Khan in July 1991, who at that time was the UN Secretary-General's executive delegate to Iraq. The relevance of his words has become more acute as the years have passed: "It remains a cardinal humanitarian principle that innocent civilians—and above all the most vulnerable—should not be held hostage to events beyond their control. Those already afflicted by war's devastation cannot continue to pay the price of a bitter peace."[5]

Notes

1. The example of Israel is relevant here. Israeli law provides considerable protection for human rights within Israeli territory (which does not include the Palestinian population in the Occupied Territories), yet Israel has been the most frequent transgressor of international law in the region.

2. The commission's report was covered in *Guardian*, 16 June 2000.

3. With these more closely targeted sanctions, there is no reason why the United Nations should not have been able to institute from the outset a quick administrative process for authorizing contracts based on lists of products to which no objection would be raised.

4. The idealism (utopianism?) of this approach must be acknowledged. In practice, support by the Western powers for the elimination of weapons of mass destruction in the Middle East does not extend to putting pressure (let alone sanctions) on Israel to give up its nuclear, chemical, and biological weapons. As Israel possesses more of such weapons than any other state in the region, a regional scheme would not be workable or acceptable unless Israel was a party to it. Neither is it likely that the Western powers would welcome human rights monitoring in the Middle East generally, due to the embarrassment it would cause to some of their key allies in the region.

5. United Nations, *Report to the Secretary-General Dated 15 July 1991 on Humanitarian Needs in Iraq*, para. 138.

PART 3

The Case
of Sudan

22

The Grounds for Sanctions

The UN sanctions imposed on Sudan in May 1996 were diplomatic sanctions. As their effects on Sudan's economy and society have been minimal, it is not necessary to cover developments in Sudan in the detail required for the cases of Iraq and Libya. The focus instead will be on the provisions contained in the sanctions resolutions, the dynamics that determined the form taken by the sanctions, and the effect that the sanctions had on Sudanese government policy.

Sanctions were imposed in response to Sudan's failure to surrender three men accused of trying to assassinate Egyptian president Husni Mubarak. The assassination attempt took place in Addis Ababa on 25 June 1995, shortly after the president had arrived for a summit meeting of the Organization of African Unity. The dynamics that led the Security Council to move toward sanctions, however, can be understood only by reference to previous events. The determination to act against Sudan was shaped by long-standing concerns within the international community about Sudanese governmental support for international terrorism. These stemmed from Sudan harboring within its territory, and allegedly giving support to, a variety of Islamist movements from other parts of the Islamic world that were intent on pursuing their struggles by violent means.

Since the military coup of June 1989 (the so-called Salvation Revolution), Sudan had been governed by what was in effect an alliance between the Islamist-oriented military leadership that had brought the regime to power and the country's civilian Islamist movement that had conspired in the coup. For six months after the coup, the role of the Islamist movement in the new regime had remained covert. This was intended to enable the regime to establish itself without the adverse reaction that an overt

199

Islamist role could be expected to provoke, regionally and internationally. The military leadership was headed by Brigadier General Umar al-Bashir, who initially served as president of the Revolutionary Command Committee before becoming national president in October 1993—within a political framework shaped by the National Charter for Political Action, which had been adopted in April 1991. The civilian Islamist involvement was headed by Dr. Hasan al-Turabi, who had led the main Islamist party, the National Islamic Front, over the parliamentary period that preceded the coup. Al-Turabi shaped government policies in conjunction with an informal Committee of Forty, most of whose members had held leading positions in the National Islamic Front prior to the new regime coming to power. Prominent Islamists also held positions in the council of ministers.

Giving other Islamist movements access to Sudan and promoting the Islamist movements internationally were prominent features of the regime's policies through the first half of the 1990s. No restrictions were placed on members of Islamist movements from other parts of the Arab world settling in Sudan, and some were actively encouraged to relocate to Sudan.[1] A substantial number of so-called Afghan Arabs—Islamists who had been recruited from various parts of the Arab world to fight against the Soviet-backed regime in Afghanistan—settled in Sudan. Among the movements that had a strong presence in Sudan in the early 1990s were the Palestinian Hamas, the Lebanese Hizballah, the Egyptian Jamaah al-Islamiyah, the Algerian Front Islamique du Salut, and the Tunisian al-Nahdah Party. Of particular significance was the arrival of the dissident Saudi businessman Usama bin Ladin in 1994 and his subsequent residence and activity in the country. Bin Ladin had played a prominent role in organizing the original recruitment of Arabs to fight in Afghanistan during the 1980s, and he effectively maintained the Afghan Arab network after the Islamists had gained power in Afghanistan. He settled in Sudan with a large number of his family and followers after being stripped of his Saudi nationality.

Little attempt was made to dissociate the regime from the use of violence in pursuit of a new international order or new national orders. Evidence of its complaisance toward, if not support for, the use of violence by nongovernment bodies was provided by the shelter and protection given to the non-Islamic guerrilla Carlos, who resided in Sudan between 1992 and 1994 before his whereabouts became known to external bodies and a Sudanese-French deal was struck for his kidnapping and transfer to France.[2]

The regime's self-perception as the coordinating point for the international Islamist movement was given institutional expression by the Popular Arab and Islamic Conferences (PAICs), of which three were held between 1991 and 1995. An official Sudanese government publication described the first conference as "the most significant event since the collapse of the Caliphate," noting that it was the "first occasion where representatives from mass movements from all over the Muslim world came together in one place."[3] Al-Turabi saw the PAIC as a vehicle for restructuring the world order, replacing the Western-dominated UN structure by a new system "comprising free platforms, egalitarian procedures and global representation."[4]

The radical line espoused by the Sudanese regime ensured that by the mid-1990s Sudan had poor relations with almost all of its neighbors. It was suspected by the Egyptian government of providing support (as well as shelter) to Egyptian Islamist groups intent on using violence against the Mubarak regime, in particular the Islamic Jihad and Jamaah al-Islamiyah; and by the Libyan leadership of supporting Libyan Islamists who were attacking government personnel and institutions in the east of Libya. The government of Saudi Arabia resented al-Turabi's critique of the Saudi system and Saudi preparedness to host U.S. troops during the Gulf War and was concerned over the facilities given to Usama bin Laden. The governments of Eritrea, Ethiopia, and Uganda all found their security compromised by the struggle between the Sudanese government and opposition forces, especially those active in southern Sudan. Sudanese government involvement in the internal affairs of the three countries, in an attempt to strike at opposition elements that had taken refuge there, was resented.[5] In 1993, Sudan had been placed on the U.S. government's list of states supporting terrorism.

It is hardly surprising, therefore, that Sudan was accused of complicity in the assassination attempt on President Mubarak almost immediately. The accusation was made by Mubarak on the day of the attack, before any reliable information about the attackers had become available. The information that subsequently emerged was based mainly on information provided by three Islamists who had taken part in the attack and who had been captured by Ethiopian security forces. The Ethiopian investigation revealed that eleven men, all Egyptian nationals, were involved in planning and/or executing the attempt on the president's life.[6] They were all members of Jamaah al-Islamiyah. Besides the three who had been captured, five others had been killed by the Ethiopian security forces during or shortly after the attempt, one other (Siraj Muhammad Hussein) had escaped and had flown to Sudan shortly after the attempt[7], and two were alleged to have coordinated the action from Sudan. The latter were named as Mustafa Hamza and Izzat Yasin. All of those who had taken part in the action had reached Ethiopia from Sudan, having previously been brought to Sudan from the Afghan Arab camps in Pakistan. They had entered Ethiopia with Sudanese or Yemeni passports, which had been given to them in Sudan. The weapons used in the attack were brought into Ethiopia on a Sudan Airways plane, apparently dispatched by the Sudanese security services.[8] Statements made by al-Turabi immediately after the assassination attempt seemed to add further credence to the suspicion that was falling on Sudan. In a speech on 5 July, al-Turabi was reported by the government news agency SUNA as having saluted the "group of mujahideen" who "grew from the Egyptian soil and hunted down the Egyptian pharaoh," adding that "Allah wishes for a revival of Islam out of Sudan and down the Nile to wipe Egypt clean."[9]

The most critical factor determining the character of the sanctions imposed on Sudan, and ensuring that these were less severe than the sanctions imposed on Iraq and Libya, was the role played by the government of Egypt. Given that Egypt was the main target of the attack and was then a nonpermanent member of the UN Security Council, it was natural for the government of Egypt to initiate the proposals for action against Sudan and to carry substantial weight in determining the form and content of the sanctions. Although the Egyptian government was eager for the government of Sudan to be chastened, it was also mindful of the damage to Egyptian interests that could ensue if there were any deepening of the political conflict in the country. Egypt's dependence on the Nile waters, and the history of close cultural and human contacts between the two countries, meant that care had to be taken to avoid rash and precipitate decisions. The dynamics affecting the imposition of sanctions imposed on Sudan were substantially different from those affecting Iraq and Libya. As will be shown, the Egyptian government was able to ensure that the sanctions imposed did not adversely affect the living conditions of the Sudanese population and did not lead to any further weakening in the (already gravely threatened) political-security infrastructure of the Sudanese state.

Notes

1. For an account of this policy see M. Kobayashi, "The Islamist Movement in Sudan: The Impact of Dr. Hassan al-Turabi's Personality on the Movement" (Ph.D. diss., University of Durham, 1996), pp. 186–245.

2. This has been left deliberately vague, insofar as the circumstances of Carlos's capture and transfer to France remain uncertain. There is no doubt, however, that his presence in Sudan had been arranged by the Sudanese authorities and

that he had contacts with senior figures in the regime during his time in the country. There are reliable reports that Carlos's presence in Sudan was leaked to the French government by elements in the Sudanese opposition. *Observer*, 14 December 1997.

3. Quoted in M. Kobayashi, "The Islamist Movement in Sudan," pp. 221–222.

4. *New Horizon*, 31 March 1995.

5. The government of Eritrea broke relations with Sudan in 1994, alleging that the Sudanese regime was training 500,000 Eritrean Islamists to fight against their government. The accuracy of the figure is highly debatable, but the existence of some training was widely acknowledged. *Observer*, 25 June 1995.

6. This information is based on an investigation by the Ethiopian ministry of internal affairs. The preliminary report of the investigation was published in *Ethiopian Herald*, 1 August 1995. The report stated that the three suspects were believed to be "in a foreign country," but it did not name Sudan. In August the Ethiopian authorities sought, without publicity, to persuade the Sudanese government to agree to the extradition of the three suspects. When these approaches failed to yield results, they issued a longer report on 1 September naming the "foreign country" as Sudan.

7. Most of those involved in the attempt were using aliases. Siraj's real name was believed to be Husain Ahmad Shabit Ali. The limited information available about the attackers who were killed or who escaped, however, suggests that even the alleged real names may not be genuine.

8. After the attack, a box of weapons bearing the markings of the general security bureau was found in one of the safehouses used by the attackers. See *Independent*, 20 March 1996. Some indication of the Sudanese government's acceptance that its security forces had given support to the assassination attempt is found in the removal from office of the head of external security (Nafi Ali Nafi) and the head of internal security (Hasan Dhahawi), announced by the Sudan News Agency on 12 August 1996. This took place eleven days after the Ethiopian authorities made public the results of their initial investigation. Whether the security forces could have acted without the agreeement of some part of the country's political leadership, however, is doubtful.

9. Quoted in *Sudan Update*, 7 August 1995.

23

The Imposition
of Sanctions

Egypt and Ethiopia, in seeking international condemnation of Sudan's alleged involvement in the assassination attempt, turned first to the Organization of African Unity. When the Ethiopian government had completed its investigation into the assassination attempt, a report was submitted on 1 September 1995 to the OAU's mechanism for conflict prevention, management, and resolution. When the committee concerned met to consider the issue on 11 September, the Egyptian foreign minister, Amr Musa, added to the case against Sudan by telling the committee that his government had unequivocal evidence that the Sudanese government was maintaining twenty training camps for terrorists inside the country.[1] The committee acknowledged and condemned Sudan's complicity in the assassination attempt, demanding at the same time that the Sudanese government hand over the three suspects identified in the Ethiopian investigation.[2] The Sudanese government responded with a complaint that it had not been able to present its own case to the committee and that the delay between the incident and the request for extradition rendered it more difficult to trace the individuals.[3] Of the three individuals, it acknowledged that Siraj Muhammad Hussein had flown to Sudan on the day of the assassination attempt but denied knowing his subsequent whereabouts. It claimed to have no information on the other two suspects. The OAU committee issued another call for Sudan to proceed with the extradition on 19 December, but with a similar lack of positive outcome.

Egypt and Ethiopia then brought the matter before the UN Security Council, with strong support from the United States. Security Council Resolution 1044, adopted on 31 January 1996, called on the government of Sudan to "undertake immediate action to extradite to Ethiopia for prosecution the three suspects sheltering in Sudan and wanted in connection with the assassination attempt," and to

> desist from engaging in activities of assisting, supporting and facilitating terrorist activities and from giving shelter and sanctuaries to terrorist elements and act in its relations with its [neighbors] and with others in full conformity with the Charter of the United Nations and with the Charter of the Organization of African Unity.[4]

The UN Secretary-General was instructed to report on the implementation of the resolution, following contacts with the government of Sudan, within sixty days. Expectations on the part of the U.S. government that a confrontation lay ahead were evident from its decision, shortly before the resolution was passed, to withdraw the remaining twenty-five U.S. diplomatic personnel from Sudan.[5] The U.S. ambassador to Sudan henceforth covered events in Sudan from the U.S. embassy in Nairobi. The Sudanese government, for its part, went through the formal motions of seeking the arrest of the three suspects. The chief public prosecutor issued the order for their arrest on 10 February, stating that "since their whereabouts are unknown to the authorities, the three suspects are required to report to the nearest police station within a time limit not exceeding one week," and calling on the public to help with the arrest.[6] The suspects did not appear.

The measures taken by the Sudanese government were not sufficient to ward off further action by the Security Council. Following the visit of a special UN envoy to Sudan in March 1996, who duly ascertained that the three suspects had not been apprehended, the UN Secretary-General reported to the Security Council that Sudan was not in compliance with Resolution 1044. Resolution 1054, passed on 26 April 1996, required UN member states to impose diplomatic sanctions on Sudan beginning on 10 May.[7] The resolution was passed under Chapter 7 of the UN Charter and was therefore mandatory. It stipulated that all countries should "significantly reduce the level and number of the staff at Sudanese diplomatic missions and consular posts and restrict or control the movement within their territory of such staff who remain," and "take steps to restrict the entry into or transit through their territory of members of the government of Sudan, officials of that government and members of the Sudanese armed forces." International and regional organizations were asked not to convene any conference in Sudan. These measures were to come into force on 10 May and to remain in place until the Council was satisfied that the requirements laid out in Resolution 1044 had been met. Both Russia and China abstained in the voting for the resolution.

The resolution reflected the Egyptian government's strategy of how to proceed, falling well short of what the U.S. government had favored. The underlying concept was that the sanctions were to constitute a warning notice to the Sudanese government, delivered in a manner that avoided any worsening of humanitarian conditions within Sudan. The initial measures would be followed by more severe sanctions if Sudan failed to heed the Security Council's demands. Decisions about this would be taken when the Sudanese government's reaction to the resolution was reviewed, sixty days after the sanctions went into effect. It was made clear, however, that Egypt would not favor sanctions on weapons imports, insofar as this might undermine the coherence of the Sudanese state.[8] The Egyptian assistant foreign minister for international and multilateral relations summed up Egyptian policy as follows:

> The Egyptian position is to increase the political pressures on the Sudanese regime so that it renounces terrorism and carries out the resolution on extraditing the suspects, without damaging the territorial integrity of Sudan or adding to the suffering of the Sudanese people.[9]

The assistant foreign minister pointed out that the regime in Sudan was temporary but that the Sudanese people and Egyptian-Sudanese relations were permanent.

The U.S. government was critical of the Egyptian approach. At an informal meeting with the nonaligned members of the Security Council, the U.S. permanent representative to the United Nations, Madeleine Albright, was reported to have "chastised Egypt for the weakness of its resolution."[10] Immediately after the resolution was passed, the U.S. deputy representative to the UN, Edward Gnehm, stated that "in failing to impose more meaningful sanctions against Sudan, we risk further insecurity and instability for the people of eastern Africa, the Middle East and the Sudan."[11]

Even the light diplomatic measures imposed on Sudan were not implemented effectively by the international community. Several countries reduced the staffing levels of Sudanese embassies in their capitals, but this mostly involved only one diplomat being asked to leave.[12] Only Egypt and Britain required three Sudanese diplomats to return to Khartoum. Even the United States, despite its criticism of the lightness of the sanctions, expelled only one Sudanese diplomat. Russia and China took no action under the resolution. The measures have had no serious economic impact on the country. The annual rate of growth of the Sudanese economy has, in fact, been slightly higher since the imposition of sanctions.[13]

At the review of sanctions in August 1996, the continued failure of the Sudanese government to hand over the three men was noted.[14] Accordingly, a new resolution was passed that envisaged the introduction of an economic dimension into the sanctions regime. Security Council Resolution 1070 called for an air embargo on Sudan, which would oblige member states to

> deny aircraft permission to take off from, land in, or overfly their territories if the aircraft is registered in Sudan, or owned, leased or operated by or on behalf of Sudan Airways or by any undertaking, wherever located or [organized], which is substantially owned or controlled by Sudan Airways, leased or operated by the government or public authorities of Sudan.[15]

The resolution, however, was not to take immediate effect. The decision as to when the measures should enter into force would not be taken until ninety days after the adoption of the resolution and would be guided by a report on Sudan's compliance with the Security Council's requirements, which the UN Secretary-General was instructed to submit by 15 November. The resolution was drafted by the nonaligned movement caucus on the Security Council and was supported by Egypt.[16] In justification of the strengthening of sanctions, Egypt's semiofficial *al-Ahram* newspaper published further information about Sudanese involvement in the assassination attempt, drawn from confessions the three Islamists held by the Ethiopian authorities had given.[17] The weapons used in the assassination attempt were reported to have been transported to the scene in a diplomatic pouch from the Sudanese embassy in Addis Ababa. The Islamists had revealed, moreover, that their housing in Sudan, travel documents, and transport to Addis Ababa had all been provided by Sudanese authorities. Despite Egypt's support for the imposition of the air embargo, however, the Egyptian government was instrumental in ensuring the inclusion of the ninety-day grace period.[18]

The tighter sanctions were in fact never applied, even though the Security Council's demand for the handover of the three suspects was not met.[19] In the months that followed the adoption of Resolution 1070, the Sudanese government launched a diplomatic offensive emphasizing the likely humanitarian effects of an air embargo. International attention was, in particular, drawn to the likely inability of the government and NGOs to channel food supplies in the event of an air embargo to areas of the southern Sudan affected by starvation. Similar concerns were expressed by some international charities.[20] The UN Secretary-General's report to the

Security Council, delivered on 14 November, itself gave some attention to the humanitarian effects that might follow an air embargo.[21] When the issue came before the Security Council on 18 November 1996, it was clear that these arguments had won some support: the Security Council delayed the application of the new sanctions for a month until a report had been compiled on the likely humanitarian effects of the sanctions.[22] The resulting report, written by the UN Department of Humanitarian Affairs, was in fact not finalized until February 1997 and was partially sympathetic to the Sudanese case. The proposed embargo, it said, could affect food production, patients seeking medical attention abroad, and the distribution of medicines. Opposition within the Security Council to any further measures against Sudan, in light of the report, ensured that the air embargo was never implemented.

The failure of the Security Council to strengthen the sanctions regime against Sudan ran strongly counter to the U.S. government's position, which had continued to favor the intensification of sanctions against Sudan.[23] After February 1997, the U.S. government effectively abandoned the attempt to impose effective multilateral sanctions on Sudan and concentrated on unilateral measures instead. Increased military assistance to Eritrea, Ethiopia, and Uganda during 1997, formally described as strengthening the ability of those countries to defend themselves against Sudan, added to the general pressure on Sudan. There was a widespread belief that some of the weaponry was intended to be passed on to the Sudanese People's Liberation Army (SPLA) and to other armed contingents controlled by the opposition National Democratic Alliance.[24] On 4 November 1997, President Bill Clinton signed an executive order stating that the U.S. government was "blocking Sudanese government property and prohibiting transactions with Sudan." A ban was placed on the import of Sudanese goods and services into the United States (excluding information and informational materials), shipments of U.S. technology to Sudan were prohibited, U.S. banks were forbidden from extending loans to Sudan, and Sudanese assets in the United States were seized.[25] A U.S. State Department official admitted that the economic sanctions were "more a statement of principle than anything else,"[26] given that there was only very limited trade and financial dealings between Sudan and the United States.[27] Perhaps more directly threatening to the survival of the Sudanese regime was the call made in December 1997 by the new U.S. secretary of state, Madeleine Albright, for a change of regime in Sudan.[28] Significantly, the call was made following a meeting she had with John Garang, the leader of the SPLA. A further direct measure against Sudan was the U.S. missile attack on a pharmaceuticals factory in Khartoum in August 1998.

Notes

1. *Observer*, 17 September 1995.

2. Economist Intelligence Unit, *Sudan: Country Report*, no. 3 (London: EIU, 1995), p.13.

3. The reference is to the time that elapsed between the incident (25 June) and the date the Ethiopian government made public the results of its preliminary investigation (1 August). As noted above, the Ethiopian government did make private approaches to Sudan during August seeking the extradition of the three suspects. The Sudanese government failed to act on the Ethiopian request. Details of the Sudanese response to the allegations made against it were laid out in letters from the Sudanese permanent representative to the United Nations to the president of the Security Council; S/1996/22 and S/1996/25, 11 and 12 January 1996.

4. United Nations, S/RES/1044, 31 January 1996.

5. The families of U.S. embassy staff, together with some nonessential personnel, had left the country after Sudan had been placed on the U.S. list of countries sponsoring terrorism.

6. *Mideast Mirror*, 12 February 1996, p. 12.

7. United Nations, S/RES/1054, 26 April 1996.

8. The concern was that a weapons embargo would lead to the breakup of Sudan. In the Security Council debate prior to the adoption of the new resolution, the Egyptian delegate stressed the need to prevent the dismemberment of Arab territories into ministates, contending that an arms embargo would enable secessionists in southern Sudan to carry out their schemes. See *al-Ahram*, 29 April 1996. For a discussion of Egyptian policy toward Sudan following the assassination attempt, see F. M. Deng, "Egypt's Dilemmas on Sudan," *Middle East Policy* 4, nos. 1–2 (September 1995).

9. *Mideast Mirror*, 3 April 1996, p. 18.

10. Ibid.

11. *Mideast Mirror*, 29 April 1996, p. 25.

12. M. A. Osman, "The United Nations and Peace Enforcement" (Ph.D. diss., University of London, 1999), pp. 225–228.

13. Economist Intelligence Unit, *Sudan: Country Profile, 1998/99* (London: EIU, 1999), p. 38.

14. The Sudanese government continued to maintain that it had no knowledge of the whereabouts of the individuals.

15. United Nations, S/RES/1070, 16 August 1996.

16. See *al-Ahram*, 19 August 1996.

17. *Al-Ahram*, 17 August 1996. The Egyptian government's willingness to see an air embargo imposed on Sudan at this time appears to have been influenced by Egyptian dissatisfaction with the outcome of security talks between Sudanese and Egyptian officials during May and June 1996. The Egyptian government claimed that there were 15,000 Egyptian Islamists in Sudan and sought the expulsion of many from the country. The Sudanese government denied that there were as many as this and was prepared to expel only forty of the principal activists. See Economist Intelligence Unit, *Sudan: Country Report,* no. 3 (London: EIU, 1996), p. 12.

18. *Al-Ahram*, 19 August 1996.

19. During 1996 the Sudanese government stressed the unreasonableness of the Security Council's basic requirement. In an address to the UN General Assembly in September 1996, the Sudanese foreign minister recalled that all of the suspects were Egyptian; Sudan had not been presented with the extradition request until thirty-two days after the attack; no evidence had been provided proving that the suspects had been in Sudan prior to the assassination attempt; Sudan had conducted exhaustive investigations, leading to the conclusion that the three suspects sought were not in its territories; one of the suspects had been shown to be currently resident in Afghanistan; and no observers were allowed to attend the trial of the captured suspects, who had then been sentenced to death. See *Sudan Focus*, 15 October 1996, p. 2.

20. Economist Intelligence Unit, *Sudan: Country Report*, no. 4 (London: EIU, 1996), p. 15.

21. United Nations, *Report of the Secretary-General to the Security Council*, S/1996/940, 14 November 1996.

22. For the account of events given here, see Economist Intelligence Unit, *Sudan: Country Report*, nos. 3 and 4 (London: EIU, 1996), and nos. 1 and 2 (London: EIU, 1997).

23. Madeleine Albright, who had recently become U.S. secretary of state, said on 24 January that U.S. policy favored the imposition of additional sanctions on Sudan. See Economist Intelligence Unit, *Sudan: Country Report*, no. 1 (London: EIU, 1997), p. 13.

24. The first reports of substantial new military assistance being planned date from November 1996. The *Washington Post*, on 10 November 1996, quoted administration officials as referring to Ethiopia, Eritrea, and Uganda as "front-line states" in the struggle to "isolate, pressure and contain Sudan." There was said to be a general acceptance in congressional circles that part of the military assistance would go to the Sudan People's Liberation Army and to the armed forces of the Sudanese National Democratic Alliance, which benefited from access to, and some facilities in, the three countries. These forces were expected to make possible a change of regime in Khartoum.

25. Economist Intelligence Unit, *Sudan: Country Report*, no. 4 (London: EIU, 1997), p. 17.

26. Quoted in ibid.

27. The principal economic loss initially appeared to be on the U.S. side. In the mid-1990s, Sudan was supplying some 70 percent of the world market for gum arabic. Some 20 percent of Sudanese production went to the United States, imported by some sixty-three U.S. companies. The trade was worth only some $9 million annually, but the paucity of alternative sources meant that the companies would have found it difficult to compensate for the loss of Sudanese supplies. For Sudan, there would not have been great difficulty in finding alternative markets. Soon after the president's executive order was signed, however, an exemption was issued permitting the import of Sudanese gum arabic into the United States.

28. For a report on the meeting at which the call was made, see *Sudan Democratic Gazette*, January 1998, p. 6.

24

The Effect
of Sanctions

The UN Security Council requirement that was initially given greatest emphasis—namely, the handing over to Ethiopia of three assassination suspects believed to be in Sudan—was not achieved. There was, in fact, never any realistic prospect that the requirement would be met. With the intensification of pressure on Sudan through late 1995, it would have been in the interests of the individuals and of the Sudanese government to ensure that refuge was found elsewhere (assuming that they were in Sudan with the knowledge of Sudanese authorities). There is no reason to disbelieve the Sudanese government's assertions, in response to Resolutions 1044, 1054, and 1070, that none of the three individuals was present in Sudan. A few days before Resolution 1054 was passed, the London-based newspaper *al-Hayat* had interviewed a man claiming to be one of the suspects, Mustafa Hamza, in Afghanistan.[1] Although the assertions of the latter that Sudan was not in any way involved in the assassination attempt may be questioned, the identity of the interviewee has generally not been challenged. He claimed responsibility for having planned the assassination attempt.

There were, however, some respects in which the sanctions achieved positive results. One of the requirements of Resolution 1054 was that Sudan should "desist from engaging in activities of assisting, supporting and facilitating terrorist activities." Between 1995 and 1997, the Sudanese government does appear to have limited, and ultimately curtailed, its support for Islamist movements operating against foreign targets. One significant move in this direction, in fact, predated sanctions (but clearly resulted from growing pressure against Sudan). Shortly after the results of the initial Ethiopian investigation into the assassination attempt were made public, the Sudanese government announced that henceforth Arab nationals would be required to have a visa in order to enter the country—on the same basis as citizens of all other countries. The announcement, on 6 August 1995, was evidently intended to bring the influx of foreign Islamists under control.[2]

After the sanctions were imposed, the government began to remove some foreign Islamists from the country. On 18 May 1996, the Saudi dissident Usama bin Ladin left Sudan, accompanied by a substantial number of his supporters, eventually settling in Afghanistan.[3] President Umar al-Bashir described the departure as being "at the request of the Sudanese authorities." In his letter to the Security Council informing it of bin Ladin's departure, the Sudanese permanent representative to the United Nations noted that his government had given consideration to "the doubts certain countries had raised concerning his position" and that the overall intent was "to take the necessary measures to prove that it did not allow terrorist activities to take place on its territory."[4] Given the crucial role that bin Ladin had played in the promotion of radical Islamism, as well as the significance of his economic investment in Sudan, the move was important. Further measures were directed toward Egyptian Islamists in response to Egyptian governmental concerns. Shortly after the adoption of Resolution 1044, the government introduced a regulation requiring all Egyptian nationals (except diplomats) in the country to register with the police. In May 1996, forty Egyptian Islamists were made to leave the country,[5] and some further removals of Egyptians continued informally and without publicity through the remainder of 1996.

Perhaps the clearest indication that the Sudanese government had moved toward satisfying those parts of Resolution 1054 that related to support for terrorism was the improvement that occurred in its relations with neighboring states. The major issue that had previously created conflict with these states had been Sudanese support for Islamist groupings opposed to the regimes concerned. In the course of 1996–1997, Sudan reestablished workable (if not unduly friendly) relations with most of its neighbors, except for Eritrea and Uganda. In early 1998, Sudanese-Egyptian relations were reported as enjoying "new-found harmony";[6] Sudan had resolved its differences with Libya and joined a new Sahelian-Saharan grouping with Libya, Chad, Niger, and Mali;[7] the presidents of Ethiopia and Sudan were reported to have agreed to normalize relations between the two countries;[8] and relations with Saudi Arabia were improving, aided not only by the expulsion of bin Ladin from Sudan but also by the Sudanese government's symbolic apology to Kuwait in 1997 for the stand it took during the Gulf War.[9] These major changes occurred before the United States imposed unilateral sanctions on Sudan.

Paradoxically, the U.S. missile strike on the al-Shifa pharmaceuticals plant in Khartoum in August 1998 also provided evidence that suspicions of continuing Sudanese support for international Islamist terrorism were unfounded. The attack came in the wake of the terrorist bombing on 7 August of the building in which the U.S. embassy in Nairobi was housed. The bombing killed more than 250 people, of whom twelve were U.S. citizens. Usama bin Ladin was suspected as having masterminded the bombing. The U.S. response was to launch missile attacks on 20 August against some of the camps used by bin Ladin in Afghanistan, as well as to strike at the al-Shifa pharmaceuticals plant in Khartoum. The U.S. government claimed, in justification of the latter attack, to have firm evidence that the plant had been producing chemical weapons (VX gas in particular) and was linked to bin Ladin's international terrorist network.[10] If Sudan were indeed involved in international terrorism, this incident could be expected to reveal evidence of that involvement.

Subsequent investigation, however, showed that the al-Shifa plant was no more than it claimed to be: a factory producing some one-third of the medicines used in Sudan. Rather than being owned by the Sudanese government's Military Industry Corporation, as U.S. officials had claimed, it was owned by Salah Idris, a Sudanese businessman with close links to Saudi Arabia's National Commercial Bank, no significant connection to Usama bin Ladin, and substantial contacts with elements of the Sudanese opposition.[11] He was in London at the time of the missile strike. The Sudanese government's request for the United Nations to send a scientific team to inspect the al-Shifa factory and any other plants that were deemed suspicious was not acted upon.[12]

The lightness of the sanctions imposed on Sudan has, furthermore, had an important consequence for domestic Sudanese developments. It has enabled the focus of the debate over the country's future to center on the critical issues of human rights and democratization. In contrast to the situations in Iraq and Libya, the sanctions to which Sudan was subject did not strengthen the regime; neither did they lead to a further weakening of the country's civil institutions and society, increase social antagonism, or give strength to disintegrative forces that would have made a negotiated settlement to the country's existing divisions even more difficult to resolve. The challenge constituted by sanctions could not be met by mobilizing national outrage at, and international sympathy over, the suffering caused by sanctions, because it was clear to all that the suffering did not stem from diplomatic sanctions. The sanctions were a symbol of international disapproval with the regime, and the only effective way for the regime to counter them was to attempt to show that its practices cohered with procedures and values maintained elsewhere.

The significance of this dimension should not be exaggerated. The actual human rights situation in Sudan has not improved (especially as regards southern Sudan and its peoples); indeed, reports produced by the rapporteur of the UN Human Rights Commission suggest that the situation has been deteriorating.[13] Nonetheless, the regime has found the need to use the discourse of human rights, cultural pluralism, and democratization. Facilities have been given for the visits of the UN human rights rapporteur, and his reports have not always been condemned as biased.[14] The divisions that opened within the regime in late 1999 between President Umar al-Bashir and Hasan al-Turabi were in part created by their differing interests as the institutional structures of the regime changed. In its public statements, the regime has had less compunction than before to use the language of liberal democracy: self-determination, democracy, multiculturalism, freedom of religious worship, and proselytization, and the like.[15] No doubt, the reality does not match the vocabulary used, but the existence of a shared vocabulary with the opposition may be of some use to the country's political future.[16]

Notes

1. *Al-Hayat*, 26 April 1996.

2. *Sudan Update*, 24 August 1995. A Palestinian Islamist in Sudan was quoted in *Guardian*, 19 October 1995, as saying aptly that "Sudan is the place you go when you have nowhere else to go." The remark related to the period before the new regulation was introduced.

3. *Independent*, 10 July 1996.

4. *Asharq al-Awsat*, 4 June 1996.

5. *Sudan Focus*, June/July 1996, p. 1.

6. Economist Intelligence Unit, *Sudan: Country Report*, no. 1 (London: EIU, 1998), p. 7.

7. Ibid., p. 14.

8. See Economist Intelligence Unit, *Sudan: Country Report*, no. 3, p. 15, and no. 4, p. 19 (London: EIU, 1997).

9. Economist Intelligence Unit, *Sudan: Country Profile, 1998/99* (London: EIU, 1999), p. 10. In mid-1998, Kuwait agreed to the gradual reopening of the Sudanese embassy in Kuwait.

10. *Guardian*, 21 August 1998.

THE EFFECT OF SANCTIONS

11. For a detailed analysis of the allegations regarding the al-Shifa plant, and a rebuttal of most of these allegations, see *Wall Street Journal*, 28 October 1998. See also *New Yorker*, October 1998; *International Herald Tribune*, 10 February 1999; and *Independent*, 15 February 1999.

12. A well-based Sudanese governmental account of the case surrounding the attack on the al-Shifa plant, including the government's legal position, was produced by the Sudanese National Scientific Committee as *Report on Al-Shifa Pharmaceutical Factory* (n.d., n.p.).

13. These reports were very much focused on conditions in those parts of the country where armed conflict was taking place. Most commentators have tended to agree, however, that the regime adopted a more relaxed attitude toward social conduct and political discussion in central Sudan in the second half of the 1990s compared to the first half. See, for example, the series of three articles written by journalist David Hirst after his visit to Sudan in mid-1997. *Guardian*, 26–28 May 1997.

14. *Sudan Democratic Gazette*, May 1997, p. 6.

15. The terms mentioned here are all drawn from the so-called Sudan Peace Agreement, signed by the government and some non-SPLA (mainstream) forces in southern Sudan. The disintegration of the peace framework in 1999 provides some evidence of the distance between pronouncement and achievement.

16. For some sophisticated opposition thinking about human rights issues in Sudan, see the unpublished papers presented to the Conference on Human Rights in the Transition in Sudan, Kampala, 8–12 February 1999.

25

A Final
Assessment

The central goal of this book, as outlined in the Introduction, has been to assess whether the UN sanctions imposed on three Arab countries contribute to, or damage, the prospects for a stable international order. Six broad conclusions on the immediate impact of sanctions emerge from the study, one of which suggests a positive contribution to the international order; the remaining five are clearly negative.

On the positive side, it is clear that sanctions can help contain a regime that might otherwise be disruptive, provided neighboring countries are prepared to work with and respect the sanctions regime. Sanctions may force the regime to concentrate on its own survival, leaving it with less time and ability to pursue aggressive or expansionist policies directed against neighboring countries or the wider international community. Sanctions that restrict the sale of weaponry will gradually weaken the military strength of the country and, hence, blunt the government's ability to wage an aggressive campaign against neighboring states. It should be noted, however, that other factors may also account for a state deciding to eschew disruptive international policies. In the case of Libya, for example, Qaddafi had been signaling a renunciation of support for extremist organizations since 1989—long before UN sanctions on Libya. The regime appears to have been responding to the changing world order, realizing that the end of the Cold War reduced the protection enjoyed by states pursuing a radical agenda. It should also be stressed that diplomatic sanctions may be as effective as economic sanctions in achieving containment: the Sudanese regime's tendency for ideological expansionism seems to have been curbed simply by the measure of international opprobrium carried by diplomatic sanctions, however insignificant the practical effects may have been.

On the negative side, the first conclusion is that sanctions do not necessarily achieve the immediate objectives sought by the Security Council. Even when states comply with the requirements, it is not clear that sanctions have been the leading factor. In Iraq and Libya, sanctions were not the critical element. In the case of Sudan, sanctions do seem to have pushed the regime to stop "assisting, supporting and facilitating terrorist activities"—but these sanctions were diplomatic. Moreover, the period that elapses while the Security Council is awaiting compliance imposes immense and prolonged suffering on the populations of states under economic sanctions. If compliance with Security Council requirements is necessary for a stable international order, therefore, economic sanctions have not proved their value.

Second, economic sanctions have tended to strengthen regimes. The assumption that sanctions will help the population by opening opportunities for civilian forces to overthrow an oppressive and undemocratic regime, therefore, is unjustified. There are three processes through which such strengthening can occur. First, the impact of the sanctions tends to make populations even more dependent on the government, mainly for provision of the basic rations needed for survival. The rationing system becomes an effective instrument for control. This has happened in both Iraq and Libya. Second, sanctions may strengthen a regime's ideological legitimacy. If the regime has projected itself to its population through an ideology built around nationalism—where external powers (especially Western powers) are seen as imperialist crusaders intent on undermining local sovereignty and indigenous interests—then the imposition of Western-orchestrated UN sanctions will reinforce the regime's central ideological message. The regime's analysis of the international order will carry conviction. The Iraqi, Libyan, and Sudanese regimes have all purveyed, from their inceptions, a nationalistic ideology. The imposition of sanctions, therefore, can be and has been used by those regimes to buttress popular acceptance of the core ideology and to mobilize popular support. Third, the regime can gain some credit domestically by deftly defending the country from an external onslaught (as perceived by the population). Its ability to maneuver successfully to build support in the international community, to withstand and circumvent a blockade, to bring in the basic goods needed by the population, and perhaps to throw doubt on the legality of what is being done to the country, can all strengthen popular support. This factor has been evident in both Iraq and Libya. Overall, the strengthening of regimes that are cavalier in their treatment of human rights is not conducive either to regional or to international stability.

Third, economic sanctions have an adverse impact on the social basis necessary for democratization. This adverse impact has two dimensions. The first stems from the social divisions opened up by sanctions—between rich and poor, and between different regional and ethnic/religious components of the population. Sanctions benefit some parts of the population and harm others or else inflict harm to varying degrees, thereby deepening intercommunal suspicion, jealousy, and antipathy. The intense competition for scarce resources encourages a narrow communal solidarity based on an individual's tribal/sectarian/regional identity, not an identification with the wider multiethnic and multireligious community. The polarization to extremes and the high tension within society prevent the development of attitudes and values essential to democracy—especially the willingness to abide by democratic procedures in determining who should be entitled to wield political power. The second dimension concerns the effect on the institutions of civil society. Under comprehensive economic sanctions (of the kind imposed on Iraq), the mass of the population is reduced to a hard struggle for immediate survival, with insufficient medicine to maintain health. People are unlikely to have the time or the energy to involve themselves in the interest groups, professional associations, and the like that constitute civil society. Yet civil society forms the basis upon which democratization processes have often been constructed. There can be little doubt that if there was an immediate change of regime in Iraq the prospects for a new regime operating a viable liberal democracy are less strong than they would have been ten years previously.

Fourth, economic sanctions undermine the long-term political stability of states, with repercussions on the stability of the wider region. The deterioration of the central infrastructure and services is crucial, for they are the elements that give the state its effective coherence. The central dynamic keeping a country together, therefore, can be critically weakened. The feeling among different population groups that they benefit from being part of the country can be destroyed. Such dangers are relevant in Iraq, but they constitute a danger in Libya as well. Where the sanctions are accompanied by Western policies that prevent the state from maintaining its control over part of the country (as in the case of the Kurdish areas in northern Iraq), the impact can be serious for long-term national integration. It may be contended that this enables states to be reformed on a more realistic basis, with autonomy or independence granted to ethnic or religious groups that do not identify their interests with the state. Yet to dismantle a state under these conditions would be problematic and disruptive to regional stability.

Fifth, sanctions delay the development of frameworks of regional cooperation (in both security and economic fields) that could underpin regional stability. As long as a state is under UN sanctions, other regional states will be constrained from seeking collaborative links with it. In some respects this involves the internationalization of a pattern of Western action that was familiar during the Cold War: regional allies were strongly discouraged from cooperating with other states closely tied to the Soviet bloc. The concerns of the regional states themselves may also, of course, inhibit cooperation—they may fear the effects of cooperating with a state that is perceived as pursuing aggressive and expansionist designs. But the external discouragement certainly acts as one more factor making regional security and economic cooperation more difficult to achieve. External powers may draw benefit from regional division, enhancing arms sales to the region and being able to treat each state individually rather than face a coordinated grouping. Yet there is a growing realization within the Arab world that the stability of individual Arab countries depends on regional structures through which security can be managed and economic interchange enhanced. Integrative links drawing Iraq into close collaboration with its Gulf neighbors, Libya into similar collaboration with the other states of North Africa, and Sudan into systems of cooperation with the Horn of Africa and with Egypt (as well as across the Red Sea) would bring substantial benefits. So would wider structures of cooperation within the Arab world, enabling the states of the region to strengthen their bargaining position vis-à-vis the large economic blocs that dominate the international economy. Economic cooperation and security cooperation are likely to be mutually reinforcing.

The central conclusion is that the international order has not yet found a satisfactory way to handle states that are accused of transgressing international law. The imposition and maintenance of economic sanctions on Iraq (through most of the 1990s and into the twenty-first century) and on Libya (between 1992 and 1999) caused substantial damage to the stability of the international order and created conditions that may well lead to long-term harm. It is encouraging to note that a realization of the failure of sanctions does seem to be spreading. The International Development Committee of the British House of Commons, in its second report on the future of sanctions, summed up the overall experience of sanctions, and the policy options that follow from it, as follows:

> Although sanctions may well represent a low-cost alternative to war in financial terms, they are all too often as damaging—in humanitarian and developmental terms—as armed conflict.

Those who should be targeted, the political leaders and elites who have flouted international law, continue to enrich themselves. Much discussion has taken place of targeted sanctions, in particular financial sanctions, as a "smarter" and more just approach. We conclude, however, that neither the United Kingdom nor the international community have made real efforts to introduce such sanctions. There has been much talk but little action. . . .

We find it difficult to believe that there will be a case in the future where the UN would be justified in imposing comprehensive economic sanctions on a country. In an increasingly interdependent world such sanctions cause significant suffering. However carefully exemptions are planned, the fact is that comprehensive economic sanctions only further concentrate power in the hands of the ruling elite. The UN will lose credibility if it advocates the rights of the poor whilst at the same time causing, if only indirectly, their further impoverishment.[1]

The problem, as the report correctly stresses, is that the sanctions issue affects the credibility of the United Nations as an organization, leading to a general loss of faith in the ability of the international order to act in the interests of those suffering from poverty and oppression. The impression created is of an international order managed exclusively in the interests of a narrow range of Western powers that have absolved themselves of responsibility for the ill effects created by their policies. The view from the underside carries considerable force; alienation from the New World Order is given added strength.

The implicit danger is that the added strength now given to perceptions from the underside may frustrate future attempts to use international organizations effectively for worthwhile international aims—the promotion of human rights, the protection of international law, the resolution of interstate conflicts, and the combating of poverty and disease. Rather than seeking to improve the instruments through which these aims can be pursued, the use of the instruments may be limited, resisted, and ultimately discarded. Resistance would come not only from those governments that fear that measures will be taken against them, but by a wider range of governments and peoples who have no faith that such instruments can be used to their own benefit. The concept of an international order that promotes humanitarian values and human rights would be abandoned.

Yet the need for international organizations to pursue worthwhile objectives is more acute than ever. What is required now, therefore, is a strategy to ensure that the instruments used in pursuing those objectives are refined and made distinct from the exclusive interests of the major Western powers. As far as UN sanctions are concerned, those against

Libya have already been suspended and in reality could not be reinstated (reinstatement of the Libyan sanctions would almost certainly be vetoed by Russia and/or China in the Security Council). Those against Iraq are under increasing criticism, and the diplomatic sanctions against Sudan no longer hold great significance. Lessons from the sanctions experience, however, need to be acknowledged internationally. The social and political repercussions from economic sanctions are widespread, and if sanctions are imposed by the Security Council, then the international community needs to take some responsibility for the harmful effects that follow; the imposition of onerous conditions, such as the reparations on Iraq, frustrates the achievement of the most critical objectives related to stability and order; the absence of any positive incentive for a regime to comply with UN requirements undermines the coherence of UN measures; the failure to link sanctions to human rights concerns leads to them being perceived (rightly) as punishment for the population in general; and diplomatic sanctions have had a better record than economic sanctions in fostering conditions favorable to international order and stability. It seems likely that human rights can best be protected, and infractions punished, through the development of international legal structures (such as the proposed International Criminal Court) functioning outside the control of the major powers.

Despite the apparent strength of the regimes in Iraq and Libya, and despite the added strength provided by sanctions, political change will come in the foreseeable future. Regimes that rely so much on one individual, where so many have personal and political grievances against the regime, have a built-in vulnerability. The effectiveness of the security services, and the tendency to use violence to suppress political dissent, do not constitute a viable basis for political survival in the long term. Yet political change in the current conditions would be problematic. The social conditions of the populations following the sanctions experience would not make transition easy. The anger and resentment that lie just below the surface, directed by individuals against individuals and by groups against groups, would pour forth. Civilian forces would be ill-suited to controlling the situation. Neither would the armed forces necessarily hold the solution: the likelihood is that they would be divided, with each section harboring its own resentments, discontents, and objectives.

The critical requirement now is for the international community to desist from measures that intensify the problems of political transition and to find frameworks within which living conditions can be improved, human rights concerns can be addressed, and regional stability can be promoted. Difficult issues need to be addressed. It seems impossible to even initiate such a process unless the major powers are willing to draw the regimes concerned into the discussion.

Note

1. House of Commons, International Development Committee, *Second Report of the Select Committee on International Development*, 1999 <http://www. publications.uk/pa/cm199900/cmselect/ cmintdev/67/6701.htm>.

Bibliography

General

Bonino, E. "The International Criminal Court: A Step Forward in Moralising International Relations." *International Spectator* (Rome) 33, no. 3 (July-September 1998).

Chomsky, N. *The New Military Humanism: Lessons from Kosovo*. London: Pluto, 1999.

———. *Year 501: The Conquest Continues*. London: Verso, 1993.

Chossudovsky, M. *The Globalization of World Poverty: Impacts of IMF and World Bank Reforms*. London: Zed Books, 1998.

Claude, R. P., and B. H. Weston (eds.). *Human Rights in the World Community*. Philadelphia: University of Pennsylvania Press, 1992.

Colclough, C., and J. Manor (eds.). *States or Markets?* Oxford: Oxford University Press, 1991.

Cox, R. W. (ed.). *The New Realism*. London: Macmillan, 1997.

Culpeper, R., A. Berry, and F. Stewart (eds.). *Global Development Fifty Years After Bretton Woods*. London: Macmillan, 1997.

Fukuyama, F. *The End of History and the Last Man*. Harmondsworth, U.K.: Penguin, 1993.

Hirst, P., and G. Thompson (eds.). *Globalization in Question*. Cambridge: Polity, 1996.

Hoogvelt, A. *Globalization and the Postcolonial World: The New Political Economy of Development*. London: Macmillan, 1997.

House of Commons, *Select Committee on International Development: Second Report*. <http://www.publications.parliament.uk/pa/cm1999000/cmselect/cmintdev/67/6701.htm>.

Ignatieff, M. *Virtual War: Kosovo and Beyond*. London: Chatto and Windus, 2000.

Kamminga, M. T. *Inter-State Accountability for Violations of Human Rights.* Philadelphia: University of Pennsylvania Press, 1992.

Lechner, F., and J. Boli. *The Globalization Reader.* Oxford: Blackwell Publishers, 2000.

Mayall, J. (ed.). *The New Interventionism.* Cambridge: Cambridge University Press, 1996.

Meron, T. (ed.). *Human Rights in International Law.* Oxford: Oxford University Press, 1984.

Roberts, A., and B. Kingsbury (eds.). *United Nations, Divided World.* Oxford: Oxford University Press, 1993.

Rodley, N. S. (ed.). *To Loose the Bands of Wickedness.* London: Brassey's, 1992.

Symonides, J. (ed.). *Human Rights: New Dimensions and Challenges.* Paris: UNESCO, 1998.

Weiss, T. G., D. P. Forsythe, and R. A. Coate. *The United Nations and Changing World Politics.* Boulder: Westview, 1997.

White, N. D. *The United Nations and the Maintenance of International Peace and Security.* Manchester: Manchester University Press, 1990.

World Bank, *World Development Indicators 1998.* Washington, D.C.: World Bank, 1998.

Iraq

Ahmad, Abd al-Ghaffur Ibrahim. *Al-Amn al-Ghiza'I fi al-Iraq* [Food Security in Iraq]. Baghdad: Bait al-Hikmah, 1999.

Alani, M. "Saddam's Support Structure." In S. McKnight, N. Partrick, and F. Toase (eds.), *Gulf Security: Opportunities and Challenges for the New Generation.* London: RUSI/Sandhurst, 2000.

Al-Khalil, S. *Republic of Fear.* London: Hutchinson Radius, 1989.

Baram, A. *Building Towards Crisis: Saddam Husayn's Strategy for Survival.* Washington, D.C.: Washington Institute for Near East Policy, 1998.

Cockburn, A., and P. Cockburn. *Out of the Ashes: The Resurrection of Saddam Husain.* New York: HarperCollins, 1999.

Committee Against Repression and for Democratic Rights in Iraq. *Iraq Since the Gulf War: Prospects for Democracy.* London: Zed Books, 1994.

———. *Saddam's Iraq: Revolution or Reaction?* London: Zed Books, 1986.

Cordesman, A., and A. Hashim. *Iraq: Sanctions and Beyond.* Boulder: Westview, 1997.

Economist Intelligence Unit. *Iraq: Country Profiles, 1989–99.* London: EIU, various years.

———. *Iraq: Country Reports, 1989–99.* London: EIU, various years.

Farouk-Sluglett, M., and P. Sluglett. *Iraq Since 1958: From Revolution to Dictatorship.* London: Routledge and Kegan Paul, 1987.

Food and Agriculture Organization. *Special Report: FAO/WFP Food Supply and Nutrition Assessment Mission to Iraq,* 3 October 1997. <http://www.fao.org/WAICENT/faoinfo/economic/giews/english/alertes/srirq997.htm>.

Gazdar, Haris. "Research and Advocacy Strategy on Iraq: A Literature Review for Save the Children Fund (UK)." London: Save the Children Fund, 2000.

Graham-Brown, S. *Sanctioning Saddam: The Politics of Intervention in Iraq.* London: I. B. Tauris, 1999.

Henderson, S. *Instant Empire: Saddam Hussein's Ambition for Iraq.* San Francisco: Mercury House, 1991.

Hopwood, D., H. Ishow, and T. Koszinowski (eds.). *Iraq: Power and Society.* Reading: Ithaca, 1993.

Human Rights Watch. *Iraq: Human Rights Developments.* <http://www.hrw.org. wr2k/Mena-05.htm>.

———. *Explanatory Memorandum Regarding the Comprehensive Embargo on Iraq: Humanitarian Circumstances in Iraq.* <http://www.hrw.org/press/ 2000/01/iraq-memo.htm>.

International Committee of the Red Cross. *Iraq: A Decade of Sanctions.* <http://www.icrc.org/Icrceng.nsf/Index/0...E49481B741412568A20030CA 99?Opendocument>.

Republic of Iraq. *Athar al-Hisar al-Iqtisadi al-Shamil ala al-Iraq* [The Effects of Comprehensive Economic Sanctions on Iraq]. Baghdad: Ministry of Foreign Affairs, 2000.

———. *Athar al-Hisar al-Ja'r ala al-Sihah wa al-Ghiza'a wa al-Turbiah wa al-Bi'ah fi al-Iraq* [The Effects of Sanctions on Health, Nutrition, Upbringing, and Environment in Iraq]. Baghdad: Ministry of Information and Culture, 1997.

———. *Child and Maternal Mortality Survey 1999: Preliminary Report.* Baghdad: Ministry of Health/UNICEF, July 1999.

———. *Distribution Plan Submitted by the Government of Iraq to the UN Secretary-General in Accordance with the MOU of 20 May 1996 and Resolution 1242 (1999).* Baghdad: Ministry of Foreign Affairs, 1999.

———. *Distribution Plan Submitted by the Government of Iraq to the UN Secretary-General in Accordance with . . . Resolution 1281 (1999).* Baghdad: Ministry of Foreign Affairs, 1999.

———. *Nutritional Status Survey of Infants in South/Centre Iraq.* Baghdad: Ministry of Health/UNICEF, November 1997.

Jabbar, F. A., A. Shikara, and K. Sakai. *From Storm to Thunder: Unfinished Showdown Between Iraq and U.S.* Tokyo: Institute of Developing Economies, 1998.

Kazemzadeh, M. "Thinking the Unthinkable: Solving the Problem of Saddam Hussein for Good." *Middle East Policy* 6, no. 1 (June 1998).

Khadduri, M. *The Gulf War.* Oxford: Oxford University Press, 1988.

Mahdi, K. "Rehabilitation Prospects for the Iraqi Economy." *International Spectator* (Rome) 33, no. 3 (July-September 1998).

Marr, P. *The Modern History of Iraq.* Boulder: Westview, 1985.

Middle East Watch. *Needless Deaths in the Gulf War.* New York: Human Rights Watch, 1991.

Nonneman, G. *Iraq, the Gulf States, and the War, 1980–86.* London: Ithaca, 1986.

Ritter, S. *Endgame.* New York: Simon and Schuster, 1999.

Rudd, G. W. "Operation Provide Comfort: Humanitarian Intervention in Northern Iraq, 1991." Ph.D. diss., Duke University, 1993.

Simons, G. *Iraq—Primus Inter Pariahs.* London: Macmillan, 1999.

———. *The Scourging of Iraq: Sanctions, Law, and Natural Justice.* London: Macmillan, 1998.

Trevans, T. *Saddam's Secrets: The Hunt for Iraq's Hidden Weapons.* London: HarperCollins, 1999.

UNICEF. *Child and Maternal Mortality Survey in Dohouk, Erbil, and Al-Suleimaniyah Governorates, 1999: Preliminary Report.* UNICEF, August 1999.

———. *Nutritional Status Survey of Infants in South/Centre Iraq.* UNICEF, 14 November 1997.

———. "Situation Analysis of Children and Women in Iraq—1997." UNICEF/IRAQ, 30 April 1998. <http://leb.net/iac/UNICEF1998.html>.

United Nations. *Distribution Plan—Phase VI.* <http://www.un.org/Depts/oip/dp6pdf/dp6toc.html>.

———. *Distribution Plan—Phase VII.* <oip/dp7pdf/dp7toc.html>.

———. *Introductory Statement by Benon V. Sevan, Executive Director of the Iraq Programme to the Report of the Secretary-General Pursuant to Paragraph 6 of Resolution 1242.* S/1999/1162. 17 November 1999. <http://www.un.org/Depts/oip/reports/bvsnov17.html>.

———. *Memorandum of Understanding Between the Secretariat of the United Nations and the Government of Iraq on the Implementation of Security Council Resolution 986.* S/1996/356. 20 May 1996.

———. *Press Briefing by Outgoing UN Humanitarian Coordinator* 1 March 2000. <http://www.un/org/News/briefings/socs/2000/20000301>.

———. *Report on Humanitarian Needs in Iraq in the Immediate Post-crisis Environment by a Mission to the Area Led by the Under-Secretary for Administration and Management, 10–17 March 1991.* S/22366. 20 March 1991.

———. *Report to the Secretary-General Dated 15 July 1991 on Humanitarian Needs in Iraq Prepared by a Mission Led by the Executive Delegate of the Secretary-General for Humanitarian Assistance in Iraq.* S/22799. 17 July 1991.

———. *Report on the Situation of Human Rights in Iraq Prepared by the Special Rapporteur of the Commission of Human Rights on the Situation of Human Rights in Iraq.* S/23685. 9 March 1992.

———. *Report of the Secretary-General on the Implementation of Security Council Resolution 986.* S/1996/1015. 9 December 1996.

———. *Report of the Secretary-General Pursuant to Paragraph 7 of Resolution 1143.* S/1998/90. 1 February 1998.

———. *Report of the Secretary-General Pursuant to Paragraph 10 of Security Resolution 1153.* S/1998/1100. 19 November 1998.

———. *Report of the Secretary-General Pursuant to Paragraph 6 of the Security Council Resolution 1210.* S/1998/187. 22 February 1999.

———. *Report of the Second Panel Established Pursuant to the Note by the President of the Security Council of 30 January 1999 (S/1999/100) Concerning the Current Humanitarian Situation in Iraq.* S/1999/356. 30 March 1999.

————. *Report of the Secretary-General Pursuant to Paragraph 6 of Security Council Resolution 1210.* S/1999/573. 18 May 1999.

————. *Report of the Secretary-General Pursuant to Paragraph 6 of Security Council Resolution 1242.* S/1999/896. 19 August 1999.

————. *Report of the Secretary-General Pursuant to Paragraph 6 of Security Council Resolution 1242.* S/1999/1162. 12 November 1999.

————. *Report of the Secretary-General Pursuant to Paragraph 32 of Security Council Resolution 1284.* S/2000/22. 14 January 2000.

————. *Report of the Secretary-General Pursuant to Paragraph 9 of Security Council Resolution 1281.* S/2000/26. 14 January 2000.

————. *Report of the Secretary-General Pursuant to Paragraph 28 and 30 of Resolution 1284 and Paragraph 5 of Resolution 1281.* S/2000/208. 10 March 2000.

————. *Review and Assessment of the Implementation of the Humanitarian Programme Established Pursuant to Security Council Resolution 986.* S/199. 28 April 1999.

————. *The United Nations and the Iraq-Kuwait Conflict, 1990–96.* New York: United Nations, 1996.

United Nations Office of the Iraq Program. *Basic Figures as 11 January 2000.* <http://www.un.org/Depts/oip/latest/basicfigures.html>.

————. *Memorandum of Understanding Between the Secretariat of the United Nations and the Government of Iraq on the Implementation of Security Council Resolution 986 (1995).* <http://www.un.org/Depts/oip/undocs/s1996356.htm>.

U.S. Congress. *Congressional Staff Report: Iraq Trip.* September 1999. <http://www.geocities...aqinfo/sanctions/sarticlre3/report.html>.

World Food Programme. *Protracted Relief and Recovery Operation—Iraq 6085.00.* 21 December 1998. WFP/EB.1/99/7-A/2. <http://www.wfp.org/eb_public/EB.1_99_English/682e98.pdf>.

World Health Organization, Division of Emergency and Humanitarian Action. *Health Conditions of the Population in Iraq Since the Gulf Crisis,* March 1996. <http://www.who.int/eha/resource/pubs/000396.html>.

Zunes, S. "Confrontation with Iraq: The Bankruptcy of U.S. Policy." *Middle East Policy* 6, no. 1 (June 1998).

Libya

Al-Hamali, Amer e Abdalla. *Al-Safwah, al-Talia'a . . . wa Zahirat Istilab Sultat al Sha'ab* [The Elite, the Vanguard . . . and the Phenomenon of Stealing Away the Power of the People]. Commentaries on *The Green Book,* no. 17. Tripoli: International Centre for Studies and Research on the Green Book, 1984.

Al-Shukry, M.F.M. "Continuity and Breakdown: The Role of Leadership in Libya's Relations with Britain, 1951–1984." Ph.D. diss., University of Manchester, 1996.

Arnold, G. *The Maverick State.* London: Cassell, 1996.

Blundy, D., and A. Lycett. *Qaddafi and the Libyan Revolution.* London: Corgi, 1988.

Davis, B. *Qaddafi, Terrorism, and the Origins of the U.S. Attack on Libya.* New York: Praeger, 1990.

Dar al-Jamahariya lil-Nashr. *Al-Thawra Libya fi 30 'Ama* [The Revolution in Libya over Thirty Years]. Tripoli: Dar al-Jamahariya lil-Nashr, 1999.

Economist Intelligence Unit. *Libya: Country Profiles, 1990–99.* London: EIU, various years.

———. *Libya: Country Reports, 1990–99.* London: EIU, various years.

El-Kikhia, M. O. *Libya's Qaddafi.* Gainesville: University Press of Florida, 1997.

ElWarfally, M. *Imagery and Ideology in U.S. Policy Toward Libya.* Pittsburgh: University of Pittsburgh Press, 1988.

Flores, C. *Shadows of Lockerbie.* Malta: Aedam Publishing House, 1997.

Haley, E. *Qaddafi and the United States Since 1969.* New York: Praeger, 1984.

Heikal, M. *The Road to Ramadan.* London: Collins, 1975.

Hinnebusch, R., and A. Ehteshami (eds.). *The Foreign Policies of Middle East States.* Boulder: Lynne Rienner, 2001.

International Monetary Fund. *Direction of Trade Statistics, 1970–80.* Washington, D.C.: IMF, various years.

Lahwej, Y. A. "Ideology and Power in Libyan-American Relations from the Revolution to the Lockerbie Affair." Ph.D. diss., University of Reading, 1998.

Management and Implementation Authority of the Great Man-Made River. *The Great Man-Made River Project.* Tripoli: MIAGMMR, 1989.

Mission of the Libyan Jamahariya to the United Nations. *Report on the Impact of UN Sanctions Against Libya.* September 1996.

Mogherbi, M. H. *Civil Society and Democratization in Libya: 1977–1992.* Cairo: Ibn Khaldoun Center for Developmental Studies, 1993.

National Corporation for Information and Documentation. *Statistical Yearbook, 1998.* Tripoli: NCID, 1998.

National Cultural Centre. *Address Delivered by Col. Mu'ammar al-Qadhafi, 16 September 1969.* Tripoli: National Cultural Centre, 1969.

———. *Al-Sijil al-Qawmi: Bayanat wa Khutab wa Ahadith Mu'ammar al-Qadhafi.* Tripoli: Markaz al-Thaqafiah al-Qawmiyah, annual publication.

National Front for the Salvation of Libya. *Libya Under Gaddafi and the NFSL Challenge.* Chicago: NFSL, 1992.

Obeidi, A.S.M. "Political Culture in Libya: A Case Study of Political Attitudes of University Students." Ph.D. diss., University of Durham, 1996.

Organization for Economic Cooperation and Development. *Monthly Statistics of Foreign Trade.* Paris: OECD, 1980–1990.

Organization for Petroleum Exporting Countries. *Statistical Bulletins,* 1990–1996.

Qaddafi, M. *The Green Book (Part One): The Solution to the Problem of Democracy.* Tripoli: Public Enterprise for Publishing, n.d.

———. *The Green Book (Part Three): The Social Basis of the Third Universal Theory.* Tripoli: Public Enterprise for Publishing, n.d.

St. John, R. *Qaddafi's World Design.* London: Saqi Books, 1987.

United Nations. *Report on the Libyan Crisis by UN Secretary-General Dr. Boutros Boutros-Ghali.* S/23574. 11 February 1992.

U.S. Congress. *Congressional Quarterly Weekly Report,* no. 40. 13 March 1982.

U.S. Department of State. *Libya Under Qadhafi: A Pattern of Aggression.* Special Report 138. Washington, D.C.: U.S. Department of State, 1986.

Vandewalle, D. *Qadhafi's Libya, 1969–1994.* New York: St. Martin's, 1995.

World Bank. *World Development Indicators.* Washington, D.C.: World Bank, 1998.

Sudan

Al-Turabi, H. *Al-Harakah al-Islamiyah fi al-Sudan.* Khartoum: n.p., 1990.

Amnesty International. *Sudan: The Military Government's First Year in Power.* London: Amnesty International, 1990.

Economist Intelligence Unit. *Sudan: Country Profiles, 1995–99.* London: EIU, various years.

————. *Sudan: Country Reports, 1995–99.* London: EIU, various years.

El-Affendi, A. *Turabi's Revolution: Islam and Power in Sudan.* London: Grey Seal, 1991.

Government of Sudan. *Dalil al-Hukm al-Ittihadi.* Khartoum: Diwan al-Hukm al-Ittihadi, n.d.

Kobayashi, M. "The Islamist Movement in Sudan: The Impact of Dr. Hassan al-Turabi's Personality on the Movement." Ph.D. diss., University of Durham, 1996.

Lowrie, A. (ed.). *Islam, Democracy, the State, and the West: A Round Table with Dr. Hassan al-Turabi.* Florida: World and Islam Studies Enterprise, 1993.

National Scientific Committee. *Report on Al-Shifa Pharmaceutical Factory.* Khartoum: n.p., 1999.

Niblock, T. *Class and Power in Sudan: The Dynamics of Sudanese Politics, 1898–1985.* London: Macmillan, 1987.

Osman, M. A. "The United Nations and Peace Enforcement." Ph.D. diss., University of London, 1999.

Taha, H. *Al-Ikhwan wa al-Askar.* Cairo: Markaz al-Hadaara al-Arabiyah, 1993.

Index

233

About the Book

UN sanctions have become an increasingly popular weapon in the political armory of the international community—a supposedly effective means, short of war, of bringing a transgressor state back in line. Tim Niblock challenges this view in a dispassionate analysis of the political, economic, and psychological impact of sanctions on the Middle East's "pariah" states.

Niblock establishes two criteria for assessing the utility of sanctions: Have they forced the countries concerned to stay within the framework of international law? How have they affected the development of those countries? He finds that sanctions, although they have contained Iraq, Libya, and Sudan in the short term, have if anything strengthened the regimes in Iraq and Libya while increasing social and religious divisions. Contrary to intentions, he cogently argues, the net effect has been damage to the long-term prospects for stability and good governance in the Middle East and for a secure international order.

Tim Niblock is professor of Middle East studies and director of the Institute of Arab and Islamic Studies at the University of Exeter. His numerous publications include *Class and Power in Sudan: The Dynamics of Sudanese Politics, 1898-1985* and *Political and Economic Liberalisation in the Middle East* (coedited).